THE VAST RIGHT-WING CONSPIRACY'S DOSSIER ON HILLARY CLINTON

THE VAST RIGHT-WING CONSPIRACY'S DOSSIER ON HILLARY CLINTON

AMANDA B. CARPENTER

Library of Congress Cataloging-in-Publication Data

Carpenter, Amanda B.
The vast right-wing conspiracy dossier on Hillary Rodham Clinton / Amanda B. Carpenter.
p. cm.
ISBN-13: 978-1-59698-014-3
ISBN-10: 1-59698-014-1
1. Clinton, Hillary Rodham—Political and social views. 2. Clinton, Hillary Rodham—Ethics. 3. United States—Politics and government—2001– I. Title.
E887.C55C37 2006
328.73092—dc22
2006028060

Published in the United States by
Regnery Publishing, Inc.
One Massachusetts Avenue, NW
Washington, DC 20001

www.regnery.com

Distributed to the trade by
National Book Network
Lanham, MD 20706

Manufactured in the United States of America

10 9 8 7 6 5 4 3 2 1

Books are available in quantity for promotional or premium use. Write to Director of Special Sales, Regnery Publishing, Inc., One Massachusetts Avenue NW, Washington, DC 20001, for information on discounts and terms or call (202) 216-0600.

CONTENTS

MEMO

TO: MEMBERS OF THE VRWC
FROM: AMANDA B. CARPENTER
RE: SEN. HILLARY RODHAM CLINTON

November 8, 2006, marks first day of Hillary Clinton's campaign to be president of the United States.

Most Americans already know how they feel about her. She is the darling of the Manhattan elite, the hope of the national Democratic Party, the MVP of the pro-choice feminist movement, the rock star of the Hollywood Left, and the favorite of the liberal media. She has even been cozying up to Rupert Murdoch in recent months.

But just as numerous, even if not nearly so well-heeled, are those who—with good reason—don't trust her. Millions of Americans disbelieve her victim act regarding her philandering husband, reject her socialist economics, and despise her radical social agenda. These are the members of the Vast Right-Wing Conspiracy.

However vast and however determined we in the VRWC are, Hillary's presidential campaign is a formidable foe. Thanks to her husband's high-priced globe-trotting speaking tours, the couple's close ties to big businesses (foreign and domestic), and her sheer star power, the Clinton campaign in 2008 will have unrivaled riches at its disposal. Throw in a friendly media and invaluable political experience, and Mrs. Clinton begins to look invincible.

Luckily, over here at the Vast Right-Wing Conspiracy, we've been keeping a file on her. The couple's scandals are so numerous and so convoluted that it's easy to forget some of the dirty deals, unsavory incidents, insane proposals, revealing comments, and outright flip-flops in Hillary's past. Also, most of the media has little interest in looking deep enough into Hillary's actions since she entered Congress.

Rather than keeping her file tucked away in the archives, we decided it was important to share with the entire VRWC the Hillary Rodham Clinton papers—specifically, the record of her activities since leaving the White House and the machinery she already has in place to return to 1600 Pennsylvania Avenue.

So, here it is—the dossier on Hillary Clinton, complete with many original documents—"exhibits," we call them. As a member of the Vast Right-Wing Conspiracy, you already know what you feel about Hillary Clinton. Here's making sure you don't forget why.

THE TRANSCRIPT

Matt Lauer: [James Carville] has said that this is war between the president and Kenneth Starr. You have said, I understand, to some close friends, that this is the last great battle, and that one side or the other is going down here.

Mrs. Clinton: Well, I don't know if I've been that dramatic. That would sound like a good line from a movie. But I do believe that this is a battle. I mean, look at the very people who are involved in this, they have popped up in other settings. This is the great story here, for anybody willing to find it and write about it and explain it, is this vast right-wing conspiracy that has been conspiring against my husband since the day he announced for president. A few journalists have kind of caught onto it and explained it, but it has not yet been fully revealed to the American public. And, actually, you know, in a bizarre sort of way, this may do it.

—Today, January 27, 1998

NAME: Hillary Rodham Clinton

Originally would not assume her husband's last name and went by Hillary Rodham. After her husband lost his re-election for Arkansas governor in 1980, Hillary changed tacks and called herself Mrs. Hillary Clinton. After becoming First Lady, she added Rodham to her title and was then known as Hillary Rodham Clinton.

DATE OF BIRTH: October 26, 1947

PLACE OF BIRTH: Chicago, Illinois

OFFICIAL ADDRESS: 15 Old House Lane, Chappaqua, NY 10514.

ALTERNATIVE ADDRESS: 3067 Whitehaven St. NW, Washington, DC 20008.

RELIGION: Methodist.

HAIR: Brown. Presently clipped short, heavily layered, bleached blond and highlighted. Designed by celebrity stylist Isabelle Goetz. Clinton paid Goetz nearly $3,000 out of her campaign cash for two appointments between April and May 2006. (Also relies on makeup artist Barbara Lacy, to whom Clinton paid $1,600 in mid-May and $1,200 two weeks later for her services. Clinton's campaign writes off these expenses as a "media production.")

EYES: Said to be hazel. Wears blue colored lenses.

HEIGHT: Approximately 5'5"-5'7."

WEIGHT: Approximately 155-165 lbs. Bottom heavy.

OTHER IDENTIFYING MARKS: Occasionally wears a diamond ring, rumored to be at least three carats, given to her by her husband for their thirtieth wedding anniversary. Always accompanied by Secret Service, who will protect her for the rest of her life, if she chooses. Favors solid-color full coverage hip-length pantsuits. Often punctuates her speech with the phrase "you know."

INCOME: $165,100 per year as base pay of U.S. senator. Has earned millions in royalties from her memoir. Donates royalties earned on some books, but keeps all profits from her much more successful memoir, Living History. Alfred A. Knopf will publish a book about "citizen activism" by Mr. Clinton that will be released in early 2008.

Mr. Clinton received a book advance rumored to be between $10 million and $12 million to write his memoir My Life from the same publisher. Mr. Clinton made over $29 million in speaking fees from 2001-2005. As a former president he earns a yearly pension of $197,000. Mr. Clinton requested a $963,000 reimbursement from the federal government for his office and staff for the fiscal year 2007.

EDUCATION: Graduated from Maine South High School in Park Ridge, Illinois, where she served as class president, student council member, and member of the National Honor Society. Graduated from Wellesley College in 1969 and served for a period of time as the president of the Wellesley chapter of College Republicans. Earned a degree from Yale Law School, where she was on the Board of Editors of the Yale Law Review and Social Action.

PROFESSIONAL CAREER: Attorney of the Children's Defense Fund, 1973-74; Counsel, U.S. House of Representatives Committee on the Judiciary, 1974; Asst. Professor, University of Arkansas School of Law, 1974-77, 1979-80; Partner, Rose Law Firm 1979-92; Chair, President's Task Force on Health Care Reform, 1993; First Lady of the United States, 1993-2001; United States Senator, 2001-present; Chairman of the Democratic Steering and Coordination Committee 2003-present; Chairman of the Democratic Leadership Council, 2006-present.

ELECTION RESULTS:

	2000 general		
Candidate	**Votes**	**Percentage**	**Money Spent**
Hillary Rodham Clinton (D):	3,747,310	55%	$41,469,989
Rick Lazio (R)	2,915,730	43%	$40,576,273
Other	116,799	2%	

COMMITTEES (SUBCOMITTEES):

- Special Committee on Aging
- Armed Services (Airland; Emerging Threats & Capabilities; Readiness & Management Support)
- Environment & Public Works (Fisheries, Wildlife & Water; Transportation & Infrastructure)
- Health, Education, Labor & Pensions (Education & Early Childhood Development; Retirement Security & Aging)

ORGANIZATIONS:

- Co-Founder, Arkansas Advocates for Children and Families
- Former Board Member, Arkansas Children's Hospital
- Former Board Member, Children's Defense Fund
- Former Board Member, La Farge
- Former Board Member, TCBY Yogurt Company
- Former Board Member, Wal-Mart

CAUCUSES/NON-LEGISLATIVE COMMITTEES:

- Former Chair, Arkansas Educational Standards Committee
- Commission on Security and Cooperation in Europe
- Co-chair, congressional E-911 Caucus
- Democratic Policy Committee
- Democratic Technology and Communications Committee
- Board Member, Legal Services Corporation
- Chair, Steering and Coordination Committee
- Senate National Guard Caucus
- Senate Steel Caucus
- Senate Rural Health Caucus
- Former Chair, Task Force of National Health Care Reform

FAVORITE SONGS: "Respect" by Aretha Franklin, "Take it to the Limit" by the Eagles, "Hey Jude" by the Beatles, "Beautiful Day" by U2

PUBLISHED BOOKS:

- It Takes a Village: And Other Lessons Children Teach Us, 1996
- The Unique Voice of Hillary Rodham Clinton: A Portrait in Her Own Words, 1997
- Dear Socks, Dear Buddy: Kids' Letters to the First Pets, 1998
- An Invitation to the White House: At Home with History, 2000
- Living History, 2003

THE LEGACY OF THE CLINTON ADMINISTRATION AS HILLARY CLINTON PRESIDED AS FIRST LADY (TAKEN FROM THE PROGRESSIVE REVIEW)

RECORDS SET:

- The first First Lady to come under criminal investigation
- The highest number of cabinet officials to come under criminal investigation
- The highest number of witnesses to flee the country or refuse to testify
- Married to the first president to be disbarred from the U.S. Supreme Court and state court
- Married to the first president sued for sexual harassment
- Married to the first president accused of rape
- Married to the only president ever impeached on grounds of personal malfeasance
- Married to the first president to establish a legal defense fund

- Largest criminal plea agreement in an illegal campaign contribution case
- Greatest amount of illegal campaign contributions
- Greatest amount of illegal campaign contributions from abroad

CRIMINAL STATISTICS:

- 47 individuals and businesses affiliated with the Clintons were convicted or pled guilty to crimes
- 33 convictions during Mrs. Clinton's tenure as First Lady
- 61 indictments and misdemeanor charges
- 122 congressional witnesses, who pleaded the Fifth Amendment, fled the country to avoid testifying, or (in the case of foreign witnesses) refused to be interviewed.

CLINTON-RELATED CRIMES FOR WHICH CONVICTIONS WERE OBTAINED

Drug trafficking (3), racketeering, extortion, bribery (4), tax evasion, kickbacks, embezzlement (2), fraud (12), conspiracy (5), fraudulent loans, illegal gifts (1), illegal campaign contributions (5), money laundering (6), perjury, obstruction of justice.

NUMBER OF TIMES MRS. CLINTON SAID SOME FORM OF "I DON'T KNOW" IN COURT OR BEFORE CONGRESS AS FIRST LADY: 250

#1 - THE FOREIGN CASH FILE

One source of Senator Clinton's vast wealth is the foreign traveling and deal-making of her husband, former president Bill Clinton. This foreign money, now Clinton family wealth, is now available to Hillary for her presidential run in 2008.

The Clintons have a long and sordid history with foreign money, presenting potential security problems, at a minimum.

Chinese Spies at the White House

Throughout the Clinton presidency, Chinese agents gained unprecedented access to sensitive parts of the executive branch. This access was not gained through outright subterfuge, but through illegal and secretive campaign contributions from Asian businessmen with ties to the Chinese military.

In the late 1990s, the Senate Governmental Affairs Committee found that top Chinese liaison Johnny Chung, later sentenced to probation for violating campaign finance laws, was given "extraordinary access to the White House and especially the First Lady's office."[1] The committee's final report said, "There can be no question that Chung's contributions to the DNC helped give him access to the president and the First Lady."

There was a direct nexus between Chung's visits to the White House and his contributions. In fact, White House officials collected money from him in the First Lady's office in exchange for permitting him to bring a delegation of clients to White House events.

Chung and his company donated a total of $366,000 to the Democratic National Convention and made at least forty-nine visits to the Clinton White House between 1994 and 1996.[2] In 1995, he told the *Los Angeles Times* that he "saw the White House like a subway: You have to put in coins to open the gates."[3]

Bill Clinton has left the White House, but he now acts as a gatekeeper controlling access to his wife the senator. In this light, Mr. Clinton's foreign activities are deserving of scrutiny.

The Intricacies of Foreign Money

Federal law prohibits foreign nationals, foreign organizations, and foreign governments from contributing to campaigns for federal office. The Clintons appear to have found a loophole to avoid these restrictions.

Money earned by a candidate's spouse does not have to be reported to the FEC, even though most married couples—including the Clintons—intertwine their finances. Thus prohibited entities such as foreign citizens or foreign governments can legally contribute to Mrs. Clinton's campaigns through donations to her husband. This could take the form, for example, of paying Mr. Clinton a large sum in exchange for a speaking engagement.

Since leaving the White House, former president Bill Clinton has earned more than $20 million in honoraria from foreign interests (see Appendix G). These monies can later be used to help finance Hillary Clinton's anticipated presidential campaign.

When asked if she would use personal money for a possible presidential campaign, Senator Clinton replied, "Oh, I have no idea."[4]

The senator's 2005 Senate financial disclosure report revealed that she and her husband held a joint Citibank deposit account containing between $5 million and $25 million, and which produced between $50,001 and $100,000 in interest. In addition, she shared a Senate Qualified Blind Trust with her husband that was also worth between $5 million and $25 million. The trust had earned between $100,000 and $1 million in interest.

Campaign finance expert Cleta Mitchell, a partner in the Foley & Lardner law firm, says that Mrs. Clinton would be entitled to at least half the funds in joint accounts held with her husband. Mitchell told me that the FEC "now treat[s] that [joint investment accounts] as joint property, and the FEC would contend that 50 percent is hers."

An FEC spokesman refused to speculate on whether Senator Clinton could liquidate jointly held assets to finance her campaign because the FEC had not issued a formal decision on the matter. The spokesman did note, however, that Senator John Kerry (D-MA) legally borrowed against the assets of his wife, Teresa Heinz, to help finance his 2004 presidential campaign. Similarly, Mrs. Clinton could borrow against the wealth her husband has accumulated in part through his honoraria to help finance her campaigns.

Former president Ronald Reagan was fiercely criticized in October 1989 when Japanese business giant Fujisankei Communications Group reportedly paid him $2 million for a nine-day visit during which Reagan gave two speeches. The *New York Times* editorialized: "[T]he Reagans' willing participation is as disturbing as their extraordinary compensation. Former presidents haven't always comported themselves with dignity after leaving the Oval Office. But none have plunged so blatantly into pure commercialism."[5]

Former president Clinton, however, has plunged more "blatantly into pure commercialism." He was paid nearly $22 million from 2001 to 2004 for 151 appearances. He usually charged at least $125,000 per appearance, and his highest single fee was $400,000. Senator Clinton's financial disclosures show that foreign-based groups paid the former president $16.04 million for eighty-nine appearances.

The foreign-based groups that paid honoraria to former president Clinton included:

- **The Australian Council for the Peaceful Reunification of China:** Chinese political dissident Wei Jingsheng publicly criticized Clinton for accepting $300,000 to speak at this organization's conference in Sydney, Australia, in 2002.[6] Jingsheng denounced the meeting as "a method from the Chinese government of promoting so-called nationalism."[7] President George W. Bush visited Taiwan that same week and pledged to "help Taiwan defend herself if provoked" by China.[8]
- **The Dabbagh Group:** The Dabbagh Group is a Saudi financial services, agricultural products, energy services, and real estate conglomerate founded in 1962 by Sheikh Abdul-

THE TRANSCRIPT

This writer asked Senator Russ Feingold (D-WI) and Representative Chris Shays (R-CT), two of the chief sponsors of the 2002 campaign finance reform laws, their opinion of Bill Clinton's foreign honoraria and the possibility of Mrs. Clinton using the funds for a political campaign. They both seemed surprised and troubled that foreign money could enter a campaign this way.[9]

Q: Former president Clinton has been traveling around the world, making $16 million in foreign money in honoraria. And he shares a joint checking account with his wife and she can legally use half for her campaign. Would this be appropriate?

Russ Feingold: You know, I've never thought about that. That's an interesting question. I don't know if we've ever looked behind the way in which individuals obtain their money, but under Supreme Court rulings people can spend their own money.

Q: Right, but candidates aren't supposed to use foreign money. I guess I'm asking you how this would work.

Feingold: Well, I mean, I'm just thinking off the top of my head, it would be an interesting and possibly troubling step to start.

* * *

Q: I wanted to talk to you because you were one of the architects of campaign finance reform. Former president Clinton has been

CONTINUED

THE TRANSCRIPT

CONTINUED

traveling all over the world getting huge speaking fees and honoraria from Saudi Arabia, China—

Chris Shays: Who is doing this?

Q: President Clinton.

Shays: All right.

Q: And he has joint checking accounts with this wife, and she's entitled to half the funds. I've talked with campaign finance lawyers. Would it be appropriate for her to use that money for her campaign?

Shays: No, I don't think so.

Q: Is there anything in the law that prevents her from doing that though?

Shays: No, but you are raising the point. My reaction is that she shouldn't use any of her funds, and she would be wise to do it. Her husband is the former president of the United States. He can raise colossal sums from all over the world. He can raise money from people who aren't even citizens of the United States and effectively take that and reconvert it to money for his wife's campaign. I think it would be wrong, and I think they should say, "We're not going to use personal funds."

lah Dabbagh, a former Saudi minister for agriculture. It was led by the sheikh's son, Amr Dabbagh, from 1991 until he was appointed by King Fahd in 2004 to become chairman of the Saudi Arabian General Investment Authority. The Dabbagh Group paid Clinton $475,000 for two speeches in 2002, one of which was for Dabbagh's charitable foundation STARS.[10]

- **Markson Sparks:** Markson Sparks is an Australian public relations firm headed by celebrity agent Max Markson. Markson paid Mr. Clinton a total of $925,000 in 2001 and 2002 to appear at seven charitable fundraisers, four of which were for children's hospitals. Patrons could buy a $1,100 ticket to Clinton's children's hospital fundraiser in Brisbane, or pay $110,000 for access to a VIP cocktail party. Markson Sparks is also a major supporter and fund raiser for the Australian Labor Party.[11]
- **CLSA Ltd.:** CLSA is a brokerage, investment, and banking group headquartered in Hong Kong but owned by French-based Credit Agricole. Clinton was paid $500,000 in 2001 and 2002 to speak at two of the company's events, where he urged investors and other corporate executives to practice "responsible investing." At one event (at which he was billed with liberal rock star/activist Bono) Clinton claimed, "Every person in every corner of the world has a vested interest in solving global problems." He asked leaders to use their power to work for the interests of the poor.[12]

New Chinese Developments—More Communist Cash?

The CEO of a Chinese company that paid Mr. Clinton a $200,000 honorarium for a thirty-minute speech in May 2002 played a prominent role in the government of Communist China.

Senator Clinton's Senate financial disclosure forms state that her husband was paid the money by DNM Strategies on behalf of the JingJi Real Estate Development Group for a speech on May 23, 2002, in Shenzhen, China. DNM Strategies produces and manages all of *BusinessWeek* magazine's events in Asia.

A *BusinessWeek* spokeswoman told this writer that JingJi is a private real estate company in Shenzhen/Southern China and that a man named Chen Hua is its CEO.

The Shenzhen Real Estate Association website described Hua as a member of the Shenzhen Standing Committee of the Chinese People's Political Consultative Conference, which is organized by the National People's Congress. According to the State Department's 2006 report on China, the National People's Congress is "the primary organ" of the Chinese Communist Party.

Neither Senator Clinton's office nor former president Clinton's office responded to inquiries about the ownership of the Chinese company that paid the former president $200,000.

Mr. Clinton's International Agenda

In June 2005, former president Clinton gave a speech calling on governments of rich countries to forgive poor countries of their debt. Clinton admonished, "You cannot approach other countries with a security policy only. Because if you believe in a world of interdependence and open borders is inevitable—a precondition for that kind of prosperity you want to build—you cannot possibly kill, imprison, or occupy all your adversaries. You must make a greater effort to make more friends and fewer enemies. That's why it's important to forgive the debt of the world's most impoverished countries."[13]

Clinton made these remarks around the time he was paid $800,000 to take a four-day trip through Mexico, Colombia, and Brazil to give four speeches for Gold Service International, a Bogota-based business

THE CLINTON PLAN FOR PEACE WITH NORTH KOREA: BUILD A PARK

DaimlerChrysler has pledged $500,000 to help former president Bill Clinton and Ted Turner build a "peace park" designed to "promote regional peace and stability" in the demilitarized zone between North and South Korea. It is unclear how a park will inspire North Korean dictator Kim Jong-il, who recently tested a missile believed capable of reaching the United States, to embrace "peace and stability." The pledge is part of the Clinton Global Initiative, which funds projects focusing on such things as "religion, conflict, and reconciliation."[14]

development company. The Associated Press reported that he was also sponsored by the Massachusetts-based Cambridge Leadership Associate, a business consultancy firm with Brazilian business interests.

Before foreign audiences, Mr. Clinton has also encouraged the United States to accept more immigrants.

He told a business leadership conference in Mexico City that allowing 250,000 more immigrants into the U.S. annually could cut "the Social Security shortfall in half."[15]

Unsurprisingly, a chief beneficiary of policies like debt forgiveness and increased immigration would be the kind of large corporations that pay Clinton's hefty honoraria.

Mr. Clinton's Corporate Partners

Former president Clinton actively recruits big businesses and billion-dollar foundations into international alliances to help carry out his global agenda.

GOOD AS GOLDMAN

Goldman Sachs, the New York–based global investment and securities firm, hired Bill Clinton to give four speeches in the course of a year. On December 3, 2004, he was paid $125,000 to speak in New York; on April 20, 2005, he received another $125,000 to appear in Kiawah, Georgia; on June 6 he spoke in Paris, France, for $125,000; and on June 13 he gave a speech in Greensboro, Georgia, for $150,000. There appears to have been no press coverage of these engagements. The Associated Press, however, ran a blurb on June 21, 2005, reporting that Clinton had flown into Charleston Executive Airport on John Island on June 20. Clinton's office refused to comment on the former president's activities there.

Clinton calls this effort the Clinton Global Initiative and claims it is his most ambitious project yet. In the CGI's first year alone, Mr. Clinton secured pledges totaling more than $3 billion to help fund his projects to alleviate poverty, climate change, and religious conflict, and to promote good governance, enterprise, and investment.[16]

The CGI revolves around an annual high-stakes networking conference. The first conference, held last September in New York City, secured over three hundred "pledges" valued at more than $2 billion. Roughly 1,000 hand-picked corporate CEOs, non-profit leaders, and top government officials participated, with each making a "commitment" to one of Clinton's causes. Participants paid a $15,000 fee to attend the conference.

Among the headliners at last year's conference were Secretary of State Condoleezza Rice, British prime minister Tony Blair, World Bank president Paul Wolfowitz, Senator Hillary Clinton, former vice president Al Gore, Goldman Sachs CEO (and current treasury secretary) Hank Paulson, King Abdullah bin Al-Hussein and Queen Rania of Jordan, and international financier George Soros.

Corporate sponsors included Citigroup, Goldman Sachs, Google, Nokia, Starbucks, Hewlett Packard, and Microsoft. Corporate spokesmen, however, were hesitant to discuss their company's involvement with CGI. A Goldman Sachs spokesman refused to speak on the record about the company's pledges, as did Starbucks representatives.

Most of the pledges Clinton raised in the first year, according to CGI's annual report, were concentrated in two areas: "alleviating world poverty," which took in $798,153,000, and "climate change," which secured $657,408,000. "Religious reconciliation" brought in $327,356,000.

Non-profits were the most generous donors, pledging $970,309,000. Corporations were second, giving $751,783,000. Individuals and foundations gave a combined total of $146,882,000, while government entities pledged $118,899,000.

Hillary Clinton's participation in the CGI, including a major address on climate change she gave at the New York conference, further illustrate the complicated, tangled web between her, her husband, and his foreign financial backers.

VRWC ACTION PLAN

Millions of dollars in foreign cash will be a tremendous asset for Hillary in her presidential run, but given the couple's past involvements with Communist Chinese businesses, it could become a serious liability.

#2 - THE CAMPAIGN CASH FILE

The Clintons are prodigious campaign fund raisers. Their methods, however, often range from the unsavory to the illegal.

The Case of Peter Paul

In 2000, Hollywood businessman Peter Paul hosted a lavish series of fundraisers for Mrs. Clinton during her first run for the U.S. Senate. The Clintons disguised the events' fundraising nature and failed to disclose all of the contributions, some of which violated campaign finance laws.

Current Pennsylvania governor Ed Rendell was the chairman of the Democratic National Committee at the time and a close friend of the Clintons. Rendell convinced Paul to bankroll two fundraisers at exclusive Hollywood locations, along with a multimillion dollar Hollywood fundraiser for Mrs. Clinton's 2000 senatorial campaign replete with a cocktail reception, eight-hour benefit concert, and dinner. Deceptively billed as the "Gala Hollywood Salute to President William Jefferson Clinton," the concert and dinner together cost couples $25,000, while individuals shelled out $1,000 just for the show.[1]

Paul hoped the fundraisers would ingratiate him not with Mrs. Clinton, but with her husband. Paul aimed to hire the former president as a spokesman for his Internet-based production and marketing company, Stan Lee Media, which Paul ran in partnership with comic book mogul Stan Lee. Paul publicly acknowledged that Rendell had suggested the Hillary fundraisers as a means to recruit her husband.

Paul was forthright with this writer about the purpose of the fundraisers:

> No one questions why I would pay money to a politician just out of the goodness of my heart. I'm not ideologically linked to the Clintons and my interest had nothing to do with Hillary's political career. It was clearly a business interest, but a legal business interest. I was merely doing what corporations do. Hire ex-presidents as rainmakers for their global companies. George Bush Sr. did it, Reagan did it, that's what ex-

presidents do. And that's what I was doing with Clinton, because he was a popular figure internationally.[2]

The Cuban Fraud Incident

The Clintons were either unaware or unconcerned that they were associating with a felon. In the late 1970s, Paul was convicted of participating in a scam coined the "Cuban Coffee Caper" by *Time* magazine.[3] As president of the Miami World Trade Center, Paul was part of a ploy to con the Cuban government into paying $8.7 million for a fictitious boatload of "Barahona" Arabic blend coffee.

According to *Time*, Paul and his cohorts planned to present the Cubans with fraudulent documents and collect the fee for the cargo, then sink an empty delivery ship and collect the insurance money as an extra payoff. The plot went awry when the crew that planned to sink the ship was prohibited from boarding in Santo Domingo, where a key bribe had not been paid. The crew that *did* man the ship apparently found something amiss and abandoned the freighter in Costa Rica, where Cuban representatives later found it without the promised coffee.

Paul offered a more conspiratorial explanation to this writer: "I was an anti-communist freedom fighter in the 1970s when I was an international corporate lawyer in Miami representing anti-Castro political leaders and governments in South America. After directing a sting operation on Castro in 1978, and because of other clandestine activities with agencies involved in undermining Castro, I was forced to plead guilty to defrauding the Cuban government and possession of cocaine by the Carter Justice Department."[4]

The Bel-Air Meeting

At Rendell's suggestion, Paul hosted two fundraising events for Hillary Clinton in 2000: a luncheon at Wolfgang Puck's illustrious

Spago restaurant in Beverly Hills, and a tea in the Bel Air home of Democratic philanthropist Cynthia Gershman. Paul says his successful organization of these events led to the ornate August gala.

Mrs. Clinton was fully aware of Paul's true intentions from the beginning. According to Paul, "When I'm sitting with her [at the Bel Air tea] I said to her, 'Listen, I'm prepared to help your campaign, if according to Ed Rendell, I can get Bill to work with me when he leaves the White House as an ex-president.' And so she said to me, she'd discuss it with him and she'd like me to help her campaign. And if I did get Bill, I'd get her with him because they're a team."

Paul claimed he was assured by Mrs. Clinton's campaign that Bill Clinton would work for Stan Lee Media after leaving office. With this assurance, said Paul, "I began writing the checks to pay for the gala. And that's how it came about. It was Jim Levin, appointed by the president to be my liaison. He worked with David Rosen [Mrs. Clinton's campaign finance manager] who moved into my offices to prepare for this event. Ed Rendell vouched for the whole thing, whom I was in touch with regularly."

Coercion

Paul claimed he planned to spend less than $500,000 on the gala, but was coerced by Mrs. Clinton's campaign into committing over $1 million. He explained:

> As we're getting into producing a miracle, which is a world-class event being produced in the backyard of a friend of mine in four weeks, in which 1,100 people showed up, and contributed $1.5 million to Hillary's campaign and all that is confirmed in the FEC report. To make it happen in four weeks, I had to write checks like crazy. First of all, an event like that would normally take six to eight months to produce. I had eight international headliners. It was the biggest private concert ever

ALL HER STAR FRIENDS

Performers at the Hillary Clinton fundraising gala, in order of appearance:

- Ian Fraser and his seventeen-piece orchestra
- Shirley MacLaine
- Patti LaBelle
- Jimmy Smits
- Sugar Ray
- Red Buttons
- Toni Braxton
- Anjelica Huston
- Melissa Etheridge
- Dylan McDermott
- Alfre Woodard
- Michael Bolton
- Whoopi Goldberg
- Cher
- Muhammad Ali
- Paul Anka
- Gregory Peck
- Diana Ross
- Ted Danson and Mary Steenburgen

Other guests included Brad Pitt, Jennifer Aniston, John Travolta, Kelly Preston, Wesley Snipes, and Patrick Swayze.

produced. The guy that produced it for me produces the Grammys and all kinds of award shows for CBS. I paid for it and as I was paying for it, it got to be ridiculous, I was complaining

> because Hillary's finance director [Rosen] was working out of my office so I complained regularly to him, and he kept saying "Well, if you don't keep paying for it, we're going to blame you for sabotaging Hillary's campaign." So after you've paid $1 million odd, you can't stop so that's how they coerced me.
>
> People say, "How can you be coerced?" It's simple. If you paid over a million bucks and people threatened that if you didn't keep paying you'd lose the million plus, you'd get bad publicity, what would you do? You don't have a choice at that point. So they kept forcing me to pay until I paid for the whole thing. And then afterwards, they forced me to pay some more. After they told everybody that they didn't know me and they wouldn't take any money from me.

The Felony Revelation

Paul's hopes of hiring the president were dashed just days after the gala—when the *Washington Post* publicized his felony conviction. In an August 15, 2000, column, Lloyd Grove revealed that Mrs. Clinton's gala organizer had served three years in prison after pleading guilty to cocaine possession and attempting to defraud the Cuban government. Grove's headline asked, "Is Hillary Clinton Soft on Crime?"

Hillary's campaign spokesman, Howard Wolfson, told Grove that Paul was only the gala's producer and had not contributed to Mrs. Clinton's campaign. "We will not be accepting any contributions from him," Wolfson insisted.

The *Post* quickly discovered that Paul, in fact, had contributed $2,000 to Hillary's campaign just six weeks before. In response, Wolfson retracted his statement and announced that Paul's check had been returned. He described Paul's other bountiful contributions to Clinton's campaign as an "an in-kind contribution . . . and not a check."

WHAT HILLARY DOESN'T WANT US TO KNOW

Barbara Olson had just completed writing The Final Days about the last scandal-filled hours of the Clinton administration when she was killed in the September 11 terrorist attacks. Olson had gained expense records related to Hillary Clinton's office at the beginning of her tenure as junior senator from New York. The documents showed that Clinton's in-state office was more than twice the size—and, at $514,148, twice the cost—of that of New York's senior senator, Charles Schumer. Olson examined that Clinton's "seventeen-year-old building, covered in peach Finnish granite, offers a terraced 154-seat auditorium with television facilities, plus two conference rooms in Hillary's suite." Taxpayers picked up the bill for the plush accommodations.[5]

Paul commented on the Clintons' attempts to minimize his role: "They want to characterize me as some serial criminal and yet I was able to host the president and First Lady in the biggest event ever for a president in Hollywood. On 25,000 invitations my name appeared along with the governor of California along with my partner as hosts of this event."

Despite the bad press, Hillary Clinton continued to pursue her lucrative relationship with Paul. Three days after the appearance of Grove's article, while her campaign was publicly treating Paul as a pariah, both she and President Clinton sent him personal thank-you notes. President Clinton thanked Paul for the "wonderful event," exclaiming "I am very grateful for the boost it gave Hillary's campaign." Mrs. Clinton expressed gratitude for Paul's friendship and conveyed her warm regards (see Appendix D).

On August 24, 2000, Hillary's campaign broke its promise not to accept Paul's money. Having already accepted more than $1.5 million from Paul, Mrs. Clinton's campaign finance director sent him a fax requesting a stock transfer worth $100,000.

Paul agreed to fork over $55,000 in stocks once he secured a brief meeting with President Clinton outside Air Force One to discuss Stan Lee Media. Paul claimed Clinton assured him at the meeting that their "deal was still on track."

Paul told this writer, "Now you can't get much more duplicitous and deceptive with the voters than vowing not to take money from somebody and then after taking $1 million and a half and then asking for another $100,000."

The Hidden Donations

Three fundraising committees had joined forces for the Hollywood gala—Clinton for Senate, the Democratic Senatorial Campaign Committee (DSCC), and the New York State Democratic Committee (NYSDC). The groups formulated a "Joint Fundraising Agreement" guaranteeing that Mrs. Clinton's campaign would be the primary beneficiary of the money raised at the gala—even though it was marketed as a tribute to her husband.

The agreement, according to the Federal Election Commission's general counsel, dictated that Clinton for Senate received the first $2,000 of each primary and general election contribution from individual donors, which was the maximum take allowed under campaign finance law. The DSCC collected the next $20,000 on individual donations larger than $2,000, and the NYSDC took in the next $3,000.[6]

Furthermore, Clinton for Senate received the first $10,000 from multi-candidate committees, again the maximum legal amount. The DSCC took the next $15,000 and the NYSDC could have the following $5,000. The DSCC put any remaining funds from individual contributors and multi-candidate committees into its non-federal account. The agreement clearly gave the Clinton campaign first dibs on the revenues from this extravagant event, which pocketed a total of $1,072,015 in direct contributions.

But staging the gala relied on over $1.1 million of in-kind contributions—goods or services given to candidates free of charge or at a special discount. Of this amount, Clinton's staff only reported about $400,000 to the FEC, even though it was legally obligated to report the entire amount.

Former Clinton aide Dick Morris explained why the Clinton campaign would under-report its in-kind contributions:

> Under the arcane rules of the Federal Election Commission at the time, campaigns could use soft money to pay for fundraising events—*provided* the gathering's costs came to 40 percent or less of the total of hard money* raised. (Soft money was far

* "Hard money" refers to direct contributions to a candidate's campaign committee. Such contributions have long been subject to strict limits. "Soft money" refers to contributions to a party or party committee, such as the Democratic National Committee or Democratic Senatorial Campaign Committee. Before the McCain-Feingold "Campaign Finance Reform" laws passed in 2001, there was no limit on the size of "soft money" contributions an individual could give. Parties legally could not use "soft money," however, to support a specific candidate, but only for broader "party building" activities.

easier to raise: Donors could give up to $25,000 of soft money, but only $1,000 of hard money.)

Hillary's Hollywood gala raised $1 million in hard money that August. This meant that the campaign could use soft money to pay for all costs up to $400,000. David Rosen conveniently reported to the campaign treasurer that the event did, indeed, cost $400,000, avoiding the necessity of spending any hard money on the affair.

Here's why he would have done it: If the real cost of the event were $1.2 million instead of $400,000, the campaign would have had to use hard money to make up the difference. The Hillary Clinton campaign would have had $800,000 less of hard money to spend running TV ads and funding get-out-the-vote operations.[7]

The FEC's general counsel investigated the gala's financing and issued a brief on July 7, 2005—almost five years after the event. The FEC found that the NYSDC failed to disclose $721,895 in in-kind contributions." The brief, which found slightly different numbers from Morris, listed the following contributions:[8]

DESCRIPTION	**REPORTED**	**UNREPORTED**
Dinner and reception in-kinds	$153,863	$109,067
Concert in-kinds	$200,000	$395,154
Travel and lodging in-kinds	—	$92,135
Printing in-kinds	$12,702	$125,539
Other in-kinds reported	$34,854	—
Direct expenses reported	$117,658	—
Total	**$519,077**	**$721,895**

According to the FEC, "the extensive concert preparations included the hiring of a professional stage designer, a large orchestra, a gospel choir (including a charter bus), and numerous talent assistants, make-up artists, audio technicians, camera and video technicians, key grips, prop technicians, electricians, and security personnel. Black Ink (the primary concert vendor) shipped in hundreds of trees and bushes; rented sophisticated lighting, sound, and video equipment; and used large generators to power the system. Publicists were also hired at a cost of over $22,000 to advertise the concert and celebrities who would be attending."

The FEC declared that the joint committee reported less than half the costs of the event. For example, the souvenir tribute journal and invitations alone cost more than $125,000, but only $12,702 was reported. Guests were also given gift bags worth $1,535 each, but the value of the 7,000 CDs included in the 1,400 gift bags weren't disclosed either.

The Rosen Indictment

David Rosen, Mrs. Clinton's national finance director at the time, was indicted in June 2002 for "underreporting" the cost of the 2000 gala. Four individuals affiliated with the event testified that Mr. Rosen was aware of unreported concert expenses. The indictment charged Rosen with four counts of facilitating the filing of false campaign finance reports to the FEC on behalf of Mrs. Clinton. Rosen's defense argued for Rosen's acquittal on the grounds that he did not personally receive any financial benefits from concealing campaign funds. He was eventually acquitted of two charges and the court dismissed the other two. One of Rosen's lawyers, Paul Mark Sandler, wrote a five-part series of articles attributing his client's acquittal to his own rhetorical prowess.

The FEC Fine

Clinton's campaign declared that Rosen's acquittal proved the campaign's innocence in the matter. Despite Rosen's acquittal, however, the FEC determined that Clinton's joint fundraising committee must have been aware of the gala's true cost. The joint committee's chairman, Andrew Grossman, was cited for underreporting contributions and the committee was fined $35,000.

Thus, incurring a mere $35,000 fine, Hillary Clinton's campaign got away with one of the largest, most fraudulent campaign contributions in political history.

And even this trifling penance may go unpaid. In January 2005 the *New York Sun*'s Josh Gerstein noted that the joint committee, with available funds of just $3,452 but facing $78,000 in legal bills, may not be able to cover the penalty.

The Deal Breaker and Hillary's Deficient Memory

Paul never got his deal with President Clinton, largely due to the maneuverings of a Japanese businessman named Tendo Oto.

Oto was president of Venture Soft Co., Ltd, a Japanese Internet-based animation company. Oto was seeking a partnership with Stan Lee Media to create a U.S.-based subsidiary of Venture Soft. According to Paul, Oto had pledged to pay half of the multimillion dollar employment package Jim Levin—Paul's liaison to Mr. Clinton—had negotiated between Paul and Mr. Clinton.

To facilitate the deal, Paul had procured for Oto special access to the Clinton White House, including an invitation to the Clinton's final state dinner at the White House and a private, midnight tour of the Oval Office.

Paul and Oto's arrangement was scrapped soon after the Hollywood gala and Paul's outing as a felon. Around four months later, in December 2000, Stan Lee Media collapsed. With Paul in disfavor, Jim Levin

WHAT WILL COME BACK TO HAUNT HER

The list of Hillary Clinton's ignoble donors is extensive.

For example, Clinton accepted at least $8,000 from a Saipan-based sweatshop operator named Willie Tan and his family.[9]

Moreover, on May 7, 2006, the *New York Times* reported that Clinton accepted $157,000 from International Profit Associates (IPA), a company owned by John Burgess, "a disbarred New York lawyer with a criminal record for attempted larceny and patronizing a sixteen-year-old prostitute." Hillary has refused to join most other politicians in returning Burgess' donations. Her husband also received $125,000 from IPA in 2001.[10]

Hillary did, however, make a public show of returning a $5,000 contribution in March 2006 from Wal-Mart. The company, a favorite target of liberal opponents of "big business," had apparently become anathema to Clinton, though she had been on the firm's board of directors in the late 1980's. Her campaign claimed Clinton had "serious differences with current company practices."[11]

Clinton later applauded a Maryland law forcing Wal-Mart to increase spending on employee health care. According to Clinton, the company had simply changed since she was affiliated with it.

simply cut Paul out and made a deal with Oto for himself. Levin incorporated his own subsidiary of Venture Soft in Chicago on November 13, 2000, appointing himself as director. The company quickly failed, dissolving on April 1, 2002.

As of this writing, Hillary Clinton has refused to speak about her relationship with Paul, save a single declaration to California's Superior Court. Clinton acknowledged meeting Paul at the Spago and Gershman fundraisers, but claimed to have no memory of their conversations and "no recollection whatsoever" of discussing his support for her campaign or his negotiations with her husband.

Continuing Developments

Paul, in cooperation with the U.S. Justice Foundation, is currently pursuing civil charges against Bill Clinton, claiming Clinton's backpedaling on his alleged agreement to represent Stan Lee Media provoked the company's demise. A trial is scheduled for March 2007 at which Paul plans to depose Hillary Clinton, whose inclusion in the lawsuit was dismissed through the invocation of an anti-SLAPP (Strategic Lawsuits Against Public Participation) law that protects public figures.

Meanwhile, there seems to be no end to Hillary Clinton's dodgy campaign financing: on May 4, 2006, the FEC warned Mrs. Clinton that she had received illegally large donations from thirty-nine individuals in the previous quarter.[12] Although the FEC called the excessive donations a "serious problem," Clinton's spokeswoman dismissed the illegal funds as "clerical cleanups."

The ImClone Scandal

Paul is not Hillary Clinton's only disreputable source of campaign cash.

On August 7, 2002, former ImClone CEO Sam Waksal was indicted for fraudulent insider trading, bank fraud, and obstruction of justice. Shortly thereafter, the *New York Post* disclosed that Waksal had contributed $27,000 to Hillary Clinton, who reeled in another $15,000 from Waksal family members and top ImClone executives.

Clinton felt no compulsion to return Waksal's funds, as politicians typically do when tainted money becomes publicized. The *Post* denounced Clinton's greed with a headline reading "HILL'S FILTHY LUCRE: HOLDS ON TO 27G FROM IMCLONE SAM." The story quoted a Clinton spokeswoman confirming that Clinton would not return Waksal's money.[13]

The *Post* then reported that Waksal had actually donated not $27,000, but a whopping $63,000 to Hillary.[14] The revelation sparked a quick about-face by Clinton, whose spokeswoman now told the *Post* that the campaign would donate Waskal's funds to charity.

Or at least some of the funds. Clinton only had $7,000 of Waskal's money left. The remaining $56,000 had been given to the Democratic Senatorial Campaign Committee, which indicated it had already spent the cash.

The $45 Million Question

The 2000 New York Senate race was the most expensive Senate race in electoral history.

Mrs. Clinton spent $29 million in the campaign, while Republican Rick Lazio paid out $24 million, yielding a record combined total of $53 million. The *New York Daily News* reported that Clinton spent $850,000 on polling alone.[15]

FEC documents show that by August 2006, Clinton had raised nearly $45 million dollars for her campaign war chest; she had $22 million on hand and zero debts.

Hillary does not need copious contributions to retain her seat in 2006, which is one of the Senate's safest. Many donors really hope their funds will help finance a presidential bid. Although Clinton has been raising money at a presidential pace in the run-up to the 2008 election, her team insists its funds are solely aimed at ensuring her re-election in New York.

HILLPAC

Senator Clinton has also generously dished out funds to party colleagues, giving over $1.2 million to congressional Democrats since 2001 through HILLPAC, a political action committee created to assist other Democrats.[16]

But Clinton's generosity has diminished as her re-election approaches; HILLPAC doled out $837,000 for the 2002 election cycle, $312,500 for 2004, and just $180,000 for 2006 as of August 2.

The Associated Press noted in March 2006: "Clinton continues to do relatively little fundraising for her political action committee, HILLPAC, generating enough money to pay the bills and slightly boost the bottom line while plowing more than $1 million a month into her Senate campaign."[17]

Methods Employed by Friends of Hillary

The committee that handles the bulk of Hillary Clinton's fundraising—that is, funds meant for Hillary's own campaigns—is called Friends of Hillary

Friends of Hillary operates an aggressive online campaign through a website, HillaryClinton.com, that collects data, organizes volunteers, registers voters and hawks Hillary-related merchandise like kitschy plastic piggy banks bearing the logo "Hillary Cares."

Friends of Hillary solicits donations through e-mails in which Clinton sometimes reveals controversial positions. For example, after staying silent for two weeks following the *New York Times*'s December 2005 revelation of the National Security Agency's terrorist surveillance program, Clinton announced her opposition to the program in an electronic donation appeal.

Clinton uses such e-mails to unleash some of her more partisan broadsides. One donation solicitation condemning the nomination of Samuel Alito to the Supreme Court declared, "Every radical activist

HER SECOND HOME

Clinton often raises funds from her $2.8 million Washington home. Her palatial residence contrasts sharply with the humble Washington abodes occupied by many other members of Congress. For example, New York's senior senator, Charles Schumer, shares a townhouse with three other congressmen, according to the 2004 Almanac of American Politics.

judge that they appoint brings our opponents one step closer to their goal: to change the law of the land and strip away our rights."

Since 1999 Clinton has also collected fees from outside organizations for mailing donation solicitations on their behalf to Clinton's own donors. This practice has netted at least $340,000, according to the *New York Daily News*.[18]

Much of Mrs. Clinton's personal fundraising occurs in her $4.2 million, seven-bedroom colonial mansion on Washington's Embassy Row. Clinton began remodeling the mansion around September 2005, just as fundraising for her 2006 re-election was kicking into high gear. The *New York Post* reported that Clinton spared no expense on the project: "Architects estimate the gutting and remodeling of the existing first floor will ring up a $560,224 tab, with the new addition off the back tallying another $273,703—a $833,927 grand total. The poolhouse cost an extra $55,000."[19]

The renovation was finished in the early summer of 2006, just in time to host lavish fundraisers during Congress's August recess.

Follow the Money

Under federal law, all political contributions over $200 must be reported to the Federal Elections Commission. Although companies are barred from donating directly to political candidates, they often have their own political action committees.

The Center for Responsive Politics estimated that as of June 30, 2006, Hillary Clinton had received $14,757,203 from the business community, including corporations, trade associations, and professional groups; $437,120 from single-issue ideological groups such as the pro-abortion EMILY's List and the environmentalist Sierra Group; and $343,165 from labor unions.

The following list itemizes the top twenty companies whose individual employees, immediate family members of employees, and employee political action committees have donated the most to Hillary Clinton's campaign since 1999.

The Corning Connection

As the new chairwoman of the Democratic Leadership Council, Senator Clinton pledged in July 2006 to increase college funding by "getting rid of wasteful business subsidies."

Nevertheless, Clinton maintains close financial ties to businesses supportive of her career. One such company is Corning, Inc., a New York–based firm that once leaned Republican, but become close to Clinton once the senator ensured for the corporation a steady stream of government subsidies.[20]

HILLARY'S MONEY TRAIL

(Contributions to Hillary from employees and PACs of top companies)

Goldman Sachs	$254,460
Citigroup Inc.	$239,050
Time Warner	$189,390
Metropolitan Life	$166,850
Corning, Inc.	$153,900
Skadden, Arps	$143,380
Morgan Stanley	$135,960
International Profit Assoc.	$129,400
Viacom, Inc.	$124,925
JP Morgan Chase & Co.	$123,230
Kushner Companies	$119,000
Cablevision Systems	$106,850
New York Life Insurance	$106,500
Ernst & Young	$103,975
UBS Americas	$96,070
Walt Disney Co.	$95,355
Akin, Gump	$85,950
General Electric	$82,105
Patton Boggs	$81,338
Intl. Brotherhood of Electrical Workers	$75,975

Individual Corning employees contributed just $15,240 to Clinton, compared to $23,500 for her opponent, Republican Rick Lazio, during the 2000 Senate campaign, according to CRP. The Corning PAC declined to fund Clinton's race at all. During the 2002 election cycle, Clinton was funded by just two Corning employees, for a total of $500.

But by 2004, the Clinton-Corning relationship had warmed up. The Corning PAC gave Clinton $10,000 that year, while individual Corning employees coughed up $51,250.

As of July 2006, Clinton had already picked up $61,359 in contributions from Corning employees for her current re-election campaign, bringing her lifetime total take from Corning employees and their PAC to $133,400. This places Clinton in the top five lifetime recipients of Corning political donations.

As Clinton has become a big recipient of Corning contributions, Corning has become a major recipient of Clinton-related legislative largesse.

WHAT WILL COME BACK TO HAUNT HER

In July 2006, U.S. Attorney Patrick Fitzgerald indicted one of the "host committee chairs" of the Clintons' 2000 gala for defrauding Chicago public schools by lying that he was contracting snow removal work to minority-owned firms. The suspect also allegedly bribed a former Chicago school employee to obtain public contracts for his companies. Josh Gerstein of the *New York Sun* identified the suspect as former strip-club owner James Levin, who had also brokered the failed deal between President Clinton and Peter Paul. Levin also served on the national finance committee for Mrs. Clinton's Senate campaign. Gerstein reported Levin and his wife had donated $12,000 to Mrs. Clinton's campaign and had been treated by the Clintons to an overnight stay in the Lincoln bedroom.

For example, the Environmental Protection Agency approved a clean air rule, called the "2007 Highway Diesel Rule," mandating that all model-year 2007 heavy-duty diesel trucks and buses reduce exhaust emissions by over 90 percent. Although older diesel trucks and buses are exempt from the law, Clinton advocates the allocation of millions of tax dollars to "retrofit" older vehicles so they too can meet the new standard. Coincidently, Corning is a leading manufacturer of the catalysts and filters used to cut emissions on older vehicles.

The EPA has further encouraged the voluntary reduction of emissions on 444,000 school buses by 2010. So Clinton inserted an earmark in the 2003 omnibus spending bill providing $5 million for a pilot program, called Clean School Bus USA, to fund schools' purchases of diesel-reduction equipment of the kind Corning makes.

A month after receiving $10,000 from Corning's PAC in 2003, Clinton traveled to Corning headquarters (at Corning's expense) to announce she would introduce legislation authorizing "hundreds of millions" of dollars in federal grants to school districts to purchase Corning-manufactured devices to improve school bus emissions. Clinton boasted that she would "create a major opportunity for Corning."

Corning vice chairman and chief financial officer James B. Flaws praised Clinton for her assistance. Flaws wrote a letter to the *Buffalo News* defending Clinton against her critics, proclaiming that "Clinton "has delivered and continues to deliver for us." He again extolled her plan to secure federal funding for the school bus retrofitting project.[21]

Since then Clinton has taken credit for substantially expanding Clean School Bus USA, as its funding has jumped from $5 million in 2003 to $10 million in 2006.[22]

Corning money began pouring into Clinton's campaign after Corning CEO James held a fundraiser for her in March 2004. Between April

Below is the General Services Administration funding request for former President Clinton for the 2007 fiscal year:

Pension	$197,000
Staff salaries	$96,000
Staff benefits	$64,000
Travel	$64,000
Rental Payments	$498,000
Telephone	$77,000
Postage	$15,000
Other Services	$113,000
Printing	$9,000
Supplies	$16,000
Equipment	$11,000
Total	**$1,160,000**

(These figures reflect an anticipated annual increase in pay rate and an additional $9,000 request from Mr. Clinton for health insurance.)

28 and June 21, thirty-five Corning employees donated a total of $48,250 to Clinton's campaign.

Clinton did Corning another service a few months later. In 2004 China's ministry of commerce, accusing Corning and eight other companies of dumping cheap optical fiber products, tacked a 16 percent tariff onto Corning's optical fiber exports.

Clinton worked furiously to get the tariff lifted. According to the *New York Times*, her activities included writing a letter to the Chinese minister, inviting a Chinese ambassador to her Capitol Hill office, and personally lobbying President Bush to become involved in the matter.

The Chinese duly lifted the tariff, but not for any other company than Corning. Corning CEO James Houghton told New York's *Elmira Star-Gazette*, "The Chinese were seemingly unaware of our reputation for integrity, so we needed a character witness. Senator Clinton provided that witness."

Corning CEO Houghton and Clinton became close allies. In March 2005, Clinton introduced legislation to designate a segment of Interstate 86 in Corning, New York, the "Amo Houghton Bypass," in honor of the former New York congressman, the CEO's brother. In November, Amo and James Houghton each sent Clinton a $1,500 check.

In 2005 Clinton co-sponsored the Diesel Emissions Reduction Act (DERA) mandating that heavy-duty diesel vehicles that are state-owned or used for work on state projects be fitted with emission-reducing technology. The law also authorized the EPA to dole out an impressive $1 billion over five years to states and localities to buy emission-reducing devices for their trucks, trains, ships, and other diesel-powered equipment.

Corning executive Timothy J. Regan was invited to testify about the DERA to the Senate Environment and Public Works Committee, on which Clinton serves. Regan unsurprisingly lobbied for the measure's approval. He also estimated that each diesel particulate-matter filter needed to retrofit diesel-powered vehicles would cost $7,500.

Clinton then cosponsored two amendments slipped into the 2005 transportation bill to provide even more money for such retrofitting. The first allowed states and local governments to access the $8.6 billion Clean Air fund to purchase emission-reducing technology for construction equipment used on federal highway projects in areas with low air quality. The second amendment authorized a $110 million expansion of the Clean School Bus USA program.

At Corning headquarters, Clinton had bragged that her plan to bring "hundreds of millions" of dollars to Corning would create jobs in New York. And in 2003 Corning did build a local, highly automated diesel plant that now employs four hundred people.

But Corning says it does not anticipate any new local hiring, despite its expectations of a vast increase in the diesel-emissions products market.

In March 2006, however, Corning announced plans for a $15 million investment to expand a Corning manufacturing plant—in China. Sixty percent of Corning's total workforce is now located outside the United States.

Corning freely attributes much of its recent good fortune to Hillary Clinton. Clinton frequently vows to slash ties between government and big business, but Corning readily admits their relationship is a two-way street. As Corning CFO James Flaws told the *Star-Gazette*, "The Clinton-Corning partnership is very rewarding for both of us."

Corning senior vice president Tim Regan more succinctly summarized Clinton's role in servicing Corning: "Senator Clinton is bigger than life."

Bountiful Personal Finances

Hillary Clinton could surely succeed as a self-funded candidate, as both she and her husband rake in huge amounts of money from their various endeavors.

Mrs. Clinton supplements her $165,100 annual salary as a U.S. senator with millions earned from her book sales. On her financial disclosure forms, Senator Clinton reported that from 1999 to 2005 she gave all royalties from her child advocacy book *It Takes a Village*—$59,124—to charity. But she kept the earnings from her memoirs, *Living History*, which brought in around $10 million since 2001.

Hillary's husband is not likely to go hungry either. He will supplement his six-figure speaking fees this year with his $183,500 presidential pension. The pension is a lifetime benefit that the National Taxpayers Union estimates will grant Mr. Clinton a total of over $7 million if he lives to his early eighties. He enjoys other official compensation as well, including up to $96,000 annually for office staff.

VRWC ACTION PLAN

In 2008, Senator Clinton will surely engage in the same sort of questionable fundraising activity that marked her 2000 race and her husband's races. Indeed, those activities have certainly already begun. The VRWC must root out her violations of the law and ethics as they occur, and expose her dirty money.

#3 - THE ECONOMICS FILE

Hillary Clinton's voting record and rare candid comments reveal an economic philosophy based on central planning, bigger government, higher and more complex taxes, and increased regulation of private industry. In general, she subscribes to the discredited belief that government is a better engine of prosperity than is a market economy.

"We're Going to Take Things Away from You"

When Hillary Clinton spoke at a private San Francisco fundraiser in 2004, an Associated Press reporter caught a particularly illuminating comment by Clinton about the 2001 tax cuts. "We're saying that for America to get back on track, we're probably going to cut that short and not give it to you," she said. "We're going to take things away from you on behalf of the common good."[1]

Her uncharacteristic frankness—perhaps reflecting the liberal audience or her possible ignorance of a reporter's presence there—allows for a penetrating view into Clinton's thinking on economic policy.

Clinton, in effect, was advocating raising taxes by undoing some of President Bush's tax cuts. Higher taxes, she argued, would "get America back on track," and serve "the common good." In Clinton's eyes, government redistribution—not private entrepreneurship—is the key to economic growth.

Her statement also revealed her view that cutting taxes is equivalent to the government giving something to taxpayers. This is a common left-wing axiom that assumes all wealth rightly belongs to the government. To the degree the government doesn't expropriate some of your money through taxes, it is *giving* you this wealth.

Clinton's vow to confiscate income from taxpayers on behalf of the "common good" further emphasized her preference for government control over private-owned wealth.

Clinton's socialistic beliefs, though rarely expressed so clearly, shine through in her activity in the Senate, where she has consistently voted against tax cuts while supporting higher government spending and strict regulation of industry. She has also displayed a particular affinity for federal subsidies in the name of "revitalization."

A Taxing Record

After Clinton assumed office in January 2001, she quickly faced the divisive issue of President Bush's tax cuts, which aimed to eliminate

ROLLCALL

Votes Against the Bush Tax Cuts

- On May 23, 2001, Clinton voted against a preliminary version of the Economic Growth and Tax Relief Reconciliation Act of 2001 (Vote #165).
- On May 26, 2001, Clinton voted against the final version of the Economic Growth and Tax Relief Reconciliation Act of 2001 (Vote #170).
- On May 15, 2003, Clinton voted against a preliminary version of the Jobs and Growth Tax Relief Reconciliation Act of 2003 (Vote #179).
- On May 23, 2003, Clinton voted against the final version of the Jobs and Growth Tax Relief Reconciliation Act of 2003 (Vote #196).

Votes Against Capital Gains Tax Cuts

- On May 21, 2001, Clinton voted against a temporary reduction of the maximum capital gains rate from 20 percent to 15 percent (Vote #115).
- On November 17, 2005, Clinton voted to raise capital gains taxes on wealthy individuals (Vote #333).
- On February 2, 2006, Clinton voted to repeal an extension of reduced tax rates for capital gains and dividends (Vote #8).
- On February 13, 2006, Clinton voted to allow the capital gains tax cuts to expire (Vote #15).

most of the marriage penalty, kill the estate tax, and reduce all income tax rates. Clinton steadfastly opposed the measures, whose passage would effectively revoke some of the tax increases approved by her husband in 1993. President Bush eventually pushed through significant tax relief, although Hillary and other like-minded senators somewhat watered down Bush's original proposals.

Senator Clinton opposed some tax cuts *candidate* Clinton had favored.

Hillary seemed to repudiate the estate tax (popularly known as the "death tax") during her 2000 Senate campaign, asserting, "You ought to be able to leave your land and the bulk of your fortunes to your children and not the government."[2]

APPARENTLY THEY DON'T WORK HARD OR PLAY BY THE RULES

At the liberal Take Back America conference in June 2006, Hillary inadvertently let loose a comical indictment of herself and her husband. She declared, "You know, my husband and I are often bewildered by the fact that it appears that the Republican majority and the president just can't do enough for us. Every time we turn around, we're getting another tax cut. And we keep looking at each other and saying, 'Wouldn't it be nice if people who worked hard and played by the rules got tax cuts?'"[3]

But once in the Senate, Clinton not only voted against President Bush's 2001 tax cut bill (H.R. 1836) that would have ended the estate tax; she also voted *for* a failed amendment to remove estate tax relief from the bill entirely.

The final version of H.R. 1836 suspended the estate tax for ten years instead of eliminating it. In June 2006, Clinton helped block a vote on a proposal by Senate Republicans to *permanently* repeal the estate tax. In sharp contrast to her campaign rhetoric, she defended her position by attacking the rich, claiming, "Repeal of the inheritance tax would have set aside $1 trillion so that the small fraction of millionaires and billionaires in this country would pay nothing when they transfer their huge estates to their heirs."[4]

These sentiments reflect Hillary's abiding belief in the government's duty to redistribute wealth. Her populist rhetoric, while popular with her party's left-wing base, ignores the reality that the richest Americans typically avoid the estate tax through clever estate planning, while the tax's onerous expense often prevents the perpetuation of family businesses from one generation to the next.

Hey, Big Spender

While opposing tax cuts, Clinton has supported hundreds of bills boosting federal spending by hundreds of billions of dollars.

Data from the National Taxpayers Union clarifies Clinton's proclivity toward big spending. During her first two years in office, Clinton sponsored or cosponsored 169 bills increasing spending by a total of $124 billion, while failing to sponsor or cosponsor a single bill to reduce spending.

In 2003 and 2004 Clinton grew even more generous with the taxpayers' dollars. She sponsored or cosponsored 211 bills to increase spending and just three bills to reduce it, yielding a total net cost of

$378 billion. This made Clinton the second most "expensive" senator during that time, according to the NTU.

Hillary's False Predictions

Since the passage of most of Bush's proposed tax cuts in 2001, Clinton has consistently argued that the president's fiscal policies are harming the economy.

In April 2003 she claimed, "There's no escaping the wrong-headed, very destructive economic policies that this administration has chosen to inflict on our country."[5] A month later Clinton warned the Senate, "We are in danger of being the first generation of Americans to leave our children worse off than we were."[6]

Hillary continued her jeremiads in January 2005, proclaiming that "the economy may be on the brink of collapse."[7] In July 2005 she further lamented, "We have not created one net new job in the last four years."[8]

With the benefit of hindsight, we now see the wild inaccuracy of Hillary's doomsday predictions. Under President Bush, the economy has enjoyed steady growth, including a 3.5 percent expansion in 2005,[9] the year that Clinton prophesized economic collapse. The Bureau of Labor Statistics found that five million new jobs were created in the past three years.

New York Blues

Clinton's plan for economic growth can be summed up in two words: *more government.*

During her campaign, Hillary Clinton promised to create 200,000 jobs in New York. Shortly after her election, she unveiled the centerpiece of her job-creation plan—a seven-piece legislative package called "New Jobs for New York."

EXPERTS REFUTE CLINTON'S ECONOMIC PESSIMISM

Prominent analysts vehemently dispute Clinton's gloomy claims about current economic growth rates, job creation, and the effectiveness of tax cuts.

"The U.S. economy isn't just producing jobs these days, it's also producing good jobs.... Management and professional occupations are employing 1.2 million more people this month than a year ago.... The construction industry continues to hammer out more than its share of new jobs." Mark Trumbull, "U.S. Economy's Latest Output: Better Jobs," ***Christian Science Monitor***, April 11, 2006.

"Critics continue to complain that President Bush's tax policies have only benefited the super-wealthy, but that would come as news to the five million Americans who were jobless before the 2003 tax cuts, and thus had no income, but now have a weekly paycheck." Editorial, "Help [Very Much] Wanted," ***Wall Street Journal***, April 10, 2006.

"The nation's booming economy, coupled with an astoundingly low 4.7 percent unemployment rate, is largely because of President Bush's tax cuts." "How Democrats Can Win Congress," ***Augusta Chronicle***, February 18, 2006.

CONTINUED

EXPERTS REFUTE CLINTON'S ECONOMIC PESSIMISM

CONTINUED

"In 2003 . . . those tax cuts [that were] much criticized, set off the boom that we are having today. . . . We're the largest growing economy among large economies in the world. We've created over nearly five million jobs and we've had a 4 percent plus growth rate. That would not have happened without the tax cuts." **Steve Forbes,** on CNBC's *Kudlow & Company*, March 20, 2006.

"[The dividend and capital gains tax cuts were] a really, really key thing for where the stock market's going from here, tells people what type of return they can expect on their investments, after tax return. Look at what happened to the market since then." ***Forbes*** magazine's Mike Ozanian, on CNBC's *Kudlow & Company*, March 1, 2006.

"The reality is that the Bush tax-cut incentives continue to propel economic growth. Just look at the outsized gains in retail sales, new home construction, and manufacturing production. Then look at the flood of new tax collections from the strong economy that has thrown off unexpected federal budget surpluses over the last two months." **Larry Kudlow,** "Big Ben's Good Beginning," National Review Online, February 17, 2006.

Three of the seven planks somehow aimed to create jobs by expanding New Yorkers' Internet access. First, Clinton proposed creating "technology bonds" to fund interest-free loans to state and local governments to improve their constituents' high-speed Internet access. Secondly, the plan called for a "Broadband Expansion Grant Initiative" to provide grants and loan guarantees directly to Internet companies to fund broadband networks in "under-served rural areas." Thirdly, Clinton sought to fund research by the National Science Foundation on expanding broadband technology in rural areas.

The plan's other four planks sought assistance for New York businesses. The first of these called for tax credits for small businesses that created jobs in smaller New York communities. The second plank proposed federal funding for "entrepreneurs who have good ideas but cannot afford lawyers and consultants to help them." Next, Clinton sought funding for the Commerce Department's Cooperative Extension Service—an agricultural program—to allow it to subsidize non-agricultural technologies. Finally, Clinton hoped to create "Regional Skills Alliances" between businesses, schools, and community colleges to provide more training for technology workers.

Clinton's efforts at job creation utterly failed. By March 2006, she had gotten only two of her centerpiece plan's seven measures signed into law; she notably failed to deliver any of her technology initiatives. Despite promising to create 200,000 jobs, during her tenure New York has lost a net 35,800 jobs, even while the nationwide economy has remarkably improved.

Clinton blamed New York's poor job performance on Republican economic policies (policies that had somehow successfully propelled the nationwide economy). She told the *Buffalo News*, "I think if we had continued the Clinton economic policies, I believe that there would have been a significant, a greater increase in employment, but you play the hand you're dealt. And we didn't win the election, and the other side got to implement their policies, which is, you know, largely tax cuts for the rich."

The Pork Platter

Hillary's belief that the government is the best agent at fostering economic growth is evident in the copious amounts of porkbarrel funds she has secured for state and local government projects aimed at stimulating New York's economy. The following are some of her gains in this realm:

2002

- **$350,000 for a regional survey by Albany's Center for Economic Growth**
  HILLARY'S EXPLANATION: "This funding will allow the Center for Economic Growth to audit the capital region's high-tech infrastructure and research and development assets and develop a master inventory of the resources available. Once the economic potential is determined, the analysis will be used as the basis for an action plan to guide future industry attraction efforts, workforce development, and infrastructure upgrades."

- **$4 million for Rochester's National Center for Excellence**
  HILLARY'S EXPLANATION: "The Center of Excellence—under the auspices of Corning, Kodak, Xerox—will work with two dozen academic institutions, including the University of Rochester, the Rochester Institute of Technology, and Monroe Community College to lock in New York's top spot in photonics, optics, and fiber optics. The federal funding will be used to build a state-of-the-art research and

development laboratory within which the photonics companies from across the state and the country will be able to work with world-class industrial and university scientists in bridging the gap between basic research and product manufacturing using photonics."

2003

- **$250,000 for the Metropolitan Development Authority of Syracuse and Central New York's "Vision 2010 Economic Development Strategy"**
  HILLARY'S EXPLANATION: "The three main goals of Vision 2010 are: the addition of 50,000 net new jobs by the year 2010, a

HILLARY'S MONEY TRAIL

Hillary Clinton's job-creation schemes seek to steer big tax dollars to technology and telecom firms. It is unsurprising, then, that she is the biggest recipient of campaign contributions from the entire communications/electronics sector for the 2006 Senate election, reeling in $1.2 million as of July 10, 2006, according to OpenSecrets.org. Within that sector, Clinton is the favorite of telecom firms, pulling in over $95,000 from that industry.

real wage growth of $4,000, a regional population increase of 1 percent per year with no erosion in the quality of life . . . the $250,000 in funding will be used to implement specific new projects and programs that will be recommended by consultants that the MDA has retained to update and revise Vision 2010."

- **$250,000 for Rural Opportunities, Inc.**
  HILLARY'S EXPLANATION: "Rural Opportunities, Inc.'s Upstate New York Community and Business Development Initiative aims to use the New Market Tax Credit program as the primary vehicle to attract private investment capital to grow and expand business opportunities within communities and neighborhoods throughout the upstate New York region."

2004

- **$250,000 for Broome-Tioga Works**
  HILLARY'S EXPLANATION: "The Broome-Tioga Workforce Development System, a unique partnership between Tioga and Broome Counties and the regional business community, is focused on helping businesses recruit and retain talented workers, assessing and responding to current and future workforce needs, and helping individuals obtain rewarding career opportunities. The $250,000 will go towards implementing their general economic development initiative program."

Central Planning in Energy

Amidst rising gas prices in June 2006, Clinton declared on *Larry King Live* that U.S. energy independence was "absolutely feasible," providing Congress created a "federal legal framework that encourages people to make the right decisions."[10]

Clinton failed to explain how the government would determine what decisions were "right" for people, or how the government would "encourage" such decisions. But the same distrust of market forces and impetus toward government control is seen in Clinton's dramatic plan for a "virtual revolution" in energy.

In May 2006, Clinton unveiled a proposal to the National Press Club to decrease the use of foreign oil by eight million barrels a day by 2025. The plan called for the creation of a $50 billion "strategic energy fund" by increasing taxes on oil companies. Clinton also suggested the government force oil firms to invest in unproven, renewable fuels like ethanol—a heavily subsidized plant-based fuel that benefits from protectionist trade policies, special tax breaks, direct subsidies, and a new federal Renewable Fuels Mandate.

Clinton, in short, sought to reallocate money from fuel that consumers *do* buy (oil) to fuel they *don't* buy (renewables).

Independent Petroleum Association of America chairman Mike Linn predicted Clinton's plan would simply chase oil companies out of the U.S. He noted, "If you have that type of tax, companies are going to sit back and say, 'Where is my best potential? Is my potential to drill domestically and pay this tax, or is my potential to go overseas and drill?"[11]

Republican senator James Inhofe of Oklahoma also condemned Clinton, who had opposed Inhofe's own proposal to sell some unused federal land to oil refineries. Instead of endorsing his market-based solution, Inhofe said, Clinton had "supported the Democrat alternative, which would essentially socialize refining capacity by placing the Environmental Protection Agency in charge of designing, constructing, and operating refineries."[12]

Clinton's plan was consistent with her tenacious opposition to any measure allowing oil companies to increase domestic drilling.

Human Events editor Terence P. Jeffrey noted, "she [Clinton] has opposed drilling in any part of the massive Artic National Wildlife Refuge. She has opposed any new drilling off our coasts. She has even opposed drilling for natural gas in New York's Finger Lakes National Forest, co-sponsoring a bill that would permanently ban such drilling."[13]

The federal government bans drilling in most of the Gulf of Mexico, except for an area off the coast of Louisiana. This ban leaves the U.S. oil supply vulnerable to a hurricane around the Louisiana coast. After Hurricane Katrina decimated this area in 2005, resulting in spiraling gas prices, Clinton rejected proposals to allow oil drilling in more diverse locations.

Ignoring the role played by federal drilling restrictions in limiting the oil supply and thus raising prices, Clinton blamed "big oil" for the post-Katrina spike in gas prices. "I want to go after oil companies and the oil speculators and the manipulators of money, because they're the ones who I think are really behind this," thundered Clinton. "I am tired of being at the mercy of people in the Middle East and elsewhere, and I'm tired frankly of being at the mercy of these large oil companies."[14]

Clinton's proposed remedy was consistent with her punitive approach to private business—she suggested the government impose "windfall" taxes on oil companies engaged in "price gouging."

The Green Cash Connection

Many of Bill Clinton's business partners stand to profit from the energy and environmental programs Senator Clinton supports. Bill's multimillion-dollar foundation has a focus area specifically devoted to "climate change."

On September 16, 2005, Senator Clinton spoke on a panel for her husband's first CGI conference titled "Promoting Prosperity with Climate Change Policy" and specifically called for the government to partner with non-profits to fight climate change.

Many major American corporations lobby for and stand to profit from policies limiting energy use, curbing carbon dioxide emissions, or otherwise addressing the issue of climate change—an issue with large uncertainties.

For example, Citigroup has invested $23 million in wind turbines and has also made significant investments in other renewable fuels. Clearly, this company stands to profit from government or business moves to promote renewable energy. Employees of Citigroup have contributed $239,050 to Mrs. Clinton's Senate runs.

Mrs. Clinton said at the CGI conference that the government needs "partners in the private and not-for-profit sector." Her record suggests that this means more subsidies for businesses that invest in renewable fuels or other efforts to reduce greenhouse gases.

Local Emissions

While opposing national policies that would decrease fuel prices like easing oil drilling restrictions, Hillary Clinton uses these high prices as an excuse to secure more porkbarrel money for her home state. Much of these funds come from the federal Low-Income Home Energy Assistance Program (LIHEAP), through which taxpayers subsidize the energy use of low-income households. Below is a listing of federal funds Clinton has acknowledged securing for energy purposes in New York:

- **January 24, 2004:** Clinton bragged that "New York will receive $36.77 million in emergency funds, more than any other state," from a $200 million LIHEAP allocation.
- **December 19, 2003:** After the Department of Health and Human Services gave New York nearly $143 in LIHEAP

funding, Clinton managed to gain an additional $46 million in additional federal funding for the state.

- **December 23, 2004:** Clinton applauded the release of $100 million in emergency low-income heating funds—$16.9 million of which went to New York—on top of the state's LIHEAP allocation.
- **November 9, 2005:** Clinton announced that the final energy and water spending bill for fiscal year 2006, which she helped write, would allocate $250,000 to a Dairy Waste Energy Program at New York's Clarkson University. The quarter million came on top of a separate $805,938 federal grant that Clinton had helped secure for the dairy waste program.

VRWC ACTION PLAN

Senator Clinton is a true believer in government control. By connecting the dots, the VRWC can destroy her attempts to position herself as a moderate.

#4 - THE PORKBARREL FILE

Specific spending items stuck in appropriations bills without prior authorization are called “earmarks” but are commonly known as “porkbarrel spending” -- or simply “pork.”

Almost all Washington lawmakers compete to deliver pork to their constituents, but Hillary Clinton has shown a special talent for it.

The Pork Dossier

Most federal spending programs are authorized by congressional committees before they are funded through appropriations bills. Unauthorized, targeted spending items are called "earmarks" or "pork." Earmarking allows individual lawmakers to micromanage the allocation of taxpayer dollars.

Earmarks are widely condemned as unfair—for example, should taxpayers in Toledo really have to pay for a bike trail in Buffalo? Another common criticism is that giving individual politicians control over billions of taxpayer dollars inevitably induces corruption. Hillary Clinton, however, has always been proud of her pork.

The following is a small sampling of earmarks supported by Senator Clinton, according to her online press archive:

2001

- $450,000 to revitalize the College Park neighborhood of Schenectady, including a recreation area
- $250,000 for a roof replacement, infrastructure upgrade, and disabled persons accommodations at the Lesbian and Gay Communities Services Center in New York City
- $200,000 to build pathways in Canandaigua's Lagoon Park

2002

- $3 million for Val-Kill's Eleanor Roosevelt Center for restoration work on historic buildings, gardens, trails, and a pond; conservation of collections' furnishings acquisitions; and creation of exhibit and auditorium space for visitor orientation

2003

- $550,000 for the "New York City Initiative: Music Educators for New York City" in cooperation with the VH1 music video network
- $720,000 to "replace a local motel that has been plagued by prostitution and other illegal activity with a Center for the Disabled" in Schenectady
- $250,000 for the Foothills Performing Arts Center to construct a 104,000-square-foot facility encompassing a grand lobby, 12,000-seat performing arts center, and a 300-seat black box theater
- $250,000 for a Binghamton indoor sports facility
- $250,000 to renovate the Auburn Schine Theater

2004

- $5 million for the "National Great Blacks in Wax" museum in Baltimore, Maryland
- $949,474 for the Grape Genetics Research and Grape Rootstock projects and Cornell's Geneva Research Park
- $2.5 million to fight Asian long-horned beetles
- $250,000 to develop an indoor sports field house in Vestal, New York
- $200,000 for the Mid-Hudson Children's Museum
- $250,000 to create "viable living and working space" for artists in Buffalo

2005

- $200,000 to double the size of the Stanley Theatre in Utica, New York; raise the roof; make all dressing rooms handicapped-accessible; modernize the theatrical equipment; and preserve the façade and interiors

- $12 million to protect the Montauk Lighthouse
- $805,938 for Clarkson University's dairy waste-to-energy project

2006

- $50,000 for the Golden Nematode project at Cornell University in Ithaca. The golden nematode (*Heterodera rostochiensis Wollenweber*) is, according to a press release from Clinton and Senator Charles Schumer, "a tiny worm that only attacks potato crops in New York State"

The Westchester County Cash

New York senators Hillary Clinton and Charles Schumer were jointly named "Porker of the Year" in 2005 by the spending watchdog group Citizens Against Government Waste. They earned the title for their extravagant abuse of a federal program called Community Development Block Grants (CDBG).

These are federal grants from the Housing and Urban Development Department (HUD) intended to address poverty and other serious community needs. But one of the program's primary beneficiaries had been Westchester County, New York—one of the richest areas in the country. The county also happens to encompass the town of Chappaqua, the site of the Clintons' official residence.

According to 2006 HUD data, the average single-person household income in Westchester County is $67,555 annually, while the median income for a family of four is $96,500. HUD assistant secretary Roy Bernardi testified to Congress in 2002 that the county boasted 2.1 times the national per capita income, but reeled in over $7 million in

THE TRANSCRIPT

"Today, New York has the largest gap between the rich and the poor of any state in the United States. Therefore, it is time for our friends in the rest of the country to return the favor and to change the way business is done in Washington and to give New York its fair share."

—Senator Clinton on *Larry King Live*, February 7, 2000

CDBG money.[1] In 2005, Westchester received $25,000 in CDBG funds for the construction of a music conservatory and another $500,000 grant for "streetscape improvements."

Westchester County is not the only part of New York to abuse CDBGs secured by the state's senators. A 2004 investigation by the *Buffalo News* found that the city of Buffalo had misspent over half a billion dollars in CDBG funds during the previous three decades.[2]

Buffalo, the paper discovered, had spent most of its aid "repaying the federal government for bad business loans and neighborhood agency employees, and less on housing and public improvement." The city spent an estimated $100 million to cover salaries and benefits for City Hall workers, compared to just $75 million for community-based organizations since the inception of the CDBG program.

Despite the program's obvious waste, both New York senators vehemently objected when President Bush proposed reducing the CDBG scheme and requiring cities to compete for grants. Schumer condemned Bush's plan as a "meat-axe approach,"[3] while Clinton extolled CDBGs as a "lifeline"[4] to New York.

VRWC ACTION PLAN

Senator Clinton can use her love of pork to win favors in New York, but nationwide, taxpayers will resent their dollars being used for her parochial purposes. The tension between local and national interests is one reason senators rarely move up to the White House. The VRWC must exploit this on a national level.

#5 - THE HEALTHCARE FILE

Hillary Clinton's maiden foray into national policymaking was a 1,342-page healthcare plan issued in 1993 that would have engulfed 14 percent of the U.S. economy. Despite the failure of "HillaryCare," as the plan became known, Clinton never abandoned her push for socialized medicine.

Medical Propaganda

In *It Takes a Village,* Hillary Clinton writes admiringly of a rural Indonesian healthcare system. The government-run neonatal care program that captured Hillary's attention had women bring their babies to be examined by healthcare providers on tables set up in an outdoor clearing.[1]

The program featured starkly collectivist elements. For example, "A large posterboard chart notes the method of birth control each family is using, so that women can compare problems and results."

Hillary was unperturbed by the program's lack of privacy. In fact, she proposed additional collectivist measures, most notably that the government broadcast medical advice instructing the masses on how to care for their children. She imagined:

> Radio and television stations could broadcast childcare tips between programs, songs, and talk-show diatribes . . . videos with scenes of common-sense baby care—how to burp an infant, what to do when soap gets in his eyes, how to make a baby with an earache comfortable—could be running continuously in doctors' offices, clinics, hospitals, motor vehicle offices, or any place where people gather and have to wait.

Not content with her dream of subjecting parents to a permanent orwellian medical propaganda campaign, Hillary advocated even greater government control over medicine. She praised systems that compel expectant mothers to participate in state-run medical programs as examples of her idealized "village." She wrote, "Examples of the village at work can be found in countries where national health care systems ensure access to pre- and postnatal care for mothers and babies. Some European countries, such as Austria and France, tie a mother's eligibility for monetary benefits to her obtaining regular medical checkups."

A Prescription for Government Meddling

In 2003, President Bush and the Republican Congress upset their conservative base by creating the largest new entitlement program since the Johnson presidency.

Hillary opposed the bill, on the grounds it was not comprehensive enough. She supported numerous amendments that would have enlarged the program and further increased government involvement in the dispensation of prescription drugs.

One of her amendments sought to order the National Institutes of Health to conduct and compile more drug studies, as well as to advise and inform patients and doctors about which drugs work best. The amendment was specifically aimed at increasing the government's role in medicine. Clinton defended it by noting, "While the FDA is responsible for determining safety and effectiveness of prescription

HILLARY'S MONEY TRAIL

The healthcare industry has been generous to Clinton. According to OpenSecrets.org, the sector has contributed over $2 million to Hillary throughout her brief career. Clinton has received the second-highest amount of donations from the health sector in the 2006 election cycle, pulling in $803,592 as of July 10, 2006.

drugs compared to a placebo, there is no government entity responsible for examining whether drug A is more effective at treating a particular condition than drug B."[2]

Republican senator Mike Enzi of Wyoming predicted that the measure "would end up as a tool for health care rationing by the bureaucrats in Washington." He warned, "This amendment would get the federal government even further into the business of making medical decisions. It would promote one-size-fits-all medicine."[3]

Universal Healthcare Starter Program

On March 8, 2006, Clinton announced that the Centers for Disease Control would give New York $75 million for first responders sickened or injured in the September 11 attacks.[4] The $75 million was part of a $125 million package Clinton secured for her state's first responders. These funds provide Clinton with unusual opportuni-

WHAT WILL COME BACK TO HAUNT HER

In an alarming example of her legislative deftness, Clinton managed to procure the $125 million for New York first responders from funds designated for victims of Hurricane Katrina. Clinton admittedly could not produce any studies or analyses justifying the $125 million figure, so her office issued a press release arguing: "any remaining funds should be used for the broader purpose of supporting the health and recovery of 9/11 responders." In other words, if $125 million was too much, she would find a use for the extra money.[5]

ties—the category of "first responders" is not precisely defined, giving Clinton broad discretion in spending the money.

Clinton used some of these funds to develop a program called the World Trade Center Medical Monitoring Program, which gives first responders medical advice and screenings before they respond to crisis scenes. Clinton is trying to expand this program into a national federally controlled healthcare system for first responders. She has already co-sponsored a Senate bill to create such a system.

David Prezant, the deputy chief medical officer for the Fire Department of New York, advocated the WTC Medical Monitoring Program's nationalization at the International Association of Fire Fighters legislative conference in April 2006, just a month after the program was first funded.

Prezant described the plan: "First responders, before arriving at a disaster site, would be able to receive health checks to ensure they can safely perform their duties" and "get answers for their questions about the risks they may face. And after they leave the disaster site, more medical checks could take place to ensure the workers receive the best care possible for any afflictions they may suffer as a result of their work."

Prezant, in other words, advocated a national plan to put the federal government in charge of the health and safety of firemen, policemen, and paramedics, as well as empower federal bureaucrats to advise first responders on health-related issues.

Unsurprisingly, Prezant is no impartial public servant. In November 2005, Prezant told New York's *Village Voice* "I am her [Clinton's] servant, damn right! The care and attention she has provided the fire department has been phenomenal."

"Care and attention" was apparently a reference to the millions of dollars in federal money Clinton has banked for New York's first responders.

HER SCARS

Clinton sometimes seems chastened by the failure of HillaryCare, remarking in a campaign ad, "A lot of people know I was involved in healthcare back in '93 and '94, and I still have the scars to show for it." But at other times she speaks with immense pride about her losing battle for socialized medicine. In response to her attempt to turn her failed healthcare scheme into a badge of honor, W. H. Von Dreele penned a short poem for *National Review* titled "Hillary's Past":

Like the spot Lady Macbeth
Famously tried to "out,"
Hillary's health history
Keeps tugging at her clout
Currently, her rhetoric
Re-casts it as a scar
Of the honorable type—
Which is har-dee-har

In Her Second Term

Clinton is showing signs that she will push for universal healthcare again in 2007. The *New York Times* observed in June 2006 that Hillary's "first major goal appears to be universal health care coverage for children, which she hopes to advance by expanding the State Children's Health Insurance Program, or SCHIP, an existing program for review in 2007."[6]

The *Times* reported: "'I have to do what the political reality permits me to do,' Mrs. Clinton said in a recent interview. She said that covering everyone remained her ultimate goal, but that Democrats would be fighting 'a lot of rear-guard actions' as long as Republicans controlled Congress."

Clinton's plan to expand SCHIP is clearly another step in her unyielding quest to introduce a European-style government-run healthcare system.

VRWC ACTION PLAN

Clinton is rarely candid about her desire for a national socialized healthcare plan. Americans are well aware of the downsides of such a program. We must remind the public of her 1993 efforts, and make it clear she has not given up on HillaryCare.

#6 - THE FAMILIES FILE

Senator Clinton holds a radical view of family life -- a view she works to promote through federal law. She stridently defends taxpayer funding of abortion and abortion on demand. However, she has deftly avoided taking a clear stance on homosexual marriage.

Hillary vs. the Traditional Family

When it comes to morality and family, Senator Clinton tends toward collectivism and government control, frequently saying: "There's no such thing as other people's children."

Human Events editor Terence P. Jeffrey parsed this phrase and examined Senator Clinton's policy proposals on the issue. Jeffrey listed her policy proposals: expand family and medical leave, fund daycare for working parents, improve child support enforcement, and offer subsidized housing for unwed mothers.[1]

Jeffrey wrote: "If, however, you are a family where 'child care' is provided by the natural mother (rather than a paid stranger), 'child support' is provided by a resident father (rather than a remote sperm donor), and every pregnant person is married, Hillary gives you zip."

FAMILY TIES

Mrs. Clinton introduces her grandmother to readers of her memoir, Living History, by describing her as "a weak and self-indulgent woman wrapped up in television soap operas and disengaged from reality."

Senator Clinton uses the tax code in a similar way. Jeffrey pointed out her promises to "fight any tax cut so big it would take us back to the bad old days" and to "fight for tax cuts to middle-income families to help with some of our biggest worries: deductions for college tuition, easing the marriage penalty, and a tax credit for the care of aging or disabled family members."

Jeffrey responded: "If, however, you are a family where the kids are too young or too old for college, where mom is an unpaid full-time homemaker (rather than a full-time highly paid lawyer), and where grandparents were prudent and frugal enough to save for their own retirement (because they realized what a rip-off Social Security is), Hillary not only gives you zip, she pledges to thwart the nondiscriminatory across-the-board tax cuts that are exactly what you need."

Jeffrey continues:

> Hillary pledges: "I'll be on your side in the fight against school vouchers that drain taxpayer dollars from our public schools." If, however, you do not send your children to government-run schools, where condoms are freely distributed, Malcolm X is mentioned more often than George Washington, and the Bible has been replaced by *Heather Has Two Mommies*, Hillary will make sure that every single penny you are forced to pay to support those public schools goes to transforming your neighbors' children—who do attend them—into aggressive ignoramuses and moral idiots.
>
> And Hillary pledges: "I'm more committed than ever to helping these children, to giving them the child care and the pre-school, the summer school, after-school, and mentoring programs they need." That means you will not only continue paying exorbitant local taxes so the public schools can corrupt the neighbor kids in first grade, but also more federal taxes, so

Hillary can corrupt them before that—and, if necessary, during summer vacation.

More Government Control

As a senator, Clinton has lived up to her campaign promises. She opposed marriage penalty relief and voted against expanding the child tax credit. She has consistently voted against reducing the marriage penalty, even though this provision as finally passed provided a larger tax cut—in absolute dollar terms—to a middle-class family who takes the standard deduction than to a millionaire couple.

Senator Clinton has voted against expanding the child tax credit, which allows families to reduce their tax bill for each dependent child, eleven times.

However, Senator Clinton does support marriage when that entails increasing government involvement in family life. She considers divorce a "public health issue" that demands government attention. Chapter Three of *It Takes a Village* says, "I admire the way the Parent Education Program in Columbus, Ohio, treats divorce as a public health issue because it constitutes a major life stress for 40 percent of American children and can put many children at risk for long-lasting difficulties that can derail their development." She wants the government to force couples to engage in "mandatory cooling-off periods, with education and counseling for partners" before being able to divorce.

The Gay Marriage Dodge

In June 2006 Senator Clinton voted against a constitutional amendment to ban gay marriage, but she has assiduously avoided making statements on the issue. When an Associated Press reporter pressed her, she refused to open up and instead assailed the amendment as part of "political machine of the White House and the Republican majority."[2]

ROLLCALL

Yes to the Marriage Penalty

- On April 5, 2001, Clinton voted against an amendment to the 2002 budget to allow for reducing the marriage penalty tax (Vote #79). Voted against the full budget that allowed for the marriage penalty cut (Vote #86).
- On May 10, 2001, Clinton voted against the final version of the budget, which included the marriage penalty cut (Vote #98).
- On May 23, 2001, Clinton voted against the tax cut bill, which reduced the marriage penalty (Vote #165).
- On May 26, 2001, Clinton voted against the final version of the tax cut, which reduced the marriage penalty (Vote # 170).

No to the Child Tax Credit

- On March 26, 2004, Clinton voted against extending the child tax credit through 2013 (Vote #106). She also voted against a sense of the Senate that the $1,000 child credit should be extended from 2011 through 2013 (Vote #108).

Since coming to Washington, Senator Clinton has remained so tight-lipped about her feelings on gay marriage that homosexual groups, historically big Hillary fans, have threatened to stop funding her.

Alan Van Capelle, executive director of the pro-gay Empire State Pride Agenda, circulated a memo in February 2006 to board members asking gays and lesbians to withhold funding to Clinton's Senate re-election campaign. The *New York Times* said the memo called Clinton a "complete disappointment" and criticized her for opposing gay marriage and supporting the Defense of Marriage Act (a federal law with very little reach). Capelle said he would not "lend my name and sell tickets" to a fundraiser for Senator Clinton. He argued that helping fundraisers for the senator would "actually hurt" homosexuals.[3]

Senator Clinton's awkward stance on this issue reflects a need to please her liberal base while not turning off culturally conservative voters—both in upstate New York and in non-coastal states she will need to carry in her presidential campaign. This tension compels her to remain as silent as possible on the issue.

Toward this end, Senator Clinton typically changes the subject as fast as she can, as she did at a fundraising luncheon in June 2006. The issue had reached a fever pitch on Capitol Hill, but she declined to talk about it, offering only, "When I travel around and speak with people whom I'm representing, they worry about everything from terrorism to gas prices to the cost of health care to energy independence."[4]

On the rare occasions when she does address the issue, her position is scattered and inconsistent. In December 2003 on CBS News, she said she opposed gay marriage, supported some form of civil unions, but was against the Federal Marriage Amendment (FMA) to the Constitution.

"I think it would be a terrible step backwards," she said. "It would be the first time we've ever amended the Constitution to deny rights to people." These words imply that she believes gay marriage is a right—yet she still opposes gay marriage.

When she talks to conservatives, Hillary says she personally opposes gay marriage, pointing to her support for the Defense of Marriage Act. The act became law by her husband's signature in 1996. It gives states the right to accept or deny same-sex marriages performed

SEND MY REGARDS TO BILL

After a video endorsement from Bill Clinton to the pro-gay Empire State Pride Agenda was shown at a dinner Mrs. Clinton appeared at, several audience members made comments about the weight Mr. Clinton had lost, rumored to be approximately thirty pounds. Mrs. Clinton laughed and said, "He's been working out. I hope you noticed." But apparently she hadn't had time to appreciate her husband's new trim figure in person, or even compliment him on it. She told them, "The next time you see him, tell him I noticed."

in other states and recognizes marriage as an act between a man and a woman for federal purposes.

Politics and Her Marriage

Hillary and Bill lack some credibility on family issues. Setting aside Bill's infidelity problems, the two do not appear to be the model couple. A *New York Times* article on May 23, 2006, found that, "Since the start of 2005, the Clintons have been together about fourteen days a month on average, according to aides who reviewed the couple's schedule." But in some months they see each other only one day. An aide told the *Times* in 2005 that Valentine's Day was the only day the couple spent time together in February.

The *Times* writer concluded, "Bill and Hillary Clinton have built largely separate lives—partly because of the demands of their distinct career paths and partly as a result of political calculations." One aide, who requested anonymity, said, "She [Mrs. Clinton] needs to be in her own separate orbit, so if something explodes in his world, she will at least have some space and distance to manage it."

The French Model

On page 211 of *It Takes a Village,* Senator Clinton lays out her ideal model of "adult authority."

Hillary asks her reader to imagine "a country in which all children between the ages of three and five attend pre-school in sparkling classrooms, with teachers recruited and trained as child care professionals. Imagine a country that conceives of child care as a program to 'welcome' children into the larger community and 'awaken' their potential for learning and growing."

This mystical land of Hillary's dreams, of course, is France.

Clinton wrote, "It may sound too good to be true, but it's not. When I went to France in 1989 as a part of a group studying the French child care system, I saw what happens when a country makes caring for children a top priority."

Clinton cheered a system that puts children in government-run schools "even before they reach the age of three" and fawned over their "modern and inviting" buildings with "bright and colorful" interiors. She then reflected, "It's no wonder that so many French parents—even mothers who do not work outside the home—choose to send their children to these government-subsidized centers."

She is resigned to the fact that the United States won't create a similar system because "the price for such generous social programs is felt across the board in higher taxes." She enviously writes, "What I do believe, however, is that the French have found a way of expressing their love and concern through policies that focus on children's needs during the earliest stages of life."

Once again, Hillary believes "love and concern" are reflected by big-government policies.

The School of Jihad

Hillary argues against school choice by warning us that vouchers will lead to a taxpayer-funded "School of Jihad."

Speaking to the South Bronx Overall Economic Development Corporation in early 2006, Hillary disparaged vouchers partly on the worry

THE TRANSCRIPT

"First family that comes and says 'I want to send my daughter to St. Peter's Roman Catholic School' and you say 'Great, wonderful school, here's your voucher,'" Clinton said. "Next parent that comes and says, 'I want to send my child to the school of the Church of the White Supremacist.' The parent says, 'The way that I read Genesis, Cain was marked, therefore I believe in white supremacy.... You gave it to a Catholic parent, you gave it to a Jewish parent, under the Constitution, you can't discriminate against me.' So what if the next parent comes and says, 'I want to send my child to the School of the Jihad?'...I won't stand for it."

—Senator Hillary Rodham Clinton, February 21, 2006,
at a breakfast of the South Bronx Overall
Economic Development Corporation

that vouchers enabling parents to send their children to parochial schools could be used to train children to become terrorists.[5]

The Clintons, however, sent their daughter to the Quaker private school Sidwell Friends in northwest D.C. without needing a voucher.

Cato Institute education expert Andrew Coulson points out that "under federal law no one would be permitted to open a school that advocates violence against the country." Thus vouchers could not go to a "School of Jihad."

Years earlier, however, Mrs. Clinton tried to play centrist on the school choice debate. In *It Takes a Village* she said she supported "choice among public schools" and talked about promoting "competition" among school systems, but subtly redefined "school choice." Instead of helping provide choice between public and private school, Clinton uses "school choice" to mean choice among public schools. She wrote "some critics of public schools urge greater competition among schools and districts, as a way of returning control from bureaucrats and politicians to parents and teachers. I find their argument persuasive, and that's why I strongly favor promoting choice among public schools."[6]

The Nominees

The loudest segment of the Democratic Party consistently opposes President Bush's nominees to the courts and to cabinet positions. Senator Clinton has worked alongside them in this battle.

Here's a list of nominations Senator Clinton opposed and some statements she made against the candidates:

Samuel A. Alito, Jr. to associate justice of the U.S. Supreme Court: Senator Clinton said if Alito became a justice, a "decade of progress would fall prey to his radical ideology, jeopardizing not only civil rights, civil liberties, health and safety, and environmental protections, but also the fundamental right to privacy."[7]

John Ashcroft to attorney general: Ashcroft had once said that African American judge Ronnie White was "pro-criminal," which led Clinton to charge that his remarks were "unjust, inflammatory, and bound to encourage racists in our society who are quick to believe the worst when they see someone of color" and that by doing so "Senator Ashcroft engaged in judicial profiling, and it was wrong." She also said his personal pro-life beliefs were "out of the mainstream."[8]

Janice Rogers Brown to U.S. Circuit Court judge for the District of Columbia: Clinton said Brown "truly sees the world in nineteenth-century terms" and said the White House was abusing power in supporting her nomination.[9]

Michael Chertoff to various positions: Senator Clinton cast the only "nay" vote against his confirmation to assistant attorney general in 2001 and again in 2003 when he became the Third Circuit Court of Appeals judge. Finally she voted in his favor when Bush appointed him to become the director of Homeland Security in 2004, rather than risk appearing soft on national defense.

Lester Crawford to Food and Drug Administration commissioner: Senator Clinton placed a hold on his nomination along with Senator Patty Murray until the FDA formally ruled on whether to make the morning-after pill available over the counter.

Dr. Andrew von Eschenbach to FDA commissioner: Senator Clinton blocked a vote along with Washington senator Patty Murray until the FDA decided about making the morning-after pill available over the counter.

Alberto Gonzales to attorney general

Porter J. Goss to director of Central Intelligence

Michael O. Leavitt to Environmental Protection Agency administrator

Gale Norton to secretary of interior: Senator Clinton said "Norton's support for self-regulation by polluters and limitations on corporate

THE TRANSCRIPT

Senator Clinton suggested in 2004 that women in Iraq have suffered major setbacks since the fall of Saddam Hussein's regime:

> I have been deeply troubled by what I hear coming out of Iraq. When I was there and met with women members of the national governing council and local governing councils in Baghdad and Kirkuk, they were starting to express concerns about some of the pullbacks in the rights they were given under Saddam Hussein. . . . On paper, women had rights. He was an equal opportunity oppressor, but on paper, women had rights. They went to school, they participated in the professions, they participated in government and in business; as long as they stayed out of his way, they had considerable freedom of movement."

A. Yasmine Rassam, the director of international policy at the Independent Women's Forum and a native-born Iraqi, slammed Senator Clinton's rhetoric. Rassam said:

> Much of the antiwar propagandists' defense of Saddam as a champion of women's rights rests on his willingness to allow women to vote (for him), drive cars, own property, get an education, and work.

CONTINUED

THE TRANSCRIPT

CONTINUED

What they choose to ignore, however, is the systematic rapes, torture, beheadings, honor killings, forced fertility programs, and declining literacy rates that also characterized Saddam's regime. A few examples can only begin to illustrate the cruelty and suffering endured by thousands of Iraqi women. One torture technique favored by Saddam's henchman and his sons involved raping a detainee's mother or sister in front of him until he talked. In Saddam's torture chambers, women, when not tortured and raped, spent years in dark jails. If lucky, their suckling children were allowed to be with them. In most cases, however, these children were considered a nuisance to be disposed of; mass graves currently being uncovered contain many corpses of children buried alive with their mothers.

responsibility for environmental damage, combined with her failure to enforce clean air and clean water laws as a state attorney general, lead me to conclude she will seek to limit, evade, and perhaps even subvert the tremendous responsibilities that reside in the office of the secretary of interior."[10]

Priscilla Owen to U.S. Circuit Court judge for the Fifth Circuit

John G. Roberts, Jr. to chief justice of the United States: Senator Clinton would not vote for him "despite John Roberts's long history of public service" because she did not believe "the judge has presented his views with enough clarity and specificity for me to in good conscience cast a vote on his behalf." Her public statement concluded that "My desire to maintain the already fragile Supreme Court majority for civil rights, voting rights, and women's rights outweighs the respect I have for Judge Robert's intellect, character, and legal skills."[11]

Michael Hayden to director of Central Intelligence: Senator Clinton opposed him because, "I believe there are unanswered questions about whether he will exercise the independence and judgment necessary to be an effective CIA director in an administration that has rejected contrary views."[12]

Brett Kavanaugh to U.S. Court of Appeals: Clinton issued no statement explaining her vote against Kavanaugh. He served as one of independent counsel Ken Starr's top aides, investigated the death of Clinton's former law partner Vince Foster, who died in a controversial suicide, and also investigated the sexual relationship between Mrs. Clinton's husband and Monica Lewinsky.

The Abortion Capital

Senator Clinton has attempted to portray herself as moderate on abortion, supposedly aiming to reduce the number of abortions. She frequently repeats her husband's line that abortion should be "safe, legal, and rare." However, she works for unlimited legal, and even subsidized, access to abortion on demand.

In an official statement on June 13, 2006, Clinton said, "Let us unite around the common goal of reducing the amount of abortions, not by making them illegal as many are attempting to do or overturning *Roe* v. *Wade* and undermining the constitutional protections that decision provided, but by preventing unwanted pregnancies in the first place through education, contraception, accessible health care services, empowering women to make decisions."[13]

But Senator Clinton has apparently failed in this effort in her home state. *New York* magazine called the Empire State the "Abortion Capital of America" in late 2005. The magazine reported: "In America, one of every ten abortions occurs in New York, and in New York, seven of every ten abortions are performed in New York City. In absolute terms, there are more abortions performed on minors, more repeat abortions, and more late abortions (over twenty-one weeks) in New York City than anywhere else in the country. In parts of the city, the ratio of abortions to births is one to one."

The piece continues, "In New York, Medicaid treats abortion no differently than any other health issue. But in twenty-nine states, the

WHAT HILLARY DOESN'T WANT US TO KNOW

Veteran reporter Robert Novak deflated the pro-contraception argument by Senators Reid and Clinton by digging deeper into the information they offered up in defense of taxpayer-funded contraception. Senators Clinton and Reid said, "a recent analysis by the nonpartisan Guttmacher Institute revealed that South Dakota is one of the most difficult states for low-income women to obtain contraceptives." Novak examined Guttmacher's files and reported in his column, "The Alan Guttmacher Institute reports that California spends more than three times as much on contraception as South Dakota for each woman who requests such services. However, California's rate of abortion per 1,000 women is 31.2 percent, nearly six times as high as South Dakota's 5.5 percent."[14]

WHAT WILL COME BACK TO HAUNT HER

Senator Clinton also voted against the "Unborn Victims of Violence Act," a bill that would charge violent offenders with two crimes in attacks made on pregnant women in which an unborn child was harmed. (March 25, 2005; Vote #63)

program is barred from funding abortions in most cases except rape, incest, or to save a woman's life. The prohibition is most effective of all state laws in preventing abortions."

In spring 2006 Senator Clinton teamed up with nominally pro-life Senate Minority Leader Harry Reid and pushed to increase federal funding to abortion providers such as Planned Parenthood in order to "increase awareness" about unintended pregnancies.[15]

Senator Clinton co-wrote an editorial with Reid titled, "Abortion Debate Shuns Prevention." The piece said, "As two senators on opposite sides of the abortion debate, we recognize that one side will not suddenly convince the other to drop its deeply held beliefs. And we believe that, while disagreeing, we can work together to find common ground."

The "common ground," was, once again, increased government—in this case government programs to promote contraception. The Prevention First Act, as they named it, would increase accessibility and "awareness and understanding" of emergency contraception, the senators argued. They aimed to ensure that sex education programs have medically accurate information about contraception and "end insurance discrimination against women." In other words, she would force all insurers and employers who offer insurance to cover the cost of contraception as healthcare.

Ramesh Ponnuru writes in *The Party of Death*: "The Democratic Party doesn't just support *Roe*; it also supports taxpayer funding. The party's 2004 platform stated: 'Because we believe in the privacy and equality of women, we stand proudly for a women's right to choose, consistent with *Roe* v. *Wade*, and regardless of her ability to pay.'"

Clinton has co-sponsored the Freedom of Choice Act. Co-sponsor Senator Barbara Boxer of California says if *Roe* were ever reversed, this bill would "supercede any law, regulation, or local ordinance that impinges on a woman's right to choose. That means a poor woman cannot be denied the use of Medicaid if she chooses to have an abortion." In other words, taxpayers would be forced to fund the abortion of an unborn child.

The Record Speaks for Itself

On March 12, 2003, Senator Clinton took to the Senate floor to oppose a bill that would outlaw partial-birth abortion, a procedure in which a late-term fetus is partly delivered and then aborted.

Below is her commentary, quoted from the congressional record, followed by a colloquy later on between her and pro-life Republican senator Rick Santorum. In the colloquy, Senator Clinton seems to imply that disabled unborn children ought to have less protection than fully healthy unborn children:

THE TRANSCRIPT

CLINTON: I am also concerned about some of the visual aids that have been used by some of my colleagues. They are as deceptive as they are heartbreaking. Because what do they show? They show a perfectly formed fetus, and that is misleading. Because if we are really going to have this debate, then we should have a chart that demonstrates the tragic abnormalities that confront women forced with this excruciatingly difficult decision. Where are the swollen heads? Where are the charts with fetuses with vital organs such as the heart and the lungs growing outside the body? Why would we choose not to demonstrate the reality of what confronts the women I know, women who come with medical diagnoses that have said the brain in the head is so swollen that the child, the fetus, your baby, is basically brain-dead?

* * *

SANTORUM: So I suggest to the senator that those in the abortion industry themselves say this is the typical procedure on the typical baby. There may be—and there are—a small number of cases that are late-term where you find out the child within the womb has a fetal abnormality and may not live. I just suggest—and you used the term—where is the brainless head? Where are the lungs outside the body? I will just say I will be happy to put a child with a disability up there. But, frankly, I don't see the difference in my mind—and I am not too sure the public does—with respect to that being any less of a child.

CONTINUED

THE TRANSCRIPT

CONTINUED

It is still a child, is it not? Maybe it is a child that is not going to live long, but do we consider—

CLINTON: Will the senator yield?

SANTORUM: In a moment. Do we consider a child that may not live long, or may have an abnormality, to be less of a child? Is this less of a human because it is not perfect? Have we reached the point in our society where because perfection is so required of us, that those who are not perfect don't even deserve the opportunity to live for however long they are ticketed to live in this country?

Are we saying we need these kinds of infanticides to weed out those who are not going to survive or those who are not perfect, and that somehow or another we have to have a method available that we only allow perfect children to be born? If that is the argument, I am willing to stand here and have that debate. If that is what you want us to show, I am willing to stand and show that.

I suggest this is the typical abortion that goes with partial-birth. That is exactly what the industry says is the case. If the senator would like me to find a child that has a cleft palate, I can do that. That doctor from Ohio performs a lot of abortions. He says he did nine in one year because of that. If she would like me to show a case of spina bifida, I can do that. That may be a reason someone has to have a late-term abortion.

I would be happy to show those, but those are the exception rather than the rule, and I think it is imperative... upon us to present the standard, the predominant case in which partial-birth

CONTINUED

THE TRANSCRIPT

CONTINUED

abortions are done, and that is what we are doing. I will be happy to yield for a question.

* * *

CLINTON: Does the senator's legislation make exceptions for serious life-threatening abnormalities or babies who are in such serious physical condition that they will not live outside the womb?

SANTORUM: No, if—

CLINTON: That is the point.

SANTORUM: I understand the senator's point. I guess my point in rebuttal is that if you want to create a separation in the law between those children who are perfect and those children who are not—

CLINTON: No—

SANTORUM: Please, let me finish. If a child is not perfect, then that child can be aborted under any circumstances. But if that child is perfect, we are going to protect that child more. I do not think the Americans with Disabilities Act would fit very well into that definition. The Americans with Disabilities Act—of which I know the senator from Iowa has been a great advocate, and I respect him greatly for it—says we treat all of God's children the same. We look at all—perfect and imperfect—as creatures of God created in his image.

What the senator from New York is asking me to do is separate those who are somehow not the way our society sees people as

CONTINUED

THE TRANSCRIPT

CONTINUED

they should be today and put them somewhat a peg below legal protection than the perfect child. I hope the senator is not recommending that because I think that would set a horrible precedent that could be extrapolated, I know probably to the disgust of the senator from Iowa, certainly to me.

No, I do not have an exception in this legislation that says if you are perfect, this cannot happen to you; but if you are not perfect, yes, this can occur. The senator is right, I do not.

CLINTON: To respond, if I could, to the senator from Pennsylvania, my great hope is that abortion becomes rarer and rarer. I would only add that during the 1990s, it did, and we were making great progress. These decisions, in my view, have no place in the law, so they should not be drawing distinctions in the law. This ought to be left to the family involved.

The very fact the senator from Pennsylvania does not have such a distinction under any circumstances, I think, demonstrates clearly the fallacy in this approach to have a government making such tremendously painful and personal and intimate decisions.

SANTORUM: I certainly respect the difference of opinion the senator and I have on the underlying issue of abortion. Again, I think people can disagree on that. I, frankly, do not agree there should be a difference between children who are "normal," in society's eyes—I do not know what that means anymore, what a society sees as normal—and those who happen to have birth defects, severe or not. I do not believe we should draw distinctions.

CONTINUED

THE TRANSCRIPT

CONTINUED

CLINTON: If the senator will yield for one final point, I want the record to be very clear that I value every single life and every single person, but if the senator can explain to me how the U.S. government, through the criminal law process, will be making these decisions without infringing upon fundamental rights, without imposing onerous burdens on women and their families, I would be more than happy to listen. But based on my experience and my understanding of how this has worked in other countries, from Romania to China, you are about to set up—

PRESIDING OFFICER: The senator from Pennsylvania has the floor.

SANTORUM: To liken a ban on a brutal procedure such as partial-birth abortion to the forced abortion policies of China is a fairly substantial stretch, and I do not accept that as an analogy. I do not think it holds up under any scrutiny.

With respect to the other issue, let the record speak for itself.

VRWC ACTION PLAN

Senator Clinton's views on abortion and the family are far outside the mainstream of American society. Bringing these views to the public's attention will weaken her ability to reach outside her liberal base.

#7 - THE MEDIA FILE

Control of information is central to the Clintons' political strategies. Hillary is perhaps the most tight-lipped senator, and has suggested government control of Internet content. Meanwhile, the couple aggressively collects information about other individuals.

Senator Clinton's Tight-Lipped Behavior

On Capitol Hill, where she works, Senator Clinton's efforts to protect herself from the media are unrivaled. Despite being such a high-profile senator, she rarely schedules press conferences and avoids the media stakeouts where reporters approach members with their questions and conduct quick, impromptu, "hallway interviews" in designated areas in the Capitol.

Most senators are accessible on Capitol Hill and regularly chat with reporters on their way to make a statement on the Senate floor or while walking from their offices to the Capitol for a roll call vote. It is not unusual to see Senator Trent Lott (R-MS) joking with journalists outside the Senate chamber long after media stakeouts or weekly policy luncheons have ended, or to find Minority Leader Harry Reid (D-NV) fraternizing with reporters while waiting for an elevator.

Hillary, as always, does things differently. Reporters have learned not to approach Senator Clinton in the halls of the Capitol. Experienced journalists have found that she answers nearly all on-the-spot questions with a variation of "I don't know"—a safe answer for her that renders the interviews useless, and prevents coverage of her views on any issues on which she has not sought coverage.

After a vote she breezes past reporters to a car waiting outside, avoiding any interviews. Clinton is not impolite, but makes it very clear she is unwilling to chat. When this writer asked her if she would use any of her personal money for her campaign (see the Foreign Money File), she completely avoided eye contact with me, although we were only a few inches from each other. Other reporters stood watching, wondering if this would be a rare occasion to get a few quotes from her.

Not only did she not answer the question, she didn't even offer a greeting. She continued walking steadily to her car. Senator Clinton

A DIFFERENT LIGHT

When Senator Clinton does schedule press conferences on Capitol Hill, they are often held in the Lyndon B. Johnson room, not the Senate Radio and TV Gallery. Instead of the harsh fluorescent lighting in regular gallery, the LBJ room is softly lit with chandeliers, sure to cast the senator in a better light.

kept her eyes straight ahead, coolly slipped on a pair of sunglasses, and said, "Oh, I have no idea."

This behavior is not normal for a senator. Reporters often wait at approved "stakeouts" for senators to pass by and briskly flag down a relevant lawmaker for a few questions. Most of the senators seem to enjoy it this, as communicating with the media is a key part of their job.

Other senators, such as Senator John McCain (R-AZ) or Senator Joe Biden (D-DE), are notorious for happily chatting up the media.

A reporter working for a conservative publication such as *Human Events* will find some liberal lawmakers unwelcoming (especially Senator Dick Durbin of Illinois), but this certainly is not standard practice. This author has had many very pleasant exchanges with most Democratic senators, particularly Senator Dianne Feinstein

(D-CA), whom our publication frequently criticizes. She never hesitates to explain her positions to me, even though I work for the "other side."

Clinton has none of this openness. Most lawmakers, after giving prepared statements, engage reporters in a lengthy question and answer period. Frequently, senators or congressmen stay until all questions are exhausted.

Not Hillary. She reliably ends the conference after only a few questions. Then her aides herd her away, inserting themselves between any persistent reporter and the senator, advising that you call her office for more information—a call that is likely to never be returned.

Hillary is steadfast in staying on message and avoiding unrehearsed answers, even when facing the most benign questions. When asked her favorite book (a question to which most senators originally answered "The Bible"), Clinton demurred. "Oh, I couldn't possibly answer that right now," she said. "My office will get back to you."

I heard one journalist sigh as she gathered her things to go Clinton's office for an interview because, as she remarked to her friend, "she'll just filibuster her way out of anything."

Clinton rarely goes anywhere on Capitol Hill without a pack of aides and her Secret Service guards. Usually, there are two officers walking near her—one a few feet in front and another just behind.

Lucky for Clinton, the mainstream media have given her many free passes. Unlucky for Senator Clinton, the visceral reaction many Americans have toward her helped spur a new media. Hillary and Bill—and their lies about the Monica Lewinsky affair—were perhaps the first victims of the blogsosphere.

Since then, the media can be seen as divided nicely into two competing camps: those who seek to protect Clinton from herself, and those who wish to expose her for what she really is—that is, the mainstream media and the alternative media, respectively.

The Code Pink Incident

Senator Clinton has demonstrated a pattern of avoiding media scrutiny by using security and Secret Service forces to keep reporters away.

At the Take Back America conference in June 2006, Clinton was protected from liberal antiwar protesters. Medea Benjamin, co-founder of antiwar feminist group Code Pink, said Senator Clinton's forces squelched Code Pink's efforts to protest what they called Hillary's pro-war record.

On the Code Pink website, Benjamin quoted her colleague and Code Pink co-founder Gael Murphy:

> Fearing that Code Pink would openly confront Clinton on her pro-war policy, the organizers of Take Back America entered into negotiations with Code Pink. . . . They pleaded with us not to protest her keynote breakfast address . . . . Instead we were told we could distribute flyers explaining Hillary's pro-war position inside and outside the hotel, and we would be called on to ask her the first question after the speech. We agreed.[1]

This arrangement was abandoned. Murphy said that morning, "burly security guards blocked us and informed us that it was a private event—that we were not welcome—and they escorted us out of the building. We telephoned the conference staff who then told us that we couldn't enter the hotel, couldn't leaflet the event, the hallways—anywhere. They went back on their word and tried to quash even peaceful, respectful dissent."

Some of the Code Pinkers did get into the event, but could not ask Senator Clinton any questions, because she decided not to take any. These few dissenters stood on their chairs, held out antiwar signs, and shouted, "What are YOU going to do to get us out of Iraq?" They were pulled down and their banner reading, "Listen Hillary: Stop Supporting the War" was taken away.

Another Code Pink cohort, Ann Wright, said leaflets that supported Clinton's primary opponent, antiwar Jonathan Tasini, were also seized.

This heavy-handed squashing of dissent strikes a contrast with the words of young Hillary Rodham, whose famed Wellesley College commencement address praised the "indispensable task of criticizing and constructive protest."

Senator Clinton offered no apologies to Code Pink, nor did she rebuff the conference's organizers for their actions.

Editing the Internet

Hillary's efforts to control the flow of information about her have extended into the Internet. In 1998, websites such as the Drudge

PRESS CORRAL

"Folks, there's security—and then there's New York senator Hillary Rodham Clinton-style security," said unimpressed *San Francisco Chronicle* political writer Carla Marinucci after Clinton headlined at a fundraiser at the St. Regis Hotel in July 2006. Marinucci described Clinton's media outreach as an "unusual corralling" of reporters who were told there would be "press availability" at the event. Not so, said Marinucci. Instead, "reporters were kept at bay in a 'safe' press room, and security ordered them to stay inside and away from doors—meaning they were barred from even seeing, much less hearing, her comings and goings," allegedly due to security reasons.[2]

Report were chiefly responsible for the publication and dissemination of information about Bill Clinton's sexual affairs, particularly with Monica Lewinsky.

During that time, Mrs. Clinton held a little-noticed briefing and forthrightly expressed her wish to "edit" the Internet.

In 1997, President Clinton announced his wife would head the "White House Millennium Program" that included an Internet-focused plan to create a "national digital library." The president even discussed the Millennium Program in his 1998 State of the Union Address as an effort to "promote America's creativity and innovation and to preserve our heritage and culture into the twenty-first century." President Clinton proposed "a public-private partnership to advance our arts and humanities."

Mrs. Clinton held a press conference on the initiative in which she suggested that the program would examine government regulation and censorship of the Internet.

Hillary said the White House "didn't have a clue about what we're going to do legally, regulatorily, technologically" about the Internet. She told reporters "there are a number of serious issues without any kind of an editing or gate-keeping function [on the Internet]."[3]

Clinton supporter Greg Papadopoulos from Sun Microsystems, a company managing Internet outreach for the Millennium Project, gave an elaborate presentation before Hillary's speech. Papadopoulos praised the Internet for democratizing information dissemination, saying:

> The information era is something very profound. That both reporting and publishing about anything has become really cheap to do. It's durable, it's pervasive. And I think it's fundamentally democratic.... Text, video, pictures, audio—as recorded—it really has an indefinite life, because you can copy

it digital. Once it's out on the Net, too, you can't take it back. So it's there.

It was in the light of these comments that a reporter questioned Mrs. Clinton on how the White House viewed the Internet's decentralizing effects. Below is portion of the briefing taken directly from US Newswire's transcript of the event.

The editors at Internet publication Wired.com and the *San Francisco Examiner* found the First Lady's comments upsetting. Wired wrote that Mrs. Clinton was looking for a new way to "deal with the Internet" because of her embarrassment over "White House sex scandal stories on the web."[4]

THE TRANSCRIPT

REPORTER: I just wanted to ask you about something that Greg said. He's obviously an Internet enthusiast. But when he talked about some of the aspects of the system—the fact that you could say something and you can't take it back, how it's so available to everyone and instantaneous, he's raised some issues that have been issues for us in the last few weeks in our business. And I wonder if you think that this new media is necessarily an entirely good thing. And also, as somebody who has been through this crucible, in the next millennium how would you like to see this new and ever more interesting—(laughter)—handled of things like the issues like the personal lives of public figures.

MRS. CLINTON: Well, Kathy, I think that's one of these issues . . . that we're going to have to really think hard about. And I think that every

CONTINUED

THE TRANSCRIPT

CONTINUED

time technology makes an advance—when you move to the railroad, or you move to the cotton gin, or you move to the automobile, or the airplane, and now certainly as you move to the computer and increasing accessibility and instantaneous information on the computer, we are all going to have to rethink how we deal with this, because there are always competing values. There's no free decision that I'm aware of anywhere in life, and certainly with technology that's the case.

As exciting as these new developments are—and I think Greg's enthusiasm is shared broadly by Americans and people around the world—there are a number of serious issues without any kind of editing function or gate-keeping function. What does it mean to have the right to defend your reputation, or to respond to what someone says?

There used to be this old saying that the lie can be halfway around the world before the truth gets its boots on. Well, today, the lie can be twice around the world before the truth gets out of bed to find its boots. I mean, it is just beyond imagination what can be disseminated. So I think we're going to have to really worry about this, because it won't be just public elected officials. We've seen some cases where somebody who had a grudge against a girl's mother because the family wouldn't let him date her put out on the Internet that the family were child abusers. Totally private people, never stuck their toe in public life. It can be done to anybody, and it can get an audience, and it can create a falsehood about somebody. And

CONTINUED

THE TRANSCRIPT

CONTINUED

certainly it's multiplied many times over if you happen to be in public life.

I don't have any clue about what we're going to do legally, regulatorily, technologically—I don't have a clue. But I do think we always have to keep competing interests in balance. I'm a big probalance person. That's why I love the founders—checks and balances; accountable power. Anytime an individual or an institution or an invention leaps so far out ahead of that balance and throws a system, whatever it might be—political, economic, technological—out of balance, you've got a problem, because then it can lead to the oppression people's rights, it can lead to the manipulation of information, it can lead to all kinds of bad outcomes which we have seen historically. So we're going to have to deal with that. And I hope a lot of smart people are going to—

REPORTER: Sounds like you favor regulation.

MRS. CLINTON: Bill, I don't know what—that's why I said I don't know what I'm in favor of. And I don't know enough to know what to be in favor of, because I think it's one of those new issues we've got to address. We've got to see whether our existing laws protect people's right of privacy, protect them against defamation. And if they can, how do you do that when you can press a button and you can't take it back. So I think we have to tread carefully.

REPORTER: One of the balances, though, in this new digital age is that you can have direct communication. You're celebrating that tonight—people can log on from anywhere. In that spirit, have you

CONTINUED

THE TRANSCRIPT

CONTINUED

thought any more about a direct and frank conversation by the president with the country about these allegations?

MRS. CLINTON: I'm not going to add anything to what the president has already said. And I think that any of you who think hard about this issue would have to agree that he's taken the right position. So I'm not going to add to that.

REPORTER: Do you think this will be indefinite, Mrs. Clinton? I mean, is there any sense that at some point he might—

MRS. CLINTON: As I said when I was on television a few weeks ago, I just wish everybody would take a deep breath. We've already seen how so much of this charge and countercharge does not withstand the scrutiny of much attention at all. And I don't anticipate that this will evaporate, but I anticipate that it will slowly dissipate over time by the weight of its own insubstantiality. And I think some of the developments of the last week or two should certainly give anybody pause about what is really going on here. Thank you very much, folks.

The *Examiner*'s Rebecca Eisenberg scolded, "It's not the Internet that needs rethinking, the Internet works fine. What needs rethinking is the drive toward closing gates, when what we need do is open them. We don't need government regulation or censorware in schools to help us find the truth.... We have a gate-keeping function already, our ability to decide for ourselves. We also have an 'editor,' a chance to disagree."[5]

Airbrushing Her Critics

In 2001, shortly after the terrorist attacks on New York City, media giant Viacom saved Senator Clinton from embarrassment by editing a live broadcast where Senator Clinton was booed offstage by a crowd of New York police and firemen in 2001.

When Senator Clinton took the stage at an October 21 appearance at the Concert for New York City, Matt Drudge reported that "VH1 cameras captured firemen and police wildly booing" her and that "anti-Clinton slurs spread and intensified throughout the Garden, with many standing near the stage lobbying profanities. 'Get off the stage! We don't want you here!' shouted one cop a few feet from the podium."[6]

Author Richard Poe of *Hillary's Secret War* watched the live broadcast and recounted the real-time Internet coverage of the program in his book. "As Hillary approached the podium," Poe wrote, "the audience erupted in boos, jeers, and catcalls, so clearly audible on our television that my wife and I turned in amazement...the jeers and catcalls came through loud and clear."[7]

The conservative blogs and message boards immediately exploded with discussion of this reaction, and soon the whole Internet was a abuzz. When Viacom rebroadcast the concert on Christmas Day that year, however, the anti-Clinton backlash had completely disappeared. Instead "thanks to the magic of digital editing" Poe wrote, "applause and cheers greeted Hillary as she walked onstage. Across America, every video and DVD on sale featured the same doctored version of the concert."

The Viacom-Hillary Cash Connection

This was not the first time Viacom had aided Hillary. At the beginning of the year, Viacom's publishing house, Simon & Schuster, extended the senator-elect an $8 million advance to write her memoir *Living History*.

WHAT HILLARY DOESN'T WANT YOU TO KNOW

Days before cops and firemen booed Clinton offstage at the Concert for New York City, a Ford conversion van rushing to deliver the senator to a fundraiser injured a police officer while blowing past a security checkpoint at Westchester County Airport. Three officers manning the station shouted at the van to stop, but their calls went unheeded. Officer Ernest Dymond was later taken to the hospital to have bruises examined, which he incurred when he slammed his shoulder into the van. "I didn't know if we had a terrorist," said Dymond. At the time, just over a month after the 9/11 attacks, the Westchester Airport was on a high security alert. Hillary's driver, a U.S. Secret Service agent, was talking on his cell phone and failed to take notice of the checkpoint. Dymond said, "And once I found out who he was, I was even more agitated that he, of all people, should have known." Dymond said Senator Clinton offered no apology for the mishap.[8]

The timing of her contract was controversial, as Clinton signed the deal just days before being sworn in as a senator. Senate ethics rules permit book advances that are "usual and customary," but the freshman senator's whopping $8 million deal was clearly unusual and uncustomary.

The Congressional Accountability Project wrote a letter to Clinton questioning whether the deal would influence her to favor Viacom within the course of her duties as a senator. CAP's letter read:

> Given Viacom's extensive efforts to affect the outcome of numerous matters pending before the Senate and federal government, if you accept the $8 million book advance from Simon & Schuster, you may violate Senate rules regarding conflicts of interest, which mandate 'no member, officer, or employee shall engage in any outside business or professional activity or employment for compensation which is inconsistent or in conflict with the conscientious performance of official duties'... the sheer size of your $8 million book advance raises questions about whether you and Senate processes may be affected by large cash payments from a major media conglomerate. This book contract, with its uniquely lavish advance for an elected official, may be, in fact, a way for that corporation to place money into your pockets, perhaps to curry favor with you.[9]

Senator Clinton's book deal was eventually approved by the Ethics Committee, and her attorney was quick to defend her to the *New York Daily News* by pointing out Clinton did not receive her entire advance upfront, but "only" $2.66 million at signing. The rest of the payments were made over the course of several years.[10]

Senator Clinton's financial disclosure reports indicate that while royalties earned from *It Takes a Village, An Invitation to the White House*, and *Dear Socks, Dear Buddy* are donated to charity, she keeps everything from her *New York Times* bestseller *Living History*.

The Database

While assiduously trying to control information about *themselves*, the Clintons are extraordinary at collecting information about everybody else. A recent effort by Clinton allies appears to be the latest push in an ongoing project of the Clintons to form an unprecedented

PORK RERUN

Citizens Against Government Waste nailed Senator Clinton for fighting for a $90 million program to research the effects of television viewing and other media on children. CAGW president Tom Schatz said, "This proposal is just one expensive rerun. For decades this issue has been studied to death, always yielding the same results."[11]

Even the American Psychiatric Association said that "The debate is over.... For the last three decades, the one predominant finding in research on the mass media is that exposure to media portrayals of violence increases aggressive behavior in children."

Senator Clinton has called sex and violence in the media "a silent epidemic" that "steals the innocence of children." Schatz suggested, "The not-so-silent epidemic Senator Clinton and her colleagues should be most concerned with is the rabid spending in Congress and the monstrous deficit created by redundant programs like this." He said "Senator Clinton in particular is clearly aware of the effects of violence in the media; she has commented on them countless times."

database of Democratic donors and voters. This project has in the past involved ethical lapses and intra-party tensions.

Harold Ickes, former deputy chief of staff in the Clinton White House and now Senator Clinton's advisor, rankled Democrats in 2006 when the *Washington Post* reported he was raising up to $11.5 million dollars, with the help of George Soros and the Democracy Alliance, to build a private voter-identification database.[12]

Traditionally, such a task is left to the national party, but Ickes expressed doubt in Democratic National Committee Chairman Howard Dean's ability to build a suitable system.

The database, called Data Warehouse, plans to sell voter information to "politically active unions and liberal interests" rather than giving it to Democratic campaigns. This has angered party loyalists because the venture is likely to divert contributions away from the DNC, thus shortchanging many Democratic candidates. The database will contain information allowing users to target voters with highly specialized messaging crafted to encourage voter turnout.

The database appears to be the fruit of an effort the Clintons began as early as 1995. As First Lady, Hillary sought to construct a $1.7 million "White House Data Base" (WhoDB) at taxpayer expense. The database would include 355,000 donor names that the administration could call on in their reelection bid.

WhoDB clashed with an 1882 law called the Hatch Act, which bans candidates from using government property, or government workers on taxpayer time, for campaign purposes.

White House aide Marsha Scott wrote a memo on WhoDB on June 28, 1994, to Hillary Clinton, Harold Ickes, and White House counsel Bruce Lindsey. The memo was titled "Recommendation for Design of New Database."

Scott wrote:

> Currently in the White House we are preparing, as you know, to implement a new database system starting August 1....
>
> My team and I are also engaged in conversations with the DNC about the new system they are proposing. We have asked that their system be modeled after whatever system we decide to use outside the White House. I need you to make very clear to them that their system must be technologically compatible, if not the same as whatever system we decide to

THE VRWC

The Boston Globe reported in June 2005 that "As far back as 1995, the Clinton White House was compiling a 331-page report meant to prove that 'right-wing think tanks,' British 'tabloids,' Republicans in Congress, the Wall Street Journal editorial page, and the Washington Times were all part of a cabal to get 'fringe stories' about Bill Clinton 'bounced into the mainstream media.'"[13]

use for our political purposes later on. These discussions are currently in progress and a clear direction from you to the DNC will eliminate much unnecessary wrangling.

The time to act is now. Cloning or duplicating database systems is not difficult if carefully planned by a good design team. We have proven that it can also be done relatively quickly and inexpensively. Therefore, I suggest that instead of continuing with an old outdated system.... that does not meet our current demands, let my team work with the DNC to help them design a system that will meet our needs and technical specifications. We can show them what do to and then clone another system for our specific uses later on. Any information stored in PeopleBase [the old database] could then be dumped

> into the new system and made available, when deemed necessary, to the DNC and other entities we choose to work with for political purposes.
>
> The time to make these decisions is now while we have the opportunity to coordinate the various projects. Please let me know your thoughts as soon as possible. In the meantime I am proceeding as if this is the plan.[14]

Scott had even been warned six months earlier such activity was forbidden. White House counsel Cheryl Mills addressed a memo to Scott and other aides on January 17, 1994, that said information stored on WhoDB was "government property" and could only be used for "official purposes." Mills also noted that, "the White House cannot provide data from the database to a non-federal entity or individual," like the DNC.[15]

White House spokesman Barry Toiv admitted to the *Los Angeles Times* that he knew about the program. He said, "The main subject of this memo is the possibility of developing a good database at the campaign and at the DNC making them compatible. Anybody interested in seeing Bill Clinton reelected presumedly would have been happy at the prospect of the best possible database being in place for reelection."[16]

Time magazine reported in February, 1997 that Texas oilman and former DNC finance chairman Truman Arnold also confirmed the White House database allowed him to give major donors "a fair share of presidential perks, a reward system of Lincoln Bedroom sleepovers, foreign trips, and governmental postings that helped the party hit a DNC fundraising record of $125 million" in 1996.[17]

Mrs. Clinton categorically denied having any knowledge of the program, telling reporters on January 30, 1997, "I'm not aware of a database and I would doubt if I was the person who ordered it...I

FIRST AMENDMENT

In *It Takes a Village*, Mrs. Clinton praised former Federal Elections Commission chairmen Newton N. Minow and Craig L. Lamay for taking "broadcasters to task for evading the consequences of their decisions and hiding behind the First Amendment."

—p. 270

certainly thought the White House needed a computer database. But the design of it, the use of it, that was for other people to figure out. I didn't know anything about that."[18]

Unfortunately for Hillary, there is a smoking gun. The very memo from Marsha Scott describing the database and calling for "coordination" between the White House and the DNC contained a handwritten endorsement from the First Lady herself. Clinton scribbled at the top of it, "Sounds promising. Please advise. HRC." (See Exhibit I)

Congressman David McIntosh, chairman of the House Government Reform and Oversight subcommittee, distributed this memo to reporters. McIntosh said, "It's now clear that Mrs. Clinton not only signed off on using taxpayer funds to create WhoDB but that she also raised no objection when Marsha Scott suggested illegally transferring Database information to the DNC. It troubles me deeply that Mrs. Clinton, who is a very bright lawyer, saw no problem with using taxpayer funds to aid the political operations of the DNC."[19]

VRWC ACTION PLAN

Senator Clinton has not succeeded in "editing" the Internet, and so the VRWC must exploit this resource to disseminate the information Senator Clinton would like to suppress. As the VRWC has done with Dan Rather, we must do with Hillary Clinton.

#8 - THE IMMIGRATION FILE

Senator Clinton supports amnesty for illegals and is less concerned about our border with Mexico than our border with Canada. As with most issues, cynical politicking shines through her policies.

The "Good Samaritan" Incident

When the immigration debate reached fever pitch on Capitol Hill in the spring of 2006, Senator Clinton enlisted God Almighty to rally support for her pro-amnesty position.

When House Judiciary chairman James Sensenbrenner introduced a measure that would make it a crime for illegal aliens to live in the United States, Senator Clinton denounced the bill as "mean spirited" and un-Christian. "It is certainly not in keeping with my understanding of the Scriptures because this bill would literally criminalize the Good Samaritan and probably even Jesus himself,"[1] she intoned. Charging that the legislation would create a police state, Clinton vowed to block the bill.

Her statement was widely dismissed as just another tactless, off-the-cuff remark from the senator, but her attack on her opponents' religion was consistent with advertisements being run by the Democratic National Committee.

The Associated Press reported that the committee was running Spanish-language radio ads that "asserted without evidence that a proposed House crackdown on illegal immigrants would criminalize 'even churches for just giving communion' to them."[2] The message

WHAT WILL COME BACK TO HAUNT HER

Mrs. Clinton voted against an amendment attached to the Senate immigration bill proposing to designate English as the "official language" of the United States. The amendment passed anyway, 64–34.

corresponded nicely with Senator Clinton's assertion that Republicans would arrest the Son of God.

Senator Clinton ultimately supported the McCain-Kennedy Senate immigration bill, which the Heritage Foundation predicted would allow more than sixty-six million immigrants into the United States over the next twenty years. As she cast her vote for the bill, Clinton wore an ornate gold cross large enough that this writer could see it from the high press gallery. It showed brilliantly for the cameras pointed at the Senate floor.

A Pattern of Amnesty Proposals

Senator Clinton often talks tough on illegal immigration. For example, in February 2003 she told WBAC Radio, "I am, you know, adamantly against illegal aliens." But her insistent efforts in the Senate to grant amnesty to illegals reveal such statements as empty rhetoric.

In March 2002 Clinton co-sponsored a bill to extend deadlines for illegal aliens living in the U.S to obtain visas. She gushed, "This is good news indeed. Instead of being forced to return to their home country to apply for permanent resident status, many immigrants will be able to seek permanent resident status while working in the U.S."[3] The bill in effect allowed illegals to wait indefinitely inside the U.S. while their applications are processed.

The following year Michelle Malkin noted in *Human Events* that while the senator was publicly warning Americans that "our approach to securing the nation is haphazard at best," she was writing legislation to protect illegal aliens from deportation. This referred to an amendment that Clinton attached to a Senate omnibus appropriations bill to prohibit the use of federal funds for removing, deporting or detaining illegal aliens related to victims of September 11.

Malkin pointed out the amendment's dangers: "The Hillary amendment would prevent the Department of Homeland Security from taking any action to deport spouses or children of September 11 victims: who crossed the border illegally; overstayed visas illegally; evaded prior deportation orders illegally; stowed away on a ship illegally; smuggled other illegal aliens; used fraudulent documents; falsely claimed U.S. citizenship; voted illegally; have a communicable disease or who failed to present documentation of having received vaccination against vaccine-preventable diseases; have a physical or mental disorder and behavior associated with a disorder that may posed, or has posed, a threat to the property, safety or welfare of the alien or others, or are likely to become a common charge."[4]

Clinton made no apology for hobbling immigration enforcement agencies. "Surviving family members should be given permanent resident status in the United States and I was proud to co-sponsor Senator Corzine's bill last year that would have done just that," she said. "Although the amendment I co-sponsored with Senator Corzine does not give these family members that status, it will at least reduce the likelihood they will be deported by prohibiting the use of federal funds to do so."[5]

Clinton has also sought to protect other "victims" who flouted U.S. immigration laws. Senator Clinton sought amnesty and welfare benefits for illegal aliens affected by Hurricanes Jeanne and Rita. In October 2003 she advocated granting temporary protected status to illegal Haitian immigrants.

Following Hurricane Katrina, she co-signed a letter in September 2005 asking Homeland Security Secretary Michael Chertoff to "terminate removal proceedings against those individuals placed in proceedings after they sought assistance" from the U.S. government.

The letter itself acknowledged that the very action it requested was unnecessary. The signatories conceded that "Department of Homeland Security officials have publicly stated that rescuers have not been asking about immigration status, and President Vicente Fox has said the United States agreed with his request not to prosecute undocumented Mexican immigrants affected by Katrina who turn to U.S. officials for help."

Hillary was merely grandstanding, but the effort by Senator Clinton and her allies would clearly weaken the Department of Homeland Security's ability to keep tabs on illegal immigrants. The letter requested "a clear statement by DHS confirming that information on undocumented immigrants will not be necessary in order to ensure the public health and safety."

Senator Clinton's benevolence toward illegals was not limited to victims of terrorism or natural disasters. The senator also cosponsored an agricultural jobs bill in September 2004 providing illegal farm workers an immediate path to citizenship.

While opposing most federal efforts to enforce the law, Senator Clinton tends to blame anonymous businesses for much of the immigration problem. According to Senator Clinton, "the current system allows unscrupulous employers to skirt the law and exploit undocumented workers in the name of cheap labor."[6]

Hillary Logic: Fake ID? No Problemo

Illegal aliens who "skirt the law" should be rewarded with citizenship, but businesses that employ them should be punished

In May 2005 the REAL ID Act—requiring drivers to provide proof of citizenship in order to obtain a license—was attached to a "must-pass" emergency defense spending bill. Clinton denounced the act as "seriously flawed."[7]

Yet in 2003, on the same radio show where she declared herself "adamantly against illegal aliens," Clinton had said she favored, "at least a Visa ID, some kind of entry and exit ID. And, you know, perhaps, although I'm not a big fan of it, we might have to move towards an ID system even for our citizens." Naturally, she declined to explain how the government could implement an identification system for its citizens without requiring some proof of citizenship.

The REAL ID Act contained provisions to prevent terrorists from abusing asylum laws; streamlined the laws on deporting immigrants for terrorism-related offenses; and authorized the construction of a three-mile fence in a section of the San Diego/Mexico border known as "Smuggler's Alley." Clinton dismissed such measures.

The REAL ID Act was eventually passed as part of a military spending bill, but Clinton continued to argue that the bill will not make America safer.

Senator Clinton doubted that a fence could improve American security. She was, however, convinced it could work for Israel.

She worked closely with Jewish leaders to oppose the International Court of Justice passing judgment on the legality of Israel's security fence. Clinton released a statement supporting the fence as a "legitimate response" to terrorist attacks.

In February 2004 Clinton stated that a suicide bombing in Jerusalem "shows the day-to-day danger that Israelis face and that has caused the Israeli government to decide that it must build a fence to protect its people."

Apparently, Senator Clinton believes border fences that can deter suicide bombers would somehow prove ineffective against Mexican labor migrants.

Hillary's Border Security Plan: More Pork for New York . . .

While opposing the allocation of security resources for the south, Clinton deemed it unjust that the northern border wasn't getting the same kind of money and attention.

HILLARY'S BLUE STATE RELIGION

It isn't unusual for Senator Clinton to invoke God for political leverage. At Tufts University in 2004 the Boston Herald reported her invocation of Jesus in a stump speech on poverty: "No one can read the New Testament of our Bible without recognizing that Jesus had a lot more to say about how we treat the poor than most of the issues that were talked about in the election," she said. This was by no means a unique line of attack for Clinton; she has been referencing God in order to impugn Republicans at least since her 1997 appearance at the National Prayer Breakfast, where she joked: "I have to confess that it's crossed my mind that you could not be a Republican and a Christian from time to time."

On April 25, 2005 she wrote a letter to Homeland Security chief Michael Chertoff seeking to boost New York's share of border security funding because "for too long, northern border security has received the short end of the stick when it comes to federal resources." In other words, giving more money to the southern border was simply unfair.

The notion of directing resources where they're most needed—in this case prioritizing the south in the distribution of border security funds—seems to have escaped Clinton. As of 2005, an estimated 78 percent of the 11.5–12 million illegal aliens living in the United States came from Mexico and Latin America.[8] In the spring of 2006, Republican senator John Kyl of Arizona and Democratic senator Dianne Feinstein of California held an alarming press conference to announce that since September 11, forty subterranean cross-border tunnels used to smuggle humans and narcotics into the United States had been discovered. Thirty-nine of them were located along the southern border.

But Clinton has always been determined to enlarge her piece of the security funding pie, regardless of the effect such reallocations may have on security elsewhere. She had boasted about getting special treatment for border security resources in 2001, when the Senate Appropriations Committee appropriated $25 million to hire additional customs personnel along the northern border. The senator's press release crowed, "Clinton worked personally at that time to ensure that the funding gives preference to New York State when deploying border agents."

. . . and No Enforcement on the Border

Senator Clinton's idea of northern border enforcement, however, is unclear. On April 10, 2005, Senator Clinton wrote to Secretary of State Condoleezza Rice and Secretary of Homeland Security Michael Chertoff charging that a proposal to require all border-crossers to show their passport when entering the U.S from Canada would, "devastate tourism on both sides of the Canadian-American border."

The junior senator suggested that revenue generated from NFL and NHL games should take precedence over security requirements. In her letter to Rice and Chertoff, Clinton noted that "the Buffalo Bills and Buffalo Sabres are dependent upon ticket sales to fans from Southern Ontario who have the option of watching the games on television rather than in person." Thus "it is imperative that your departments listen closely to the voices of my constituents and consider all feasible alternatives that will both enhance security and facilitate commerce."

And Clinton asked the House and Senate appropriations chairmen to block funding for this border enforcement.

Hillary's La Raza Connection

In 2005 Clinton gave a speech to members of the National Council of La Raza ("The Race"), an open-borders advocacy group that lobbies for driver's licenses, in-state tuition rates and free healthcare for illegal aliens, as well as bilingual requirements for state agencies and voting ballots. Clinton told the group's members, "You are doing your part to make sure that every child and every American family has access to the tools necessary to live out their dreams, to have a piece of the American dream, but I don't know that your government is doing its part right now—I'm not sure we are doing everything to make your job easier, to make sure that the opportunities in society are alive and well for everyone."[9]

Speaking in support of the DREAM Act, which would grant illegal aliens in-state tuition rates(rates that are almost always much lower than those paid by out-of-state U.S. citizens), Clinton proclaimed, "We need to open the doors of college to immigrant children who came here, did well, and deserve to go on with their education."[10]

Affiliations with Illegal Immigrants

In 2006, Clinton appeared with Senators Kennedy, McCain, and Schumer before a group of illegal Irish immigrants who came to Capitol Hill to lobby the U.S. government for amnesty. Clinton celebrated the illegals' presence in America, telling them, "It is so heartening to see you here. You are really here on behalf of what America means, America's values, American's hopes."

VRWC ACTION PLAN

Hillary will try to sound tough on border security, but her record is one of amnesty for illegals, disdain for border security, and support for radical immigration groups like La Raza. This is a major vulnerability.

#9 - THE 9/11 FILE

After the terrorist attacks of September 11, Washington politics changed dramatically. Senator Clinton did not.

September 11 spurred her to win pork -- large federal grants for her well-heeled corporate campaign donors and pipelines of money for boondoggles in New York -- and dodge the tough issues in order to maintain her political viability.

The $20 Billion "First Installment"

Two days after the attacks, as Ground Zero was still smoking, Senator Clinton and Senator Chuck Schumer marched into the Oval Office and demanded President Bush give New York $20 billion—the largest federal aid package in history. President Bush quickly approved. What the Vast Right-Wing Conspiracy suspected, America learned months later: millions of these dollars were routed to big business and pet political projects.

The $20 billion was not designated for actual damage estimates. It was a near-arbitrary figure invented by New York's senators and governor, along with the city's mayor.

Clinton justified the expense in a biographical video for her 2006 Senate re-election campaign. "We need at least as much as is being asked for everything else. We need $20 billion," she said.

Schumer concurred: "To ask for more than $20 billion—more for New York for all the military, and the rest of the country—would seem excessive," he explained to the *Daily News.* "But to ask for less than $20 billion would be derelict in my duties as a New York senator. So I figured, 'Let's match it, $20 billion for the rest and $20 billion for New York.'"

And so it was matched.

That week on *Face the Nation*, Senator Clinton praised the president for quickly approving the aid, but indicated she considered it only a "first installment." Still, she told *Today Show* host Katie Couric she was "absolutely delighted" about the cash. Some corporations close Senator Clinton were likely "delighted" as well.

The Goldman Sachs Connection—Hillary Helps the Rich Get Richer

The *Daily News* published a scathing seven-part investigative series near the end of 2005 exposing the gross misuse of 9/11 funds

HILLARY'S MONEY TRAIL

Senator Clinton has benefited from Goldman's profits. Between her two campaigns, the PAC and employees of the investment giant have contributed $254,460 to Hillary's campaigns. That is more than she has received from any other company's employees.

and documenting how huge corporations and wealthy real estate moguls got the lion's share of recovery allocations.[1]

The *Daily News* had long been on the case. The tabloid began sounding the alarm in 2002, reporting that "about $500 million is being funneled in grants to 145 big corporations that promise not to quit downtown. By comparison, thousands of families struggling to pay their rent and mortgage have received less than $75 million from the Federal Emergency Management Agency."

One beneficiary of this federal largess was Goldman Sachs, a global investment banking and securities firm. Ranking forty-first on the *Fortune 500* in 2006, Goldman Sachs is worth $43.3 billion and turned a $5.6 billion profit in 2005.

Goldman Sachs received a $25 million grant in 2005 from the Job Creation and Retention program. According to the *Daily News*,

Goldman Sachs "agreed to stay downtown only after forcing Governor Pataki to abandon a West St. tunnel near the entrance to Goldman's planned $2.4 billion headquarters across from Ground Zero."

The jobs program, funded by the Department of Housing and Urban Development and administered by the Empire State Development Corporation (ESDC), dispensed $320 million to seventy-five recipients that "employed 200 or more people that were displaced from their workplace and are committed to keeping jobs in New York City for seven years." An ESDC spokeswoman admitted to the *Daily News* that grants were "awarded to firms to stay downtown even when they were not at risk" of leaving. And Goldman Sachs, to be sure, was highly unlikely to leave its prestigious Manhattan address.

HILLARY SUPPORTS CORPORATE WELFARE

Business tycoon Donald Trump pocketed a portion of Hillary's $20 billion in federal cash for a property he lauded in his 2004 book *How to Get Rich*. Trump claimed 40 Wall Street was "one of the best deals I ever made," bragging "I make a great deal from 40 Wall Street." He sure does. According to his application for federal aid, that business earned $26.8 million per year; it received $150,000 in 9/11 assistance. Other corporations also reeled in some easy money. A downtown office of the Ford Models agency, which generated $19.9 million in revenue, received $100,000 in aid; a Morgan Stanley property was granted $300,000; and two Rockefeller group subsidiaries that are owned by the Mitsubishi Estate Group got $234,397 each.

On November 29, 2005, Clinton spoke at the groundbreaking ceremony in Lower Manhattan of Goldman Sachs's new forty-three-story corporate headquarters, a resplendent building partially financed with government recovery grants.

According to a Goldman Sachs press release, Clinton declared, "Following the tragic events of September 11, I was proud to have worked with my colleagues in Congress to secure $20 billion in federal aid for New York. Major employers like Goldman Sachs needed to know they had a partner in government to ensure that Lower Manhattan could sustain their business in the area."

And this was not the end of the government's benevolence toward Goldman Sachs. According to New York City's Independent Budget Office, the company also saved a whopping $9 million in interest payments when it received a $1.65 billion "Liberty Bond," a federally funded, tax-exempt, private activity bond program made available to New York after September 11.[2]

Capitol Corruption

In 2001, Congress authorized the Small Business Administration (SBA) to dispense up to $4.5 billion in Supplemental Terrorist Activity Relief (STAR) loans to small businesses that were "adversely affected" by the September 11 attacks. Senator Clinton, who helped create the program, expressed shock when news broke that the SBA was being abused by out-of-state businesses. But Senator Clinton, in fact, was intimately familiar with SBA abuse.

In December 2005, the Office of Inspector General (OIG) produced a report revealing the program's enormous waste. The investigation found that only 15 percent of STAR loan recipients had been qualified to receive their loans.

To qualify for a loan, an applicant had to provide documentation proving to the SBA that his business was "adversely affected" by

September 11. But, according to the Inspector General report, "Lenders were actually advised they would not be required to provide their justification for prior SBA approval."

This allowed many out-of-state businesses to get cheap federal loans on the flimsiest of pretexts.

New York Post correspondent Geoff Earle reported that a semiprivate golf course in Texas received a $640,000 loan by claiming that his business was harmed by the 9/11 terrorist attacks because, "People were more interested in staying home and watching coverage of the attack on television than playing golf."[3]

Earle also described how a Las Vegas tanning salon earned a $584,000 loan with its sob story of losses stemming from local showgirls who, having been laid off after September 11, were no longer tanning themselves.

Abuses of the STAR program abounded. A single liquor store in Georgia received over $1 million, while two California gas stations procured $732,000 and $1,460,000 respectively. A Florida dry cleaner pocketed a hefty $450,000.

Following these revelations, Clinton claimed she was infuriated that federal funds she had helped allocate were so grossly misspent.

She fired off a letter to the president in December 2005, declaring, "I am particularly incensed by the finding included in the SBA's Inspector General's report that despite the fact that in the months following September 11th, while many New York businesses struggled to just to stay afloat, SBA undertook efforts to promote the program by advising lenders that virtually any small business qualified and assuring them that SBA would not second guess their justifications."[4]

But Clinton had not always been so skeptical toward the organization. In fact, she had reacted to previous Republican attempts to reign in the SBA by extolling it as a noble, innocent victim of Republican greed and cruelty.

At a September 2004 speech to the National Press Club, Senator Clinton urged the president to keep SBA programs fully funded, since reducing the organization would allegedly favor wealthy CEOs. Hillary took a shot at the president. "The president has cut funding for the Small Business Administration by 25 percent, the largest percentage cut of any federal agency," she said, defending the wasteful spending she would later deplore.

FROM THE MEMORY FILE

Mrs. Clinton is indeed intimately familiar with SBA waste, fraud, and abuse scandals. After all, Susan McDougal, the Clintons' partner in the Whitewater venture, was convicted for embezzling a $300,000 SBA loan.

Clinton also sat in on a clemency hearing for four Hasidic men in New Square, New York. Charged with stealing more than $40 million in education grants, small business loans, and housing grants by creating a fake parochial school, Clinton's husband pardoned the men in the final fevered hours of his presidency. The AP pointed out the likely motive for Mrs. Clinton's presence at the clemency hearing: "Mrs. Clinton traveled to New Square, in suburban Rockland County, during her Senate campaign and met Grand Rabbi David Twersky. Many Hasidic communities tend to vote in blocs, and because of that, politicians aggressively court their leaders." On Election Day, "Mrs. Clinton received 1,400 votes in New Square; her Republican opponent, Rick Lazio, received 12."

HILLARY CLINTON: CONSPIRACY THEORIST

In 2003 she blasted the president for allegedly "misleading" New Yorkers into believing the air was safe, claiming "There seems to have been a deliberate effort at the direction of the White House to provide unwarranted reassurances to New Yorkers about whether their air was safe to breathe." Democratic congressman Jerry Nadler took Clinton's conspiracy theory to its logical conclusion, proclaiming that "President Bush may have killed more people on September 11 than the terrorists" due to Bush's alleged lies about the safety of New York air.

The Paths of Waste Lead to Hillary

Another boondoggle was the September 11 clean air program. This scheme apparently made every last New Yorker eligible to receive up to $1,750 in federal funds to purchase air conditioners, purifiers, and vacuum cleaners. Hillary, from her seat on the senate Committee on Environment and Public Works, supported the program.

The program, originally estimated at $15 million, ended up costing at least $129.7 million. Only 5,000 New Yorkers were expected to participate, but 118,591 ultimately won approval for free appliances, including 5,211 applicants in Flushing, Elmhust, Hillcrest, and Rego Park in Central Queens—areas that the plume of noxious air from the blasts did not reach—were approved to get $6.3 million in appliances. Eight miles from Ground Zero in Starrett City, where residents were likewise unaffected by soot, one in every ten households applied for clean-air freebies. In that city, a total of residents hauled in $633,495 from federal taxpayers.

The situation brought to mind the famous image of the "magic bullet" theory of President Kennedy's assassination. "New Yorkers by tens of thousands received free air conditioners, air purifiers, and other clean-air devices in such an illogical pattern that the toxic plume from the smoldering World Trade Center would have had to travel like a wild tornado, arbitrarily touching down here and there throughout the city," reported the *Daily News*. "The size and scope of abuse in the FEMA-funded program dwarfs any fraud and misuse allegations that have surfaced in disaster aid programs for hurricanes in Florida, wildfires in California, and floods in Detroit."[5]

The *Daily News* found a staggering total sum was spent on clean air equipment:

Air conditioners	83,656	$37.7 million
Air purifiers	119,872	$43.0 million
Air filters	96,609	$18.3 million
Vacuums	164,794	$30.7 million
Total:		**$129.7 million***

*This total differed from FEMA's estimate of $131 million.

Hillary's Pizzas for Arabs

One of Senator Clinton's favorite mental health programs was used to buy pizzas for Arab immigrants and assist them with their immigration applications in the aftermath of September 11.

The $154.9 million Project Liberty grief counseling program was created to help New Yorkers cope emotionally with the terrorist attacks. Clinton had worked hard to fund the program since its inception. In an October 2004 press release Clinton declared, "Project Liberty has provided crucial mental health services to so many people who might not have asked for it." The statement emphasized that "Clinton has been working to secure continued funding for mental health counseling since the attacks of September 11, 2001."

The program ended up funding Brooklyn's Arab-American Family Support Center, an organization dedicated to helping "Arab-speaking immigrants in New York adapt to life in the United States and its culture." Emira Habiby-Brown, former head of the Brooklyn Center, told the *Daily News* she used her organization's $75,000 Liberty mental health grant to help "hundreds of our men" waiting outside a nearby immigration office by assisting them in filling out forms, interpreting for them, and even buying them pizza. Habiby-Browne commented that the Liberty funds—designed strictly for mental health assistance—were "used it in a way that was helpful to our community at the time."[6]

Ben Hindell also got cash. Hindell is an artist, but he landed a job as a school counselor thanks to a $740,000 federal grant to a nonprofit called Leap. The money was supposed to help children cope with the terrorist attacks. By 2003 and 2004, Hindell admitted, "a lot of people who counseled lost track that it was about 9/11 and it just kinda became helping kids with whatever they were struggling with."[7]

Hindell's boss, Ila Gross, indicated that Leap was encouraged to spend money regardless of the level of need. "A lot of people were seduced that there was suddenly an enormous amount of funding available. Everyone was pushing us to get out there, get out there."

Senator Clinton is still pushing this grief cash today. When President Bush's 2006 fiscal year budget proposed eliminating these funds, Clinton fought to include $75 million in similar programs for ostensibly disconsolate New Yorkers in the Hurricane Katrina emergency spending bill.

Hillary's Federal Aid for Robert DeNiro

Large sums of recovery money helped finance pet projects that included street beautification, an "I Love NY" tourism campaign and Robert DeNiro's Tribeca Film Festival in Manhattan.

The Alliance for Downtown New York may be the champion at plundering recovery funds. The Alliance convinced the Lower Manhattan Development Corporation (LMDC), which controlled $2.7 billion in recovery money, to grant it $5.4 million. Nearly all of this money was used to pay for projects that, before September 11, were privately financed by a group of downtown property owners.

Bill Bernstein, vice president of the Alliance, said his group approached the LMDC for money to complete its $20 million "streetscape program." The project began in 1998 to "reconstruct sidewalks, install benches and trash cans, improve lighting and signs along Broadway from City Hall to the Battery, and install metal inserts commemorating parades along the Canyon of Heroes." After September 11 the government started picking up this tab, apparently viewing events like ticker-tape parades for the Yankees as a vital government interest.

Bernstein recalled to the *Daily News* that securing funding for DeNiro's film festival was initially difficult. The Department of Housing and Urban Development (HUD) "had a lot of bizarre requirements," he said.[8]

But HUD does not appear to be strict about handing out money. The following is a partial list of projects that did receive monies after meeting HUD's "bizarre requirements":

- $90 million to buy the Deutsche Bank building at Ground Zero

- $45 million to decontaminate and demolish that very building
- $30 million to enhance sixteen city parks
- $19 million for an "I Love NY" tourism campaign
- $4 million for the beautification of four blocks on Broadway's Canyon of Heroes
- $3 million to promote fifteen museums
- $3 million for actor Robert De Niro's Tribeca Film Festival
- $220,000 to cover Zagat's downtown guide booklets that were distributed for free to workers below Houston Street
- $250,000 toward a three-day film festival for Italian artisans

HILLARY'S MONEY TRAIL

To Hillary's two campaigns so far, the Securities and Investment industry had contributed $2,651,069 by July 10, 2006. For her 2006 race, Senator Clinton had brought in more than $1.6 million by July, which made her the top recipient of Wall Street money in 2005–2006. She brought in more contributions from this sector than the top two Republican recipients combined.

- $100,000 to Pace University to design the largest roof in the northeast to be made out of live plants
- $328,000 for consultations on exhibits for the World Trade Center memorial competition

The "Bush Knew" Claim

On September 12, 2001, Senator Clinton joined President Bush in his condemnation of the terrorist attacks, warning the killers they would soon feel the fury of the United States.

She declared, "We will also stand united behind our president as he and his advisers plan the necessary actions to demonstrate America's resolve and commitment. Not only to seek out and exact punishment on the perpetrators, but to make very clear that not only those who harbor terrorists, but those who in any way aid or comfort them whatsoever will face the wrath of our country."[9]

Within a few months, however, her tune had changed. Senator Clinton turned against the president, even accusing him of having prior knowledge of the attacks.

On May 16, 2002, the cover of the *New York Post* blared: "Bush Knew." According to the *Post*, the Bush administration "believed bin Laden was merely plotting a 'traditional' hijacking," but "evidence has surfaced in recent weeks that intelligence and law-enforcement officials had evidence something bigger might have been in the works."[10]

Senator Clinton scrambled to be the first to react publicly. On the floor of the Senate, she exclaimed, "We have learned that President Bush had been informed last year, before September 11, of a possible plot by those associated with Osama bin Laden to hijack a U.S. airliner."[11]

White House spokesman Ari Fleischer told the press corps that Senator Clinton "did not call the White House, did not ask if [the *Post* headline] was accurate or not. Instead, she immediately went to the floor of the Senate, and I'm sorry to say that she followed that headline and divided."[12]

On the Senate floor, Clinton demanded that classified intelligence discussed in the story be made public. She added, "I also support the call by the distinguished majority leader, Mr. Daschle, for the release of the Phoenix FBI memorandum and the August intelligence briefing to congressional investigators."

This referred to a memo written before September 11 by FBI Special Agent Kenneth Williams that had raised suspicions about foreign flight students in the U.S., including Hani Hanjour, who would later pilot Flight 77 into the Pentagon. A December 2002 report by a joint congressional intelligence committee concluded that Williams's memo had been ignored by his superiors in the intelligence community—not by the president. The director of Central Intelligence at the time of the Phoenix memo was George Tenet, appointed by Senator Clinton's husband.

The Wiretapping Dodge

During the debate about reauthorizing the Patriot Act, the *New York Times* printed a story on December 16, 2005, claiming that "President Bush secretly authorized the National Security Agency to eavesdrop on the communications of Americans and others inside the United States to search for evidence of terrorist activity without court-approved warrants ordinarily required for domestic spying." Liberals on Capitol Hill were outraged, but Senator Clinton said nary a word.

Three days later, Attorney General Alberto Gonzales and General Michael Hayden, the principal deputy director of national intelligence, held a press briefing to explain the terrorist surveillance program. They said a communication monitored through the program had to meet three standards: there had to be "a reasonable basis" to

WHAT WILL COME BACK TO HAUNT HER

Senator James Inhofe responded to Clinton's remarks on the Senate floor: "I take a moment to add my voice to those who were outraged and offended last week at these idle attempts by some members of Congress to impugn the integrity of our president, George W. Bush. Sure, they all now will deny that was their intent because they have been home and they have heard from their people, and the people do not believe it. They know it is cheap politics."

Inhofe also entered into the congressional record a *Washington Times* article titled "Demogauging September 11." The piece reported that as First Lady, Mrs. Clinton had "wined and dined" members of the American Muslim Council that included Hamas apologist Abdulrahman Alamoudi and allowed the group to organize a reception at the White House. The group also allegedly provided Mrs. Clinton with talking points for her syndicated newspaper column and speeches.

conclude that one party to the communication was affiliated with al Qaeda, one of the communicating parties had to be located outside the U.S., and the communication had to be otherwise unavailable to the government. The Left howled that the program violated civil liberties. Democratic senator Russ Feingold of Wisconsin, a potential 2008 presidential candidate, introduced a resolution to censure the president. Senator Clinton was silent, neither supporting nor condemning Feingold's resolution.

In support of censure, Senator Feingold declared, "This president exploited the climate of anxiety after September 11, 2001, both to push for overly intrusive powers in the Patriot Act, and to take us into a war in Iraq that has been a tragic diversion from the critical fight against al Qaeda and its affiliates. In both of those instances, however, Congress gave its approval to the president's actions, however mistaken that approval may have been. That was not the case with the illegal domestic wiretapping program authorized by the president shortly after September 11. The president violated the law, ignored the Constitution and the other two branches of government, and disregarded the rights and freedoms upon which our country was founded."[13]

Senator Feingold had thrown down the gauntlet. President Bush was a duplicitous scoundrel, and his tactics in the war on terror were un-American. Where would Senator Clinton come down?

As it turned out—nowhere.

The Capitol Hill press gaggle clamored to get Senator Clinton's reaction to Feingold's statement, but she and her colleagues conspicuously fled from reporters waiting outside of their weekly policy luncheon.

In an interview with National Public Radio, *Washington Post* national political reporter Dana Milbank described how Clinton even tried to use the four-foot, eleven-inch Senator Barbara Mikulski as a shield to keep reporters at bay. Why does Hillary not join her party in demagoguing against these intelligence programs? However much it annoys her liberal base, Hillary needs to pose as a candidate who believes in strong national security. (The VRWC should exploit this tension.)

The Homeland Security Gambit

In a January 2003 speech at the John Jay College of Criminal Justice in New York, Senator Clinton ridiculed the Department of

Homeland Security and criticized President Bush for his alleged weakness on defense. "We have relied on the myth of homeland security—a myth written in rhetoric, inadequate resources, and is a new bureaucracy, instead of relying on good old fashioned American ingenuity, might, and muscle," she claimed. "Homeland Security is not simply about reorganizing existing bureaucracies," she explained, but rather "about having the right attitude, focus, policy and resources."

Hillary's "right attitude," included repealing tax cuts (that is, raising taxes) to give more federal money to New York, and increasing the bureaucracy. She introduced the Provide for the Common Defense Act that would increase spending and the size of government as well as help pay for state-run programs that New York was not funding. The bill called for two additional security coordinators inside the Department of Homeland Security dedicated to New York, a $3 billion "counter-technology fund" to pay for city-based security measures, more security regulations for certain industries, and money to track medical records of first responders.

The "Federal Interoperable Communications Act"

In March 2006, the Democrats with great fanfare unveiled their new "National Security Strategy," proposing, among other ideas, to catch Osama bin Laden. Nearly all the prominent party members attended the ceremony—except Senator Clinton.

The event, held at Union Station, featured a bevy of law enforcement officials stationed for prime photo opportunities with Senate and House minority leaders Harry Reid and Nancy Pelosi, senators John Kerry, Dick Durbin, Barak Obama, Debbie Stabenow, House member Steny Hoyer, and even retired general Wesley Clark and former secretary of state Madeleine Albright, among others. Participants crowded onto an elevated platform in front of slickly produced signs that read "Real Security."

GREEN: THE COLOR OF MONEY

Meghan French, government relations director of New York City's Pace University, said university president David Caputo thought the old, ugly roof of the university's main building "would be a great place for a green roof."

In addition to the $100,000 grant mentioned above, the plant topper project received $650,000 from the Department of Education, $60,000 from the Environmental Protection Agency, and $150,000 from Pace's local city council.

Pace had been getting the green treatment from Senator Clinton since 2001. On November 9, 2001, Clinton announced along with Democratic congresswoman Nita Lowey and Senator Charles Schumer that Pace was getting $130,000 in that year's Agriculture Appropriations bill to "assist communities fighting urban sprawl." Clinton also advocated giving Pace University an additional $4.1 million in FEMA money to rebuild Pace's World Trade Institute.

It was unlike Clinton to miss such an opportunity for publicity, but the reason soon became clear. Two months later, through the Democrats' "Steering and Outreach" committee (which she chairs), Clinton scheduled a day-long security summit to unveil *her own* plans. The conference was ostensibly organized to help the party refine its agenda and rhetoric on national security, but Clinton used the occasion to promote a new piece of legislation she had crafted, lining up several supporters to advocate her plan.

She proposed the Federal Interoperable Communications and Safety Act (FICS). She would create a new undersecretary for emergency communications and an "interoperability czar" to lead an

Office of Emergency Communications. Her bill would also require all state and local governments to implement statewide communications programs in order to be eligible for some Department of Homeland Security grants.

Technology Daily, one of the few publications to cover the conference—because it was closed to the press—reported that most speakers supported Clinton's ideas. Robert Atkinson, president of the Information Technology and Innovation Foundation, Michael O'Hanlon of the Brookings Institution, Delaware governor Ruth Ann Minner, 9/11 Commissioner Jamie Gorelick, and other panelists discussed the need for a federally funded interoperable communications program.

Former Democratic senator Bob Kerrey, another member of the 9/11 Commission and president of the New School, who had previously told *New York Magazine* that Clinton was a "rock star," delivered the keynote address. Harold Schaitberger of the International Association of Fire Fighters, who regularly endorses Democrats, was also a featured speaker.

This was another example of Hillary ditching her party in order to better position herself for a presidential run.

The Dubai Connection: How Bill Cashed In

One of the Clintons' strengths is their ability to play two sides of an issue. Sometimes this is called "triangulation." Sometimes it is called cashing in and demogoguing.

When the Bush administration signed a $6.8 billion contract with United Arab Emirates–owned Dubai Ports World in early 2006, Senator Clinton came out against the accord because, she claimed, it would compromise America's security and "fiscal sovereignty." She wrote a letter to Senate Majority Leader Bill Frist insisting that"[t]his sale will create an unacceptable risk to the security of our ports. We therefore request that emergency legislation we are introducing to ban foreign governments from controlling port operations be slated for immediate consideration when the Senate convenes on February 27."

Meanwhile her husband, who had approved a deal in 1999 allowing control of both ports of the Panama Canal to fall to Hutchinson Whampoa—a company with close ties to the Chinese military—had other ideas.

Mr. Clinton enjoyed a lucrative relationship with Dubai. Mrs. Clinton reported in her own senatorial disclosure forms that her husband had earned $600,000 giving speeches there.[14] The UAE had also

LABOR UNIONS TRUMP A SAFER HOMELAND

President Bush's Homeland Security bill, proposed by Democratic senator Joe Lieberman, consolidated twenty-two federal agencies and 170,000 workers into a single organization: the Department of Homeland Security. Labor unions objected to the bill, and Senator Clinton took up their cause. Clinton said the bill would "strip workers of their collective bargaining rights through a waiver authority." She continued, "I must say that we have every reason to believe that this administration will take advantage of this authority. It has already taken away these rights from secretaries at the U.S. Attorney's offices. And I fully expect that it will use this authority—if it is granted—to strip away the rights from the more than 50,000 workers who will make up the newly formed Department of Homeland Security." Despite this inflammatory speech, Clinton voted in favor of the bill she herself claimed would "strip" workers' rights.

contributed between $500,000 and $1 million to his presidential library in Arkansas. Furthermore, "Yucaipa, an American company that has Bill Clinton as a 'senior adviser' and pays him a percentage of its profits, formed a partnership with the Dubai Investment Group to form DIGL, Inc., a company dedicated to managing the sheik's personal investments," according to former Clinton adviser Dick Morris.[15]

In fact, as Senator Clinton was accusing the White House of "trying to hand over U.S. ports" to unreliable foreigners and exclaiming that "we cannot concede sovereignty over critical infrastructure like our ports," her bedmate was trying to land his former press secretary, Joe Lockhart, a job lobbying the U.S. government on behalf of DP World—the very company slated to take over the six U.S. ports. Veteran journalist Robert Novak reported, "according to well-placed UAE sources, the former president made the suggestion [to hire Lockhart as a lobbyist] at the very highest level of the oil-rich state." Lockhart ultimately failed to land the job; UAE officials claim he asked for too much money, while Lockhart maintains he declined the position.

During the Dubai ports controversy, Mr. Clinton publicly extolled the UAE as a "good ally to America." Moreover, Dubai officials consulted with Mr. Clinton as to how to ensure that the ports deal went through. On March 2, 2006, Clinton's spokesman told the *Financial Times*, "the Dubai leaders called him [Mr. Clinton] and he suggested that they submit to the full and regular scrutiny process and that they should put maximum safeguards and security into any port proposal" to ameliorate congressional concerns over the deal.

The following day, the *New York Post* reported that Mrs. Clinton was unaware that her husband was advising the very Dubai officials she was warning would undermine our security and fiscal sovereignty. She stammered, "That's . . . I mean, as far as I know, he supports my position and has said so publicly."

VRWC ACTION PLAN

Hillary's reaction to the terrorist attacks—seeking pork to aid her corporate allies and attacking the president—were typical of the no-holds-barred politics she practices. The VRWC must stay on guard for this sort of ruthlessness, and highlight her cynical behavior.

#10 - THE IRAQ FILE

Senator Clinton's stance on the Iraq war constantly changes. To justify her flip-flops, she has misrepresented President Bush's position and dissembled about her own.

A Vote for War—For Now

On October 11, 2002, Senator Clinton voted "Yea" on House Joint Resolution 114, authorizing the president to wage war against Iraq.

The bill specified the justification for war. In voting for the resolution, Hillary agreed to all its assertions, which including the following:

- "Iraq had large stockpiles of chemical weapons and a large-scale biological weapons system."
- Iraq had "an advanced nuclear weapons development program that was much closer to producing a nuclear weapon than intelligence reporting had previously indicated."
- "Iraq, in direct and flagrant violation of the cease-fire, attempted to thwart the efforts of weapons inspectors to identify and destroy Iraq's weapons of mass destruction stockpiles and development capabilities."
- "In 1998 Congress concluded that Iraq's continuing weapons of mass destruction programs threatened vital United States interests and international peace and security, declared Iraq to be in 'material breach of its international obligations' and urged the president to 'take appropriate action, in accordance with the Constitution and relevant laws of the United States, to bring Iraq into compliance with its international obligations.'"
- "Iraq poses a continuing threat to the national security of the United Sates and international peace and security in the Persian Gulf region and remains in material and unacceptable breach of its international obligations by, among other things, continuing to possess and develop significant chemical and biological weapons capability, actively seek-

ing a nuclear weapons capability, and supporting and harboring terrorist organizations."

- "The current Iraq regime has demonstrated its continuing hostility toward, and willingness to attack, the United States, including by attempting in 1993 to assassinate former president Bush and by firing on many thousands of occasions on United States and Coalition Armed Forces engaged in enforcing the resolutions of the United Nations Security Council."
- "Members of al Qaeda, an organization bearing responsibility for the attacks on the United States, its citizens, and its interests, including the attacks that occurred on September 11, 2001, are known to be in Iraq."
- "Iraq's demonstrated capability and willingness to use weapons of mass destruction, the risk that the current Iraqi regime will either employ those weapons to launch a surprise attack against the United States or its Armed Forces or provide them to international terrorists who would do so and the extreme magnitude of harm that would result to the United States and its citizens from such an attack, combine to justify action by the United States to defend itself."

The day before the Senate vote, Senator Clinton delivered a hawkish speech on the Senate floor that included the following remarks:

THE TRANSCRIPT

"In the four years since the inspectors, intelligence reports show that Saddam Hussein has worked to rebuild his chemical and biological weapons stock, his missile delivery capability, and his nuclear program. He has also given aid, comfort and sanctuary to terrorists, including al Qaeda members, though there is apparently no evidence of his involvement in the terrible events of September 11, 2001. It is clear, however, that if left unchecked Saddam Hussein will continue to increase his capability to wage biological and chemical warfare and will keep trying to develop nuclear weapons. Should he succeed in that endeavor, he could alter the political and security landscape of the Middle East which, as we know all too well, affects American security. This much is undisputed."

—Senator Hillary Rodham Clinton on the Senate floor, October 10, 2002

She then discussed demands by some that the United States take no action without United Nations approval. Hillary clearly understood that the UN would likely handcuff U.S. military action:

> The United Nations is an organization that is still growing and maturing. It often lacks cohesion to enforce its own mandates. And when the Security Council members use the veto on occasion for reasons of narrow national interest, it cannot act.... In the case of Iraq, recent comments indicate that one or two Security Council members might never approve forces against Saddam Hussein until he has actually used chemical, biological, or God forbid, nuclear weapons.

Revisionist History

But Hillary quickly backed off from her pro-war orientation, instead using the war as a political weapon against the president and the Republican Party.

By 2005 Clinton's rhetoric on the war was markedly different from the sentiments expressed in her Senate speech. In November 2005 she wrote an open letter to her constituents (see Exhibit A) claiming she had supported the war "on the basis of the evidence presented by the administration, assurances they gave that they would first seek to resolve the issue of weapons of mass destruction peacefully through United Nations–sponsored inspections, and the argument that the resolution was needed because Saddam Hussein never did anything to comply with his obligations that he was not forced to do."

She omitted any reference to Saddam Hussein's aid to al Qaeda and the shortfalls of the United Nations that she had emphasized three years earlier. Clinton further claimed that she had been "publicly and privately assured" the administration would seek international support for inspections in Iraq.

Nothing in the Iraqi War Resolution, however, mandated that the administration seek UN approval for its actions in Iraq.

By voting for that resolution, Clinton had clearly supported the unilateral enforcement of UN resolutions by the United States.

In fact, the war resolution specifically authorized "all necessary means"—not UN means—to force Iraqi compliance. Asserting that "Iraq's suppression of the civilian population violates the United Nations Security Council Resolution 698," the resolution declared that Congress "supports the use of all necessary means to achieve the goals of the United Nations Security Council Resolution 688."

The resolution reiterated President Bush's commitment to "work with the United Nations Security Council to meet our common challenge" in Iraq. But the bill made clear that the U.S. itself was taking responsibility to ensure that "the Security Council resolutions will be enforced, and the just demands of peace and security will be met, or action will be unavoidable."

Hillary's letter strangely interpreted the promise to "work with" the UN as a demand that the U.S. must "first seek to resolve the issue of weapons of mass destruction peacefully through the United Nations." In other words, cooperation with the UN was replaced with U.S. subordination to it.

Hillary's letter also implied that President Bush had promised in late 2002 to defer to the UN. "Before I voted in 2002," Senator Clinton wrote, "the administration publicly and privately assured me that they intended to use their authority to build international support in order to get the UN weapons inspectors back in Iraq, as articulated by the president in his Cincinnati speech on October 7, 2002."

This statement mischaracterizes the president's remarks. Here is what the president actually said in Cincinnati about UN weapons inspections:

> Clearly, to actually work, any new inspections, sanctions, or enforcement mechanisms will have to be very different. America wants the UN to be an effective organization that helps keep the peace. And that is why we are urging the Security Council to adopt a new resolution setting out tough, immediate requirements. Among those requirements: the Iraqi regime must reveal and destroy, under UN supervision, all existing weapons of mass destruction. To ensure that we learn the truth, the regime must allow witnesses to its illegal activities to be interviewed outside the country—and these witnesses must be free to bring their families with them so that they are beyond the reach of Saddam Hussein's terror and murder. And inspectors must have access to any site, at any time, without pre-clearance, without delay, without exceptions.

Demanding that inspections be "different" and given "tough, immediate requirements," and insisting that the Iraqi regime immediately destroy its weapons of mass destruction under UN supervision is quite different from a pledge "to build international support in order to get the UN inspectors back in Iraq," as Hillary interpreted it.

But President Bush's speech went even further, dismissing the likely effectiveness of further weapons inspections. "Some believe we can address this danger by simply resuming the old approach to inspections," the president said, "and applying diplomatic and economic pressure. Yet this is precisely what the world has tried to do since 1991. The UN inspections program was met with systematic deception."

Hillary argued that "the Bush administration short-circuited the UN inspectors" and abandoned efforts to secure "a larger international coalition." Once again, Hillary held the Bush administration accountable for promises it never made. President Bush never vowed to assemble a "larger coalition" before going to war, nor did he imply any country, group of countries or organization would have a veto over U.S. foreign policy.

"Many nations are joining us in insisting that Saddam Hussein's regime be held accountable," President Bush said. "They are committed to defending the international security that protects the lives of both our citizens and theirs. And that's why America is challenging all nations to take the resolutions of the UN Security Council seriously."

More Hillary Flip-Flops

Even when she still supported the war before American audiences, Hillary furiously distanced herself from this position while overseas. In March 2003, commentator Ann Coulter reported that Hillary had insisted on an Irish TV program that UN inspectors be given more time, denouncing any U.S. action against Iraq as "precipitous."

Coulter commented, "No one in the United States saw Hillary's interview on Irish TV, so she is now secretly on the record against the war, which will come in handy if the war goes badly. But if the war goes well, she is also officially on the record as being for the war, allowing the *New York Times* to call her a 'moderate.'"[1]

The same day Coulter's column appeared the Associated Press found Hillary at the Watervliet Arsenal, a government-owned weapons facility in Watervliet, New York. Back in front of U.S. reporters, the war against Iraq suddenly didn't seem so "precipitous."[2] Hillary declared to reporters: "I fully support the policy of disarming Saddam Hussein. She continued, "it is preferable that we do this in a peaceful manner through coercive inspection but if it's more of the same equivocation and prevarication we've had from him [Hussein] before at some point we have to be willing to uphold the United Nation resolutions [on disarmament]."

In September 2003, six months after Saddam's forces were routed in a lightning U.S. invasion, Hillary was showing a new, ultra-hawkish side. She defended her vote for the war resolution and defended the validity of the facts it cited. The *Washington Times* reported that "she [Clinton] said the intelligence she saw leading up to the war was consistent with intelligence from previous administrations and she checked out information with trusted Clinton administration officials."

Hillary even credited her husband for the war's success. The *Times* continued: "She noted after the 1991 Gulf War, Dick Cheney, who was defense secretary and is now vice president said wars are won with the prior administration's military, and therefore he should have written a thank-you note to Ronald Reagan." Mrs. Clinton responded, "I don't think he's done that to my husband yet. I'd be happy to deliver it personally."[3]

But a month later, as the U.S. struggled to suppress a fierce insurgency in Iraq, Hillary again turned against the war, condemning

Bush's foreign policy as "aggressive unilateralism," according to the *New York Daily News*.[4] Notwithstanding her previous defense of the intelligence assessments on Iraq, she now blasted Bush for going to war "as a first resort against perceived threats, not as a necessary final resort." A *New York Post* editorial noted that "the senator has both voted for the use of military force and criticized Bush's security policies. Talk about playing both ends against the middle!" The article justly asked, "So, is Hillary a hawk or a dove? Or is she playing New Yorkers for bird brains?"[5]

An Accomplice or a Liar

In November 2005, when Senate Minority Leader Harry Reid alleged that President Bush had "manufactured and manipulated intelligence" to mislead Americans into war, Hillary withheld comment. After all, Hillary's husband appointed George Tenet to head the CIA. And it was Tenet, still leading the CIA during the run-up to the Iraq War, who famously claimed intelligence on Iraqi weapons of mass destruction was a "slam dunk," as revealed by Bob Woodward's *Plan of Attack*.

Tenet based his assessment on the National Intelligence Estimate compiled for Democratic senator Richard Durbin, who requested in September 2002 a comprehensive report on Iraqi weapons of mass destruction and the likelihood of Saddam sharing such weapons with terrorist organizations.

Tenet's report found that Iraq was reconstituting its nuclear program; possessed chemical and biological weapons; was developing unmanned aerial vehicles that could possibly deliver biological warfare agents; that all key aspects of Iraq's offensive biological weapons program were active; and that the technology of most of these elements had significantly advanced since the Gulf War.

This was no "cherry picking" of intelligence by the Bush administration, as war protesters insist—the document was Tenet's alone.

The Senate Intelligence Committee specified that the NIE was "the Director's estimate and its finding are his."

Tenet was no Bush insider; he had risen through liberal ranks, serving as a member of former president Clinton's national security staff and working as an Intelligence Committee aide for former Intelligence Committee chairman Democratic senator David Boren of Oklahoma and Democratic senator Patrick Leahy of Vermont.

When this writer asked Hillary point blank whether she believed Tenet had intentionally falsified any evidence in his report, Hillary evaded the question, responding, "You know, I have nothing to say about that. It's one of the complicated issues surrounding intelligence that I think need to be looked into by the committee."

Bad Timing

In early 2005 Hillary rejected a deadline for withdrawing troops from Iraq, claiming a deadline "just gives a green light to the insurgents and the terrorist, that if they just wait us out they can basically have the country. It's not in our interests, given the sacrifice we've made."

Nevertheless, a few months later she supported a failed amendment to a defense bill requiring the president to establish precisely such a deadline. By 2006 Hillary no longer had any discernable opinion on the question of withdrawing U.S. troops from Iraq. In a speech at the liberal Take Back America conference in June, she said, "I do not think it is a smart strategy either for the president to continue with his open-ended commitment," but "nor do I think it's a smart strategy to set a date certain" to withdraw troops.

Hillary's one constant in Iraq has been to say whatever seems politically expedient.

VRWC ACTION PLAN

Senator Clinton has tried to position herself between her party's pro-UN, antiwar stance and the president's aggressive strategy toward Iraq. The result is waffling and hypocrisy as well as potential clashes with her party. There is no telling what position Hillary will take in her White House bid, but this issue provides a great opportunity for the VRWC to exploit her indecisiveness and the split in her party.

EXHIBIT A

Hillary Clinton's Financial Disclosure Forms

UNITED STATES SENATE PUBLIC FINANCIAL DISCLOSURE REPORT
FOR ANNUAL AND TERMINATION REPORTS

Last Name	First Name and Middle Initial	Annual Report — Calendar Year Covered by Report:	Senate Office / Agency in Which Employed
CLINTON	HILLARY RODHAM	2000	U.S. SENATE
Senate Office Address *(Number, Street, City, State, and ZIP Code)*	**Senate Office Telephone No.** *(Include Area Code)*	**Termination Report** — Termination Date (Mo., Day, Yr.):	**Prior Office / Agency in Which Employed**
476 RUSSELL SENATE OFFICE WASHINGTON, D.C. 20510	202-224-4451		

AFTER READING THE INSTRUCTIONS - ANSWER EACH OF THESE QUESTIONS AND ATTACH THE RELEVANT PART

Did any individual or organization make a donation to charity in lieu of paying you for a speech, appearance, or article in the reporting period? If yes, Complete and Attach PART I.	YES [ ] NO [X]	Did you, your spouse, or dependent child receive any reportable travel or reimbursements for travel in the reporting period (i.e., worth more than $260 from one source)? If yes, Complete and Attach PART VI.	YES [ ] NO [X]
Did you or your spouse have earned income (e.g., salaries or fees) or non-investment income of more than $200 from any reportable source in the reporting period? If yes, Complete and Attach PART II.	YES [X] NO [ ]	Did you, your spouse, or dependent child have any reportable liability (more than $10,000) during the reporting period? If yes, Complete and Attach PART VII.	YES [X] NO [ ]
Did you, your spouse, or dependent child receive unearned or investment income of more than $200 in the reporting period or hold any reportable asset worth more than $1,000 at the end of the period? If yes, Complete and Attach PART IIIA and/or IIIB.	YES [X] NO [ ]	Did you hold any reportable positions on or before the date of filing in the current calendar year? If yes, Complete and Attach PART VIII.	YES [ ] NO [X]
Did you, your spouse, or dependent child purchase, sell, or exchange any reportable asset worth more than $1,000 in the reporting period? If yes, Complete and Attach PART IV.	YES [ ] NO [X]	Do you have any reportable agreement or arrangement with an outside entity? If yes, Complete and Attach PART IX.	YES [X] NO [ ]
Did you, your spouse, or dependent child receive any reportable gift in the reporting period (i.e., aggregating more than $260 and not otherwise exempt)? If yes, Complete and Attach PART V.	YES [ ] NO [X]	If this is your FIRST Report: Did you receive compensation of more than $5,000 from a single source in the two prior years? If yes, Complete and attach Part X.	YES [ ] NO [X]

File this report and any amendments with the Secretary of the Senate, Office of Public Records, Room 232, Hart Senate Office Building, U.S. Senate, Washington, D.C. 20510. $200 Penalty for filing more than 30 days after due date.

This Financial Disclosure Statement is required by the Ethics in Government Act of 1978, as amended. The statement will be made available by the Office of the Secretary of the Senate to any requesting person upon written application and will be reviewed by the Select Committee on Ethics. Any individual who knowingly and willfully falsifies, or who knowingly and willfully fails to file this report may be subject to civil and criminal sanctions. (See 5 U.S.C. app. 6, 104, and 18 U.S.C. 1001.)

Certification	Signature of Reporting Individual	Date *(Month, Day, Year)*
I CERTIFY that the statements I have made on this form and all attached schedules are true, complete and correct to the best of my knowledge and belief.	Hillary Rodham Clinton	May 15, 2001

For Official Use Only - Do Not Write Below This Line

	Signature of Reviewing Official	Date *(Month, Day, Year)*
It is the opinion of the reviewer that the statements made in this form are in compliance with Title I of the Ethics in Government Act.		

For Official Use Only - Do Not Write Below This Line

SECRETARY OF THE SENATE
01 MAY 15 PM 3:00

Previous Editions Cannot Be Used

Revised 3/00

Exhibit A

Reporting Individual's Name: HILLARY RODHAM CLINTON

PART II. EARNED AND NON-INVESTMENT INCOME

Page Number: 2

Report the source (name and address), type, and amount of earned income to you from any source aggregating $200 or more during the reporting period. For your spouse, report the source (name and address) and type of earned income which aggregate $1,000 or more during the reporting period. No amount needs to be specified for your spouse (see page 3, Part B of the Instructions). Do not report income from employment by the U.S. Government for you or your spouse.

Individuals not covered by the Honoraria Ban:
For you and/or your spouse, report honoraria income received which aggregates $200 or more by exact amount, give the date of, and describe the activity (speech, appearance or article) generating such honoraria payment. Do not include payments in lieu of honoraria reported on Part I.

	Name of Income Source	Address (City, State)	Type of Income	Amount
Example:	JP Computers MCI (Spouse)	EXAMPLE Wash., D.C. Arlington, VA	EXAMPLE Salary Salary	$15,000 Over $1,000
1	SIMON & SHUSTER, INC.	LIVONIA, MI	BOOK ROYALTIES	$8,534*
2				
3	*Senator Clinton donates the entire amount to			
4	charitable organizations.			
5				
6				
7				
8				
9				
10				
11				
12				
13				
14				

Previous Editions Cannot Be Used

Revised 3/00

Reporting Individual's Name: HILLARY RODHAM CLINTON

PART IIIA. PUBLICLY TRADED ASSETS AND UNEARNED INCOME SOURCES

Page Number: 3

BLOCK A — Identity of Publicly Traded Assets and Unearned Income Sources

Report the complete name of each publicly traded asset held by you, your spouse, or your dependent child (see page 3, Part B of the instructions), for production of income or investment which:
(1) had a value exceeding $1,000 at the close of the reporting period; and/or
(2) generated over $200 in "unearned" income during the reporting period.
Include on this Part IIIA a complete identification of each public bond, mutual fund, publicly traded partnership interest, excepted investment funds, bank accounts, excepted and qualified blind trusts, and publicly traded assets of a retirement plan.

BLOCK B — Valuation of Assets
At close of reporting period. If none, or less than $1,001, check the 1st column.

BLOCK C — Type and Amount of Income
If "None (or less than $201)" is checked, no other entry is needed in Block C for that item. This includes income received or accrued to the benefit of the individual.

	Block A	None (or less than $1,001)	$1,001 - $15,000	$15,001 - $50,000	$50,001 - $100,000	$100,001 - $250,000	$250,001 - $500,000	$500,001 - $1,000,000	Over $1,000,000***	$1,000,001 - $5,000,000	$5,000,001 - $25,000,000	$25,000,001 - $50,000,000	Over $50,000,000	Dividends	Rent	Interest	Capital Gains	Excepted Investment Fund	Excepted Trust	Qualified Blind Trust	Other (Specify Type)	None (or less than $201)	$201 - $1,000	$1,001 - $2,500	$2,501 - $5,000	$5,001 - $15,000	$15,001 - $50,000	$50,001 - $100,000	$100,001 - $1,000,000	Over $1,000,000***	$1,000,001 - $5,000,000	Over $5,000,000	Actual Amount Required if "Other" Specified
S DC J	Example: IBM Corp. (stock) NYSE			x		EXAMPLE								x		EXAMPLE							x			EXAMPLE							
	Example: Keystone Equity Fund (widely diversified)				x		EXAMPLE											x	EXAMPLE						x		EXAMPLE						
1 J	BANK OF AMERICA - PERSONAL	X																				X											
2 J	CITIBANK - CHECKING ACCOUNT				X																	X											
3 DC	FIRST STAR CD (FORMERLY MERCANTILE BANK)			X												X							X										
4 DC	U.S. SAVINGS BONDS		X																			X											
5 DC	VERIZON COMMON (FORMERLY BELL ATLANTIC COMMON)			X										X									X										
6 DC	BELLSOUTH COMMON			X										X									X										
7	NORTHWESTERN MUTUAL LIFE INSURANCE (CASH VALUE)			X												X									X								
8 S	NORTHWESTERN MUTUAL LIFE INSURANCE (CASH VALUE)			X												X									X								
9 S	ARKANSAS PUBLIC EMPLOYEES RETIREMENT SYSTEM		X																			X											
10 S	OGE CERTIFIED & SENATE QUALIFIED BLIND TRUST					X														X						X							

EXEMPTION TEST *(see instructions before marking box)*: If you omitted any asset because it meets the three-part test for exemption described in the instructions, please check here. ☐

*** This category applies only if the asset is/was held independently by the spouse or dependent child. If the asset is/was either held by the filer or jointly held, use the other categories of value, as appropriate.

Previous Editions Cannot Be Used

Revised 2/01

Exhibit A

Reporting Individual's Name: HILLARY RODHAM CLINTON

PART IIIA. PUBLICLY TRADED ASSETS AND UNEARNED INCOME SOURCES

Page Number 4

BLOCK A — Identity of Publicly Traded Assets and Unearned Income Sources

Report the complete name of each publicly traded asset held by you, your spouse, or your dependent child (see page 3, Part B of the instructions), for production of income or investment which:

(1) had a value exceeding $1,000 at the close of the reporting period; and/or

(2) generated over $200 in "unearned" income during the reporting period.

Include on this Part IIIA a complete identification of each public bond, mutual fund, publicly traded partnership interest, excepted investment funds, bank accounts, excepted and qualified blind trusts, and publicly traded assets of a retirement plan.

BLOCK B — Valuation of Assets At close of reporting period. If none, or less than $1,001, check the 1st column.

BLOCK C — Type and Amount of Income If "None (or less than $201)" is checked, no other entry is needed in Block C for that item. This includes income received or accrued to the benefit of the individual.

	Block A	None (or less than $1,001)	$1,001 - $15,000	$15,001 - $50,000	$50,001 - $100,000	$100,001 - $250,000	$250,001 - $500,000	$500,001 - $1,000,000	Over $1,000,000***	$1,000,001 - $5,000,000	$5,000,001 - $25,000,000	$25,000,001 - $50,000,000	Over $50,000,000
Example:	IBM Corp. (stock) NYSE			x		EXAMPLE							
Example:	Keystone Equity Fund (widely diversified)				x		EXAMPLE						
1	OGE CERTIFIED & SENATE QUALIFIED BLIND TRUST							X					
D 2	OGE CERTIFIED & SENATE QUALIFIED BLIND TRUST				X								
D 3	AT&T COMMON		X										
D 4	LUCENT TECHNOLOGY COMMON		X										
5	"IT TAKES A VILLAGE" (1)(2) SIMON & SHUSTER, INC. (ALSO	X											
6	REPORTED PART II)												
7	THE RIGGS BANK OF WASHINGTON DC (CHECKING ACCOUNT)		X										
8	HENRY G. FREEDMAN, JR PIN MONEY FUND (2)	X											
D 9	STATE STREET CORPORATION		X										
10													

Block C — Type of Income

	Block A	Dividends	Rent	Interest	Capital Gains	Excepted Investment Fund	Excepted Trust	Qualified Blind Trust	Other (Specify Type)
Example:	IBM Corp. (stock) NYSE	x	EXAMPLE						
Example:	Keystone Equity Fund (widely diversified)					x	EXAMPLE		
1	OGE CERTIFIED & SENATE QUALIFIED BLIND TRUST							X	
D 2	OGE CERTIFIED & SENATE QUALIFIED BLIND TRUST							X	
D 3	AT&T COMMON								
D 4	LUCENT TECHNOLOGY COMMON								
5	"IT TAKES A VILLAGE" (1)(2) SIMON & SHUSTER, INC. (ALSO								BOOK ROYALTIES
6	REPORTED PART II)								
7	THE RIGGS BANK OF WASHINGTON DC (CHECKING ACCOUNT)								
8	HENRY G. FREEDMAN, JR PIN MONEY FUND (2)								ANNUITY
D 9	STATE STREET CORPORATION								
10									

Block C — Amount of Income

	Block A	None (or less than $201)	$201 - $1,000	$1,001 - $2,500	$2,501 - $5,000	$5,001 - $15,000	$15,001 - $50,000	$50,001 - $100,000	$100,001 - $1,000,000	Over $1,000,000***	$1,000,001 - $5,000,000	Over $5,000,000	Actual Amount Required if "Other" Specified
Example:	IBM Corp. (stock) NYSE		x		EXAMPLE								
Example:	Keystone Equity Fund (widely diversified)				x	EXAMPLE							
1	OGE CERTIFIED & SENATE QUALIFIED BLIND TRUST								X				
D 2	OGE CERTIFIED & SENATE QUALIFIED BLIND TRUST					X							
D 3	AT&T COMMON	X											
D 4	LUCENT TECHNOLOGY COMMON	X											
5	"IT TAKES A VILLAGE" (1)(2) SIMON & SHUSTER, INC. (ALSO												$8,534
6	REPORTED PART II)												
7	THE RIGGS BANK OF WASHINGTON DC (CHECKING ACCOUNT)	X											
8	HENRY G. FREEDMAN, JR PIN MONEY FUND (2)												$12,000
D 9	STATE STREET CORPORATION	X											
10													

EXEMPTION TEST *(see instructions before marking box)*: If you omitted any asset because it meets the three-part test for exemption described in the instructions, please check here. ☐

(1) NO ROYALTIES DUE AND OWING AS OF 12/31/00. FUTURE VALUE NOT ASCERTAINABLE.

*** This category applies only if the asset is/was held independently by the spouse or dependent child. If the asset is/was either held by the filer or jointly held, use the other categories of value, as appropriate.

(2) EACH YEAR MRS. CLINTON CONTRIBUTES THE ENTIRE AMOUNT TO CHARITABLE ORGANIZATIONS.

Previous Editions Cannot Be Used | Revised 8/01

Reporting Individual's Name: HILLARY RODHAM CLINTON

PART VII. LIABILITIES

Page Number: 5

Report liabilities over $10,000 owed by you, your spouse, or dependent child (see page 3, Part B of the Instructions), to any one creditor at any time during the reporting period. Check the highest amount owed during the reporting period. **Exclude:** (1) Mortgages on your personal residences unless rented; (2) loans secured by automobiles, household furniture or appliances; and (3) liabilities owed to certain relatives listed in Instructions. See Instructions for reporting revolving charge accounts.

SP, DC, or J	Name of Creditor	Address of Creditor	Type of Liability		Interest Rate		Category of Amount of Value (x): $10,001 - $15,000		$50,001 - $100,000		$250,001 - $500,000		Over $1,000,000***		$5,000,001 - $25,000,000		Over $50,000,000
Example:	First District Bank	Washington, D.C. EXAMPLE	Mortgage on undeveloped land EXAMPLE		13%				x		EXAMPLE						
	John Jones	Washington, D.C. EXAMPLE	Promissory note EXAMPLE		10%						x		EXAMPLE				
1 J	WILLIAMS & CONNOLLY	WASHINGTON, DC	LEGAL FEES	1998-2000										X			
2 S	SKADDEN ARPS	WASHINGTON, DC	LEGAL FEES	1998										X			
3 S	WRIGHT LINDSEY & JENNINGS	LITTLE ROCK, AR	LEGAL FEES	1998				X									
4 S	WILSON, ENGSTROM, CURUM & COULTER	LITTLE ROCK, AR	LEGAL FEES	2000				X									
5 S	MAYER, BROWN & PLATT	WASHINGTON, DC	LEGAL FEES	1998							X						
6																	
7																	
8																	
9																	
10																	
11																	
12																	
13																	
14																	

EXEMPTION TEST *(see instructions before marking box):* If you omitted any liability because it meets the three-part test for exemption described in the Instructions, please check here. ☐

***This category applies only if the obligation was solely that of the spouse or dependent child. If the obligation was the filer's or a joint obligation with the spouse or dependent child, use the other categories, as appropriate.

Previous Editions Cannot Be Used

Revised 3/00

Exhibit A

Reporting Individual's Name: HILLARY RODHAM CLINTON

PART IX. AGREEMENTS OR ARRANGEMENTS

Page Number: 6

Report your agreements or arrangements for future employment (including agreements with a publisher for writing a book), leaves of absence, continuation of payment by a former employer (including severance payments), or continuing participation in an employee benefit plan. See Instructions regarding the reporting of negotiations for any of these arrangements or benefits.

	Status and Terms of any Agreement or Arrangement	Parties	Date
Example:	Pursuant to partnership agreement, will receive lump sum payment of capital account & partnership share calculated on services performed through 11/9X and retained pension benefits (diversified, independently managed, fully funded, defined contribution plan)	Jones & Smith, Hometown, USA **EXAMPLE**	1/83
1	PUBLISHING AGREEMENT REGARDING THE LITERARY WORK "IT TAKES A VILLAGE" (WILL RECEIVE ROYALTY PAYMENTS	SIMON & SHUSTER, INC.	1/4/96
2	PURSUANT TO USUAL AND CUSTOMARY TERMS OF THE TRADE)		
3	PUBLISHING AGREEMENT FOR AUTOBIOGRAPHICAL LITERARY WORK APPROVED BY SELECT COMMITTEE ON ETHICS (WILL RECEIVE	SIMON & SHUSTER, INC.	1/2/01
4	ROYALTY PAYMENTS PURSUANT TO USUAL AND CUSTOMARY TERMS OF THE TRADE)		
5	PUBLISHING AGREEMENT REGARDING THE LITERARY WORK "DEAR SOCKS, DEAR BUDDY" (ROYALTY PAYMENTS ASSIGNED TO	SIMON & SHUSTER, INC.	9/98
6	NATIONAL PARK FOUNDATION)		
7	CHARITABLE GIFT ASSIGNMENT REGARDING THE LITERARY WORK "DEAR SOCKS, DEAR BUDDY" (ROYALTY PAYMENTS ASSIGNED TO	NATIONAL PARK FOUNDATION	9/98
8	NATIONAL PARK FOUNDATION AND PAID DIRECTLY BY PUBLISHER)		
9	PUBLISHING AGREEMENT REGARDING THE LITERARY WORK "INVITATION TO THE WHITE HOUSE" (ROYALTY PAYMENTS	SIMON & SHUSTER, INC.	12/99
10	ASSIGNED TO WHITE HOUSE HISTORICAL SOCIETY)		
11	CHARITABLE GIFT ASSIGNMENT REGARDING THE LITERARY WORK "INVITATION TO THE WHITE HOUSE" (ROYALTY PAYMENTS	WHITE HOUSE HISTORICAL SOCIETY	12/99
12	ASSIGNED TO THE WHITE HOUSE HISTORICAL SOCIETY AND PAID DIRECTLY BY PUBLISHER)		
13			
14			
15			
16			

Previous Editions Cannot Be Used

Revised 2/01

UNITED STATES SENATE FINANCIAL DISCLOSURE REPORT
FOR ANNUAL AND TERMINATION REPORTS

Last Name	First Name and Middle Initial	Annual Report Calendar Year Covered by Report:	Senate Office / Agency in which Employed
CLINTON	HILLARY RODHAM	2001	U. S. SENATE
Senate Office Address (Number, Street, City, State, and ZIP Code)	Senate Office Telephone Number (Include Area Code)	Termination Report Termination Date (mm/dd/yy)	Prior Office / Agency in which Employed
476 RUSSELL OFFICE BLDG., WASHINGTON, DC 20510	202-224-4451		

AFTER READING THE INSTRUCTIONS - ANSWER EACH OF THESE QUESTIONS AND ATTACH THE RELEVANT PART	YES	NO
Did any individual or organization make a donation to charity in lieu of paying you for a speech, appearance, or article in the reporting period? If Yes, Complete and Attach PART I		X
Did you or your spouse have earned income (e.g., salaries or fees) or non-investment income of more than $200 from any reportable source in the reporting period? If Yes, Complete and Attach PART II.	X	
Did you, your spouse, or dependent child receive unearned or investment income of more than $200 in the reporting period or hold any reportable asset worth more than $1,000 at the end of the period? If Yes, Complete & Attach PART IIIA and/or IIIB	X	
Did you, your spouse, or dependent child purchase, sell, or exchange any reportable asset worth more than $1,000 in the reporting period? If Yes, Complete and Attach PART IV		X
Did you, your spouse, or dependent child receive any reportable gift in the reporting period (i.e., aggregating more than $260 and not otherwise exempt)? If Yes, Complete and Attach PART V		X
Did you, your spouse, or dependent child receive any reportable travel or reimbursements for travel in the reporting period (i.e., worth more than $260 from one source)? If Yes, Complete and Attach PART VI		X
Did you, your spouse, or dependent child have any reportable liability (more than $10,000) during the reporting period? If Yes, Complete and Attach PART VII.	X	
Did you hold any reportable positions on or before the date of filing in the current calendar year? If Yes, Complete and Attach PART VIII.		X
Do you have any reportable agreement or arrangement with an outside entity? If Yes, Complete and Attach PART IX	X	
If this is your FIRST Report: Did you receive compensation of more than $5,000 from a single source in the two prior years? If Yes, Complete and Attach PART X.		

File this report and any amendments with the Secretary of the Senate, Office of Public Records, Room 232, Hart Senate Office Building, U.S. Senate, Washington, DC 20510. $200 Penalty for filing more than 30 days after due date.

This Financial Disclosure Statement is required by the Ethics in Government Act of 1978, as amended. The statement will be made available by the Office of the Secretary of the Senate to any requesting person upon written application and will be reviewed by the Select Committee on Ethics. Any individual who knowingly and willfully falsifies, or who knowingly and willfully fails to file this report may be subject to civil and criminal sanctions. (See 5 U.S.C. app. 6, 104, and 18 U.S.C. 1001.)

Certification	Signature of Reporting Individual	Date (Month, Day, Year)
I CERTIFY that the statements I have made on this form and all attached schedules are true, complete and correct to the best of my knowledge and belief.	Hillary Rodham Clinton	May 15, 2002
	For Official Use Only - Do Not Write Below This Line	
It is the Opinion of the reviewer that the statements made in this form are in compliance with Title I of the Ethics in Government Act	Signature of Reviewing Official	Date (Month, Day, Year)

FOR OFFICIAL USE ONLY
Do Not Write Below this Line

SECRETARY OF THE SENATE
MAY 15 PM 3:34

(11)
A

Exhibit A

PART II. EARNED AND NON-INVESTMENT INCOME

Reporting Individual's Name	HILLARY RODHAM CLINTON	Page Number	2

Report the source (name and address), type, and amount of earned income to you from any spouse aggregating $200 or more during the reporting period. For your spouse, report the source (name and address) and type of earned income which aggregate $1,000 or more during the reporting period. No amount needs to be specified for your spouse. (See p.3, CONTENTS OF REPORTS Part B of Instructions.) Do not report income from employment by the U.S. Government for you or your spouse.

Individuals not covered by the Honoraria Ban:
For you and /or your spouse, report honoraria income received which aggregates $200 or more by exact amount, give the date of, and describe the activity (speech, appearance or article) generating such honoraria payment. Do not include payments in lieu of honoraria reported on Part I.

	Name of Income Source	Address (City, State)	Type of Income	Amount
Examples	*JP Computers*	*Wash., DC* *Example*	*Salary* *Example*	*$15,000*
	MCI (Spouse)	*Arlington, VA* *Example*	*Salary* *Example*	*Over $1,000*
1	Morgan Stanley Dean Witter & Co. (Spouse)	New York, NY	Speech - 02/05/01	$125,000
2	Aventura-Turnberry Jewish Center (Spouse)	Aventura, FL	Speech - 02/10/01	$150,000
3	Oracle Corporation (Spouse)	Redwood Shores, CA	Speech - 02/19/01	$125,000
4	Credit Suisse First Boston (Spouse)	New York, NY	Speech - 02/27/01	$125,000
5	Asian American Hotel Owners Association (Spouse)	Atlanta, GA	Speech - 03/08/01	$125,000
6	Jim Pattison Group (Spouse)	Vancouver, British Columbia Canada	Speech - 03/09/01	$150,000
7	Decision Makers InterAction (Spouse)	Maastricht, The Netherlands	Speech - 03/12/01	$150,000
8	Media Control GmbH on behalf of Media Peace Prize Committee (Spouse)	Baden Baden, Hausanschrift, Germany	Speech - 03/13/01	$250,000
9	Borsen Executive Club (Spouse)	Copenhagen, Denmark	Speech - 03/14/01	$150,000
10	Salem State College Foundation (Spouse)	Salem, MA	Speech - 03/26/01	$125,000
11	Old York Road Temple Beth Am (Spouse)	Abington, PA	Speech - 04/22/01	$125,000
12	Morgan Firestone Foundation (Spouse)	Oakville, Ontario Canada	Speech - 05/02/01	$125,000
13	Fortune Magazine Forum (Spouse)	New York, NY	Speech - 05/10/01	$250,000

PART II. EARNED AND NON-INVESTMENT INCOME

Reporting Individual's Name ☞	HILLARY RODHAM CLINTON	Page Number ☞	3

Report the source (name and address), type, and amount of earned income to you from any spouse aggregating $200 or more during the reporting period. For your spouse, report the source (name and address) and type of earned income which aggregate $1,000 or more during the reporting period. No amount needs to be specified for your spouse. (See p.3. CONTENTS OF REPORTS Part B of Instructions.) Do not report income from employment by the U.S. Government for you or your spouse.

Individuals not covered by the Honoraria Ban:
For you and /or your spouse, report honoraria income received which aggregates $200 or more by exact amount, give the date of, and describe the activity (speech, appearance or article) generating such honoraria payment. Do not include payments in lieu of honoraria reported on Part I.

	Name of Income Source	Address (City, State)	Type of Income	Amount
Examples	*JP Computers*	*Wash., DC* Example	*Salary* Example	*$15,000*
	MCI (Spouse)	*Arlington, VA* Example	*Salary* Example	*Over $1,000*
1	CLSA Ltd. (Spouse)	Hong Kong, PRC	Speech - 05/10/01	$260,000
2	Dinamo Norge (Spouse)	Lysaker, Norway	Speech - 05/14/01	$150,000
3	The Talar Forum (Spouse)	Stockholm, Sweden	Speech - 05/15/01	$183,333
4	Wirtschafts Blatt (Spouse)	Vienna, Austria	Speech - 05/16/01	$183,333
5	Puls Biznesu, Bonnier Business (Polano) (Spouse)	Warsaw, Poland	Speech - 05/17/01	$183,333
6	Fundacion Rafael Del Pino (Spouse)	Madrid, Spain	Speech - 05/18/01	$250,000
7	Independent News & Media (Spouse)	Dublin, Ireland	Speech - 05/21/01	$150,000
8	The Sunday Times Hay Festival (Spouse)	Hay-on-Wye, England	Speech - 05/26/01	$150,000
9	Paris Golf & Country Club (Spouse)	Paris, France	Speech - 06/05/01	$150,000
10	Yorkshire International Business Convention (Spouse)	Leeds, Yorkshire, England	Speech - 06/08/01	$200,000
11	Success Events International, Inc (Spouse)	Tampa, FL	Speech - 06/12/01	$125,000
12	Radio & Records (Spouse)	Los Angeles, CA	Speech - 06/15/01	$125,000
13	Success Events International, Inc (Spouse)	Tampa, FL	Speech - 06/19/01	$126,000

Exhibit A

PART II. EARNED AND NON-INVESTMENT INCOME

Reporting Individual's Name ☞	HILLARY RODHAM CLINTON	Page Number ☞	4

Report the source (name and address), type, and amount of earned income to you from any spouse aggregating $200 or more during the reporting period. For your spouse, report the source (name and address) and type of earned income which aggregate $1,000 or more during the reporting period. No amount needs to be specified for your spouse. (See p.3, CONTENTS OF REPORTS Part B of Instructions.) Do not report income from employment by the U.S. Government for you or your spouse.

Individuals not covered by the Honoraria Ban:
For you and /or your spouse, report honoraria income received which aggregates $200 or more by exact amount, give the date of, and describe the activity (speech, appearance or article) generating such honoraria payment. Do not include payments in lieu of honoraria reported on Part I.

	Name of Income Source	Address (City, State)	Type of Income	Amount
Examples	*JP Computers*	*Wash., DC* *Example*	*Salary* *Example*	*$15,000*
	MCI (Spouse)	*Arlington, VA* *Example*	*Salary* *Example*	*Over $1,000*
1	Canadian Society for Yad Vashem (Spouse)	Toronto, Ontario Canada	Speech - 06/25/01	$125,000
2	The McCarthy Group (Spouse)	London, England	Speech - 07/07/01	$200,000
3	The Varsavsky Foundation (Spouse)	Madrid, Spain	Speech - 07/10/01	$175,000
4	Valor Economico S.A. (Spouse)	Sao Paolo, Brazil	Speech - 07/11/01	$150,000
5	infoUSA, Inc. (Spouse)	Omaha, NE	Speech - 07/27/01	$200,000
6	SFX Sports Group on behalf of Magna International (Spouse)	Aurora, Ontario Canada	Speech - 08/20/01	$125,000
7	MIKI Corporation (Spouse)	Tokyo, Japan	Speech - 08/21/01	$150,000
8	MIKI Corporation (Spouse)	Tokyo, Japan	Speech - 08/22/01	$160,000
9	MIKI Corporation (Spouse)	Tokyo, Japan	Speech - 08/23/01	$150,000
10	Fundacao Armando Alvares Penteado (Spouse)	Sao Paolo, Brazil	Speech - 08/27/01	$260,000
11	Markson Sparks' on behalf of the Children's Hospital at Westmead (Spouse)	Sydney, Australia	Speech - 09/08/01	$150,000
12	Markson Sparks' on behalf of Labor Council of New South Wales (Spouse)	Sydney, Australia	Speech - 09/09/01	$160,000
13	J.T. Campbell & Co. Pty. Limited (Spouse)	Melbourne, Australia	Speech - 09/10/01	$150,000

PART II. EARNED AND NON-INVESTMENT INCOME

Reporting Individual's Name	HILLARY RODHAM CLINTON	Page Number	5

Report the source (name and address), type, and amount of earned income to you from any spouse aggregating $200 or more during the reporting period. For your spouse, report the source (name and address) and type of earned income which aggregate $1,000 or more during the reporting period. No amount needs to be specified for your spouse. (See p.3, CONTENTS OF REPORTS Part B of Instructions.) Do not report income from employment by the U.S. Government for you or your spouse.

Individuals not covered by the Honoraria Ban:
For you and /or your spouse, report honoraria income received which aggregates $200 or more by exact amount, give the date of. and describe the activity (speech, appearance or article) generating such honoraria payment. Do not include payments in lieu of honoraria reported on Part I.

	Name of Income Source	Address (City, State)	Type of Income	Amount
Examples:	*JP Computers*	*Wash., DC* *Example*	*Salary* *Example*	*$15,000*
	MCI (Spouse)	*Arlington, VA* *Example*	*Salary* *Example*	*Over $1,000*
1	VNU Business Media on behalf of Online Learning 2001 Conf. and Exposition (Spouse)	Minneapolis, MN	Speech - 10/01/01	$125,000
2	El Paso Holocaust Museum & Study Center (Spouse)	El Paso, TX	Speech - 10/03/01	$125,000
3	Greater Washington Society of Association Executives (Spouse)	Washington, DC	Speech - 10/09/01	$125,000
4	Economic Club of Southwestern Michigan (Spouse)	St. Joseph, MI	Speech - 10/11/01	$125,000
5	Kushner Companies (Spouse)	Florham Park, NJ	Speech - 10/17/01	$125,000
6	Colonial Life Ins. Co. (Trinidad) Ltd. (Spouse)	Trinidad Tobago, West Indies	Speech - 10/22/01	$200,000
7	Comitato per il Congresso Nazionale della Pubblicita (Spouse)	Milano, Italy	Speech - 10/25/01	$350,000
8	Seeliger Y Conde (Spouse)	Barcelona, Spain	Speech - 10/29/01	$200,000
9	Renaissance Calgary (Spouse)	Calgary, Alberta Canada	Speech - 11/08/01	$125,000
10	Pinpoint Knowledge Management, The Portables (Spouse)	Richmond, British Columbia Canada	Speech - 11/09/01	$125,000
11	America Israel Chamber of Commerce (Spouse)	Chicago, IL	Speech - 11/11/01	$125,000
12	Galeries Lafayette - Monoprix (Spouse)	Paris, France	Speech - 11/14/01	$250,000
13	Hebrew Home and Hospital, Inc. (Spouse)	West Hartford, CT	Speech - 12/02/01	$125,000

Exhibit A

PART II. EARNED AND NON-INVESTMENT INCOME

Reporting Individual's Name	HILLARY RODHAM CLINTON	Page Number	6

Report the source (name and address), type, and amount of earned income to you from any spouse aggregating $200 or more during the reporting period. For your spouse, report the source (name and address) and type of earned income which aggregate $1,000 or more during the reporting period. No amount needs to be specified for your spouse. (See p.3, CONTENTS OF REPORTS Part B of Instructions.) Do not report income from employment by the U.S. Government for you or your spouse.

Individuals not covered by the Honoraria Ban:
For you and /or your spouse, report honoraria income received which aggregates $200 or more by exact amount, give the date of, and describe the activity (speech, appearance or article) generating such honoraria payment. Do not include payments in lieu of honoraria reported on Part I.

	Name of Income Source	Address (City, State)	Type of Income	Amount
Examples	JP Computers	Wash., DC Example	Salary Example	$15,000
	MCI (Spouse)	Arlington, VA Example	Salary Example	Over $1,000
1	International Profit Associates, Inc. (Spouse)	Buffalo Grove, IL	Speech - 12/08/01	$125,000
2	Jewish National Fund (Spouse)	Glasgow, Scotland	Speech - 12/10/01	$133,334
3	Jewish National Fund (Spouse)	Manchester, England	Speech - 12/11/01	$133,333
4	Jewish National Fund (Spouse)	London, England	Speech - 12/12/01	$133,333
5	The London School of Economics and Political Science (Spouse)	London, England	Speech - 12/13/01	$ 28,100
6	British Broadcasting Corporation (Spouse)	London, England	Speech - 12/14/01	$ 75,000
7	Scherer Consulting Group and Jorg Lohr Training (Spouse)	Freising, Germany	Speech - 12/16/01	$150,000
8	Random House, Inc. (Spouse)	New York NY	Book Royalties	Over $1,000
9	Simon & Schuster, Inc - literary work	Parsippany, NJ	Book Royalties	$2,845,190
10	Simon & Schuster, Inc - It Takes a Village - (No royalties due and owing at 12/31/01 Future value not ascertainable)*	Parsippany, NJ	Book Royalties	$ 6,847
11	*Senator Clinton donates the royalties from this book to charity. In 2001 the Clintons donated in excess of $800,000 to charity including $800,000 to the Clinton Family Foundation, a Section 501(c)(3) entity			

PART IIIA. PUBLICLY TRADED ASSETS AND UNEARNED INCOME SOURCES

Reporting Individual's Name ☞ HILLARY RODHAM CLINTON

Page Number ☞ 7

BLOCK A
Identity of Publicly Traded Assets and Unearned Income Sources

Report the complete name of each publicly traded asset held by you, your spouse, or your dependent child (See p 3, CONTENTS OF REPORTS Part B of Instructions) for production of income or investment which:

(1) had a value exceeding $1,000 at the close of the reporting period, and/or
(2) generated over $200 in "unearned" income during the reporting period

Include on this PART IIIA a complete identification of each public bond, mutual fund, publicly traded partnership interest, excepted investment funds, bank accounts, excepted and qualified blind trusts, and publicly traded assets of a retirement plan.

BLOCK B
Valuation of Assets
At the close of reporting period
If None, or less than $1,001, Check the first column.

BLOCK C
Type and Amount of Income
If "None (or less than $201)" is Checked, no other entry is needed in Block C for that item. This includes income received or accrued to the benefit of the individual

S, DC or J	Block A	B: None (or less than $1,001)	B: $1,001 - $15,000	B: $15,001 - $50,000	B: $50,001 - $100,000	B: $100,001 - $250,000	B: $250,001 - $500,000	B: $500,001 - $1,000,000	B: Over $1,000,000***	B: $1,000,001 - $5,000,000	B: $5,000,001 - $25,000,000	B: $25,000,001 - $50,000,000	B: Over $50,000,000	C Type of Income: Dividends	Rent	Interest	Capital Gains	Excepted Investment Fund	Excepted Trust	Qualified Blind Trust	Other (Specify Type)	C Type and Amount of Income: None (or less than $201)	$201 - $1,000	$1,001 - $2,500	$2,501 - $5,000	$5,001 - $15,000	$15,001 - $50,000	$50,001 - $100,000	$100,001 - $1,000,000	Over $1,000,000***	$1,000,001 - $5,000,000	Over $5,000,000	Actual Amount Required if "other" Specified
Example	*IBM Corp (stock)*				X									X							*Example*		X										*Example*
Example	*Keystone Fund*					X												X			*Example*				X								*Example*
1	Bank of America - Checking Account (J)	X																				X											
2	Citibank - (Deposit Accounts) (J)										X					X													X				
3	First Star - CD (DC)			X												X							X										
4	U.S. Savings Bonds (DC)		X																			X											
5	Verizon - Common (DC)			X										X									X										
6	Bellsouth - Common (DC)		X											X									X										
7	Northwestern Mutual Life Ins. (cash value) (S)			X												X									X								

Exhibit A

PART IIIA. PUBLICLY TRADED ASSETS AND UNEARNED INCOME SOURCES

Reporting Individual's Name ☞ HILLARY RODHAM CLINTON | **Page Number** ☞ 8

BLOCK A — **Identity of Publicly Traded Assets and Unearned Income Sources**

Report the complete name of each publicly traded asset held by you, your spouse, or your dependent child (See p.3, CONTENTS OF REPORTS Part B of Instructions) for production of income or investment which:

(1) had a value exceeding $1,000 at the close of the reporting period; and/or
(2) generated over $200 in "unearned" income during the reporting period.

Include on this PART IIIA a complete identification of each public bond, mutual fund, publicly traded partnership interest, excepted investment funds, bank accounts, excepted and qualified blind trusts, and publicly traded assets of a retirement plan.

BLOCK B — **Valuation of Assets**
At the close of reporting period
If None, or less than $1,001, Check the first column

BLOCK C — **Type and Amount of Income**
If "None (or less than $201)" is Checked, no other entry is needed in Block C for that item. This includes income received or accrued to the benefit of the individual

#	Block A	None (or less than $1,001)	$1,001 - $15,000	$15,001 - $50,000	$50,001 - $100,000	$100,001 - $250,000	$250,001 - $500,000	$500,001 - $1,000,000	Over $1,000,000***	$1,000,001 - $5,000,000	$5,000,001 - $25,000,000	$25,000,001 - $50,000,000	Over $50,000,000	Type of Income: Dividends	Rent	Interest	Capital Gains	Excepted Investment Fund	Excepted Trust	Qualified Blind Trust	Other (Specify Type)	Type and Amount of Income: None (or less than $201)	$201 - $1,000	$1,001 - $2,500	$2,501 - $5,000	$5,001 - $15,000	$15,001 - $50,000	$50,001 - $100,000	$100,001 - $1,000,000	Over $1,000,000***	$1,000,001 - $5,000,000	Over $5,000,000	Actual Amount Required if "other" Specified
S, DC or J Example	*IBM Corp (stock)*				X									X							*Example*		X										*Example*
S, DC or J Example	*Keystone Fund*					X												X			*Example*				X								*Example*
1	Northwestern Mutual (cash value)			X												X									X								
2	Senate Qualified Blind Trust (J and DC)									X										X		X											Net Loss
3	Arkansas Public Employees Ret System (S)		X																			X											
4	AT&T Common (DC)		X																			X											
5	Riggs Bank of Wash DC (checking acct)		X																			X											
6	State Street Corporation Common (DC)		X																			X											

PART IIIA. PUBLICLY TRADED ASSETS AND UNEARNED INCOME SOURCES

Reporting Individual's Name ☞	HILLARY RODHAM CLINTON	Page Number ☞	9

BLOCK A
Identity of Publicly Traded Assets and Unearned Income Sources
Report the complete name of each publicly traded asset held by you, your spouse, or your dependent child (See p.3, CONTENTS OF REPORTS Part B of Instructions) for production of income or investment which:

(1) had a value exceeding $1,000 at the close of the reporting period and/or
(2) generated over $200 in "unearned" income during the reporting period.

Include on this PART IIIA a complete identification of each public bond, mutual fund, publicly traded partnership interest, excepted investment funds, bank accounts, excepted and qualified blind trusts, and publicly traded assets of a retirement plan

BLOCK B
Valuation of Assets
At the close of reporting period.
If None, or less than $1,001, Check the first column.

BLOCK C
Type and Amount of Income
If "None (or less than $201)" is Checked, no other entry is needed in Block C for that item. This includes income received or accrued to the benefit of the individual

BLOCK B — Valuation of Assets

	BLOCK A	None (or less than $1,001)	$1,001 - $15,000	$15,001 - $50,000	$50,001 - $100,000	$100,001 - $250,000	$250,001 - $500,000	$500,001 - $1,000,000	Over $1,000,000***	$1,000,001 - $5,000,000	$5,000,001 - $25,000,000	$25,000,001 - $50,000,000	Over $50,000,000
S, DC or J / Example	IBM Corp (stock)				X								
S, DC or J / Example	Keystone Fund					X							
1	Lucent Technology Common (DC)	X											
2													
3													
4													
5													
6													
7													
8													
9													

BLOCK C — Type of Income

	BLOCK A	Dividends	Rent	Interest	Capital Gains	Excepted Investment Fund	Excepted Trust	Qualified Blind Trust	Other (Specify Type)
S, DC or J / Example	IBM Corp (stock)	X							*Example*
S, DC or J / Example	Keystone Fund					X			*Example*
1	Lucent Technology Common (DC)								
2									
3									
4									
5									
6									
7									
8									
9									

BLOCK C — Type and Amount of Income

	BLOCK A	None (or less than $201)	$201 - $1,000	$1,001 - $2,500	$2,501 - $5,000	$5,001 - $15,000	$15,001 - $50,000	$50,001 - $100,000	$100,001 - $1,000,000	Over $1,000,000***	$1,000,001 - $5,000,000	Over $5,000,000	Actual Amount Required if "other" Specified
S, DC or J / Example	IBM Corp (stock)		X										*Example*
S, DC or J / Example	Keystone Fund				X								*Example*
1	Lucent Technology Common (DC)	X											
2													
3													
4													
5													
6													
7													
8													
9													

EXEMPTION TEST *(see instructions before marking box)*: If you omitted any asset because it meets the three-part test for exemption described in the instructions, please check box to the right

*** This category applies only if the asset is/was held independently by the spouse or dependent child. If the asset is/was either held by the filer or jointly held, use the other categories of value, as appropriate.

Exhibit A

PART VII. LIABILITIES

Reporting Individual's Name	HILLARY RODHAM CLINTON	Page Number	10

Report liabilities over $10,000 owed by you, your spouse, or dependent child (See p.3 CONTENTS OF REPORTS Part B of Instructions), to any one creditor at any time during the reporting period. Check the highest amount owed during the reporting period. Exclude: (1) Mortgages on your personal residences unless rented; (2) loans secured by automobiles, household furniture or appliances; and (3) liabilities owed to certain relatives listed in Instructions. See Instructions for reporting revolving charge accounts.

S, DC or J	Name of Creditor	Address	Type of Liability	Date Incurred	Interest Rate	Term if Applicable	$10,001 - $15,000	$15,001 - $50,000	$50,001 - $100,000	$100,001 - $250,000	$250,001 - $500,000	$500,001 - $1,000,000	Over $1,000,000 ***	$1,000,001 - $5,000,000	$5,000,001 - $25,000,000	$25,000,001 - $50,000,000	Over $50,000,000
							Category of Amount of Value (x)										
Example	First District Bank	Wash., DC	Mortgage on undeveloped land	1981	13%	25yrs			X		E	x	a	m	p	l	e
Example	John Jones	Wash., DC	Promissory Note	1989	10%	on dmd				X	E	x	a	m	p	l	e
1	Williams & Connolly (J)	Wash., DC	Legal Fees	1998 to 2000										X			
2	Mayer Brown & Piatt (S)	Wash., DC	Legal Fees	1998							X						
3	Skadden Arps (S)	Wash., DC	Legal Fees	1998					X								
4																	
5																	
6																	
7																	
8	NOTE: In 2001 the Clintons paid in excess of $1,300,000 in legal fees for themselves and former staff members																
9																	

PART IX. AGREEMENTS OR ARRANGEMENTS

Reporting Individual's Name ☞ HILLARY RODHAM CLINTON | **Page Number** ☞ 11

Report your agreements or arrangements for future employment (including agreements with a publisher for writing a book or sale of other intellectual property), leaves of absence, continuation of payment by a former employer (including severance payments), or continuing participation in an employee benefit plan. See Instructions regarding the reporting of negotiations for any of these arrangements or benefits

	Status and Terms of any Agreement or Arrangement	Parties	Date
Example	*Pursuant to partnership agreement, will receive lump sum payment of capital account & partnership share calculated on services performed through 11/9X and retained pension benefits (diversified, independently managed, fully funded, defined contribution plan)*	*Jones & Smith, Hometown, USA* Example	*1/83*
1	Publishing agreement regarding the literary work "It Takes A Village" (will receive royalty payments pursuant to usual and customary terms of the trade)	Simon & Shuster, Inc.	1/4/96
2	Publishing agreement for autobiographical literary work approved by Select Committee on Ethics (will receive royalty payments pursuant to usual and customary terms of the trade)	Simon & Shuster, Inc.	1/2/01
3	Publishing agreement regarding the work "Dear Socks, Dear Buddy" (royalty payments assigned to National Parks Foundation)	Simon & Shuster, Inc.	9/98
4	Charitable gift assignment regarding the literary work "Dear Socks, Dear Buddy" (royalty payments assigned to National Parks Foundation and paid directly by the publisher)	National Parks Foundation	9/98
5	Publishing agreement regarding the literary work "Invitation to the White House" (royalty payments assigned to the White House Historical Society)	Simon & Shuster, Inc.	12/99
6	Charitable gift assignment regarding the literary work "Invitation to the White House" (royalty payments assigned to the White House Historical Society and paid directly by the publisher	White House Historical Society	12/99
7			
8			
9			
10			
11			
12			
13			
14			

Exhibit A

PART VII. LIABILITIES

Reporting Individual's Name	HILLARY RODHAM CLINTON	Page Number	10

Report liabilities over $10,000 owed by you, your spouse, or dependent child (See p 3 CONTENTS OF REPORTS Part B of Instructions), to any one creditor at any time during the reporting period. Check the highest amount owed during the reporting period. Exclude: (1) Mortgages on your personal residences unless rented, (2) loans secured by automobiles, household furniture or appliances; and (3) liabilities owed to certain relatives listed in Instructions. See Instructions for reporting revolving charge accounts.

S, DC or J		Name of Creditor	Address	Type of Liability	Date Incurred	Interest Rate	Term if Applicable	$10,001 - $15,000	$15,001 - $50,000	$50,001 - $100,000	$100,001 - $250,000	$250,001 - $500,000	$500,001 - $1,000,000	Over $1,000,000 ***	$1,000,001 - $5,000,000	$5,000,001 - $25,000,000	$25,000,001 - $50,000,000	Over $50,000,000
	Example	First District Bank	Wash., DC	Mortgage on undeveloped land	1981	13%	25yrs			X		F	x	a	m	p	l	e
	Example	John Jones	Wash., DC	Promissory Note	1989	10%	on dmd				X	E	x	a	m	p	l	e
1		Williams & Connolly (J)	Wash., DC	Legal Fees	1998 to 2001										X			
2		Mayer Brown & Platt (S)	Wash., DC	Legal Fees	1998							X						
3		Skadden Arps (S)	Wash., DC	Legal Fees	1998								X					
4																		
5																		
6																		
7																		
8		NOTE: In 2001 the Clintons paid in excess of $1,300,000 in legal fees for themselves and former staff members.																
9																		

UNITED STATES SENATE FINANCIAL DISCLOSURE REPORT
FOR ANNUAL AND TERMINATION REPORTS

Last Name	First Name and Middle Initial	Annual Report / Calendar Year Covered by Report	Senate Office / Agency in which Employed
CLINTON	HILLARY RODHAM	2002	U.S. SENATE
Senate Office Address (Number, Street, City, State, and ZIP Code)	Senate Office Telephone Number (Include Area Code)	Termination Report / Termination Date (mm/dd/yy):	Prior Office / Agency in which Employed
476 RUSSELL OFFICE BUILDING, WASHINGTON, DC 20510	202-224-4451		

AFTER READING THE INSTRUCTIONS - ANSWER EACH OF THESE QUESTIONS AND ATTACH THE RELEVANT PART		YES	NO
Did any individual or organization make a donation to charity in lieu of paying you for a speech, appearance, or article in the reporting period?	If Yes, Complete and Attach PART I	☐	☒
Did you or your spouse have earned income (e.g., salaries or fees) or non-investment income of more than $200 from any reportable source in the reporting period?	If Yes, Complete and Attach PART II.	☒	☐
Did you, your spouse, or dependent child receive unearned or investment income of more than $200 in the reporting period or hold any reportable asset worth more than $1,000 at the end of the period?	If Yes, Complete & Attach PART IIIA and/or IIIB.	☒	☐
Did you, your spouse, or dependent child purchase, sell, or exchange any reportable asset worth more than $1,000 in the reporting period?	If Yes, Complete and Attach PART IV.	☐	☒
Did you, your spouse, or dependent child receive any reportable gift in the reporting period (i.e., aggregating more than $285 and not otherwise exempt)?	If Yes, Complete and Attach PART V.	☐	☒
Did you, your spouse, or dependent child receive any reportable travel or reimbursements for travel in the reporting period (i.e., worth more than $285 from one source)?	If Yes, Complete and Attach PART VI	☐	☒
Did you, your spouse, or dependent child have any reportable liability (more than $10,000) during the reporting period?	If Yes, Complete and Attach PART VII.	☒	☐
Did you hold any reportable positions on or before the date of filing in the current calendar year?	If Yes, Complete and Attach PART VIII.	☐	☒
Do you have any reportable agreement or arrangement with an outside entity?	If Yes, Complete and Attach PART IX.	☒	☐
If this is your FIRST Report: Did you receive compensation of more than $5,000 from a single source in the two prior years?	If Yes, Complete and Attach PART X.	☐	☐

File this report and any amendments with the Secretary of the Senate, Office of Public Records, Room 232, Hart Senate Office Building, U.S. Senate, Washington, DC 20510. $200 Penalty for filing more than 30 days after due date.

This Financial Disclosure Statement is required by the Ethics in Government Act of 1978, as amended. The statement will be made available by the Office of the Secretary of the Senate to any requesting person upon written application and will be reviewed by the Select Committee on Ethics. Any individual who knowingly and willfully falsifies, or who knowingly and willfully fails to file this report may be subject to civil and criminal sanctions. (See 5 U.S.C. app. 6, 104, and 18 U.S.C. 1001.)

FOR OFFICIAL USE ONLY
Do Not Write Below this Line

SECRETARY OF THE SENATE
03 MAY 15 PM 2:27

Certification	Signature of Reporting Individual	Date (Month, Day, Year)
I CERTIFY that the statements I have made on this form and all attached schedules are true, complete and correct to the best of my knowledge and belief.	HR Clinton	5/15/03

For Official Use Only - Do Not Write Below This Line

	Signature of Reviewing Official	Date (Month, Day, Year)
It is the Opinion of the reviewer that the statements made in this form are in compliance with Title I of the Ethics in Government Act.		

A (10)

Exhibit A

PART II. EARNED AND NON-INVESTMENT INCOME

Reporting Individual's Name ☞	HILLARY RODHAM CLINTON	Page Number ☞	2

Report the source (name and address), type, and amount of earned income to you from any spouse aggregating $200 or more during the reporting period. For your spouse, report the source (name and address) and type of earned income which aggregate $1,000 or more during the reporting period. No amount needs to be specified for your spouse. (See p.3, CONTENTS OF REPORTS Part B of Instructions.) Do not report income from employment by the U.S. Government for you or your spouse.

Individuals not covered by the Honoraria Ban:
For you and /or your spouse, report honoraria income received which aggregates $200 or more by exact amount, give the date of, and describe the activity (speech, appearance or article) generating such honoraria payment. Do not include payments in lieu of honoraria reported on Part I.

	Name of Income Source	Address (City, State)		Type of Income		Amount
Examples	*JP Computers*	*Wash., DC*	*Example*	*Salary*	*Example*	*$15,000*
	MCI (Spouse)	*Arlington, VA*	*Example*	*Salary*	*Example*	*Over $1,000*
1	University of Judaism (Spouse)	Universal City, CA.		Speech 1/14/02		$125,000
2	The Dabbagh Group on behalf of STARS (Spouse)	Dubai, United Arab Emirates		Speech 1/17/02		$300,000
3	Future Generation Foundation (Spouse)	Cairo, Egypt		Speech 1/18/02		$175,000
4	The Dabbagh Group on behalf of the Jeddah Economic Forum (Spouse)	Jeddah, Saudi Arabia		Speech 1/20/02		$300,000
5	Ness Technologies, Inc. (Spouse)	Tel Aviv, Israel		Speech 1/21/02		$150,000
6	Stree - Global Investments in Women (Spouse)	Palo Alto, CA		Speech 1/29/02		$125,000
7	Educational Institute of The AHLA (Spouse)	Santa Barbara, CA		Speech 1/31/02		$125,000
8	WIZO (Spouse)	Miami Beach, FL		Speech 2/7/02		$125,000
9	Group Vivendi Universal (Spouse)	Sundance, UT		Speech 2/11/02		$150,000
10	Long Island Association, Inc. (Spouse)	Woodbury, NY		Speech 2/15/02		$125,000
11	ORT Montreal (Spouse)	Montreal, Quebec Canada		Speech 2/18/02		$125,000
12	Austrailian Council for the Promotion of Peaceful Reunification of China (Spouse)	Sydney, Australia		Speech 2/22/02		$300,000
13	Markson Sparks on behalf of Princess Margaret Children's Hospital, Perth (Spouse)	Perth, Australia		Speech 2/23/02		$125,000

PART II. EARNED AND NON-INVESTMENT INCOME

Reporting Individual's Name ☞	HILLARY RODHAM CLINTON	Page Number ☞	3

Report the source (name and address), type, and amount of earned income to you from any spouse aggregating $200 or more during the reporting period. For your spouse, report the source (name and address) and type of earned income which aggregate $1,000 or more during the reporting period. No amount needs to be specified for your spouse. (See p.3, CONTENTS OF REPORTS Part B of Instructions.) Do not report income from employment by the U.S Government for you or your spouse.

Individuals not covered by the Honoraria Ban:
For you and /or your spouse, report honoraria income received which aggregates $200 or more by exact amount, give the date of, and describe the activity (speech, appearance or article) generating such honoraria payment. Do not include payments in lieu of honoraria reported on Part I.

	Name of Income Source	Address (City, State)		Type of Income		Amount
Examples:	*JP Computers*	*Wash., DC*	*Example*	*Salary*	*Example*	*$15,000*
	MCI (Spouse)	*Arlington, VA*	*Example*	*Salary*	*Example*	*Over $1,000*
1	Markson Sparks on behalf of The Women and Children's Hospital, Adelaide (Spouse)	Adelaide, Australia		Speech 2/25/02		$125,000
2	Australian Information Industry Association (Spouse)	Adelaide, Australia		Speech 2/26/02		$250,000
3	Markson Sparks on behalf of The Microsurgery Foundation, Melbourne (Spouse)	Melbourne, Australia		Speech 2/27/02		$125,000
4	Markson Sparks on behalf of The Royal Children's Hospital Foundation, Brisbane (Spouse)	Brisbane, Australia		Speech 3/1/02		$125,000
5	Markson Sparks on behalf of The Prince of Wales Medical Research Institute, Sydney (Spouse)	Sydney, Australia		Speech 3/2/02		$125,000
6	Tufts University (Spouse)	Medford, MA		Speech 3/13/02		$125,000
7	One Family - Israel Emergency Solidarity Fund (Spouse)	New York, NY		Speech 3/14/02		$125,000
8	Maruri Communications Group (Spouse)	Guayaquil, Equador		Speech 3/16/02		$200,000
9	Listin Diario (Spouse)	LaRomana, Dominican Republic		Speech 3/18/02		$250,000
10	Personal Dynamics on behalf of Provente.com (Spouse)	Montreal, Quebec Canada		Speech 4/5/02		$125,000
11	EPC International on behalf of Workshop Ischgl-Club of the Alps (Spouse)	Ischgl, Austria		Speech 4/13/02		$245,000
12	Warburg Pincus (Spouse)	New York, NY		Speech 4/15/02		$125,000
13	Hunter College Foundation (Spouse)	New York, NY		Speech 5/6/02		$ 35,000

Exhibit A

PART II. EARNED AND NON-INVESTMENT INCOME

Reporting Individual's Name	HILLARY RODHAM CLINTON	Page Number	4

Report the source (name and address), type, and amount of earned income to you from any spouse aggregating $200 or more during the reporting period. For your spouse, report the source (name and address) and type of earned income which aggregate $1,000 or more during the reporting period. No amount needs to be specified for your spouse. (See p.3, CONTENTS OF REPORTS Part B of Instructions.) Do not report income from employment by the U.S. Government for you or your spouse.

Individuals not covered by the Honoraria Ban:
For you and /or your spouse, report honoraria income received which aggregates $200 or more by exact amount, give the date of, and describe the activity (speech, appearance or article) generating such honoraria payment. Do not include payments in lieu of honoraria reported on Part I.

	Name of Income Source	Address (City, State)	Type of Income	Amount
Examples:	*JP Computers*	*Wash., DC* *Example*	*Salary* *Example*	*$15,000*
	MCI (Spouse)	*Arlington, VA* *Example*	*Salary* *Example*	*Over $1,000*
1	Compuware Corporation (Spouse)	Dana Point, CA	Speech 5/10/02	$125,000
2	Gruner & Jahr Publishing USA on behalf of The American Jewish Committee (Spouse)	New York, NY	Speech 5/15/02	$125,000
3	Global Artists on behalf of Nihon University (Spouse)	Tokyo, Japan	Speech 5/21/02	$200,000
4	CLSA Ltd (Spouse)	Hong Kong, PRC	Speech 5/22/02	$250,000
5	dnmStrategies on behalf of JingJi Real Estate Development Group (Spouse)	Shenzhen, PRC	Speech 5/23/02	$200,000
6	Success Resources Pte Ltd. (Spouse)	Singapore	Speech 5/24/02	$250,000
7	BMW Group of New Zealand (Spouse)	Auckland, New Zealand	Speech 5/27/02	$137,500
8	Protocol Resource and Operation Services (Spouse)	Dublin, Ireland	Speech 6/6/02	$200,000
9	Aripaeva Kirjastus (Spouse)	Tallin, Estonia	Speech 6/10/02	$150,000
10	The American University in Dubai (Spouse)	Dubai, United Arab Emirates	Speech 6/11/02	$150,000
11	Nordstrom International APS on behalf of World Celebrity Golf (Spouse)	Stockholm, Sweeden	Speech 7/6/02	$300,000
12	Ahmet San Productions on behalf of TUSIAD (Spouse)	Istanbul, Turkey	Speech 7/6/02	$250,000
13	Toranto Hadassah - WIZO (Spouse)	Toranto, Ontario Canada	Speech 7/29/02	$125,000

PART II. EARNED AND NON-INVESTMENT INCOME

Reporting Individual's Name ☞	HILLARY RODHAM CLINTON	Page Number ☞	5

Report the source (name and address), type, and amount of earned income to you from any spouse aggregating $200 or more during the reporting period. For your spouse, report the source (name and address) and type of earned income which aggregate $1,000 or more during the reporting period. No amount needs to be specified for your spouse. (See p.3, CONTENTS OF REPORTS Part B of Instructions.) Do not report income from employment by the U.S. Government for you or your spouse.

Individuals not covered by the Honoraria Ban:
For you and /or your spouse, report honoraria income received which aggregates $200 or more by exact amount, give the date of, and describe the activity (speech, appearance or article) generating such honoraria payment. Do not include payments in lieu of honoraria reported on Part I.

	Name of Income Source	Address (City, State)	Type of Income	Amount
Examples	*JP Computers*	*Wash., DC* *Example*	*Salary* *Example*	*$15,000*
	MCI (Spouse)	*Arlington, VA* *Example*	*Salary* *Example*	*Over $1,000*
1	PeopleSoft, Inc. (Spouse)	New Orleans, LA	Speech 8/29/02	$125,000
2	The German Union of Small and Medium-Sized Compaines (Spouse)	Munich, Germany	Speech 10/4/02	$100,000
3	Media Control GmbH (Spouse)	Baden Baden, Germany	Speech 10/05/02	$100,000
4	American Friends of the Rabin Medical Center (Spouse)	New York, NY	Speech 10/27/02	$125,000
5	London Drugs (Spouse)	Mississauga, Ontario Canada	Speech 11/4/02	$125,000
6	The Abraham Fund (Spouse)	New York, NY	Speech 11/6/02	$125,000
7	Celebrity Forum II (Spouse)	San Jose, CA	Speech 11/11/02	$100,000
8	MPSF, Inc. (Spouse)	Oakland, CA	Speech 11/12/02	$100,000
9	MPSF, Inc. (Spouse)	San Mateo, CA	Speech 11/13/02	$100,000
10	MPSF, Inc. (Spouse)	San Rafael, CA	Speech 11/14/02	$100,000
11	Celebrity Forum II (Spouse)	Cupertino, CA	Speech 11/15/02	$100,000
12	University of California - Davis (Spouse)	Davis, CA	Speech 11/17/02	$100,000
13	Mito City Political Research Group (Spouse)	Mito City, Japan	Speech 11/19/02	$400,000

Exhibit A

PART II. EARNED AND NON-INVESTMENT INCOME

Reporting Individual's Name ☞	HILLARY RODHAM CLINTON	Page Number ☞	6

Report the source (name and address), type, and amount of earned income to you from any spouse aggregating $200 or more during the reporting period. For your spouse, report the source (name and address) and type of earned income which aggregate $1,000 or more during the reporting period. No amount needs to be specified for your spouse. (See p.3, CONTENTS OF REPORTS Part B of Instructions.) Do not report income from employment by the U.S. Government for you or your spouse.

Individuals not covered by the Honoraria Ban:
For you and /or your spouse, report honoraria income received which aggregates $200 or more by exact amount, give the date of, and describe the activity (speech, appearance or article) generating such honoraria payment. Do not include payments in lieu of honoraria reported on Part I.

	Name of Income Source	Address (City, State)		Type of Income		Amount
Examples:	*JP Computers*	*Wash., DC*	*Example*	*Salary*	*Example*	*$15,000*
	MCI (Spouse)	*Arlington, VA*	*Example*	*Salary*	*Example*	*Over $1,000*
1	Global Artists (Spouse)	Tokyo, Japan		Speech 11/21/02		$100,000'
2	Value Grupo Financiero (Spouse)	Monterrey, Mexico		Speech 12/2/02		$175,000
3	National Society for the Prevention of Cruelty to Children (Spouse)	Lancashire, England		Speech 12/7/02		$100,000
4	Temple Beth Avodah (Spouse)	Newton, MA		Speech 12/9/02		$125,000
5	GBD Group (Spouse)	Rotterdam, The Netherlands		Speech 12/13/02		$250,000
6	United Israel Appeal of Geneva (Spouse)	Geneva, Switzerland		Speech 12/14/02		$150,000
7	RDM Group (Spouse)	Rotterdam, The Netherlands		Speech 12/15/02		$125,000
8	European Travel Commission (Spouse)	New York, NY		Speech 12/18/02		$125,000
9	Info USA, Inc. (Spouse)	Omaha, NE		Nonemployee Compensation		Over $1,000
10	Simon & Schuster, Inc. - literary work	Parsippany, NJ		Book Royalties		$1,149,621
11	Simon & Schuster, Inc. - It Takes a Village (no royalties due and owing at 12/31/02. Future value not ascertainable)*	Parsippany, NJ		Book Royalties		$1,237
12	*Senator Clinton donates the royalties from this book to charity.					
13						

PART IIIA. PUBLICLY TRADED ASSETS AND UNEARNED INCOME SOURCES

Reporting Individual's Name ☞ HILLARY RODHAM CLINTON — **Page Number** ☞ 7

BLOCK A
Identity of Publicly Traded Assets and Unearned Income Sources

Report the complete name of each publicly traded asset held by you, your spouse, or your dependent child, (See p.3, CONTENTS OF REPORTS Part B of Instructions) for production of income or investment which:

(1) had a value exceeding $1,000 at the close of the reporting period; and/or
(2) generated over $200 in "unearned" income during the reporting period.

Include on this PART IIIA a complete identification of each public bond, mutual fund, publicly traded partnership interest, excepted investment funds, bank accounts, excepted and qualified blind trusts, and publicly traded assets of a retirement plan.

BLOCK B
Valuation of Assets

At the close of reporting period.
If None, or less than $1,001, Check the first column.

#	S, DC, or J / Asset	None (or less than $1,000)	$1,001 - $15,000	$15,001 - $50,000	$50,001 - $100,000	$100,001 - $250,000	$250,001 - $500,000	$500,001 – $1,000,000	Over $1,000,000***	$1,000,001 - $5,000,000	$5,000,001 - $25,000,000	$25,000,001 - $50,000,000	Over $50,000,000
Ex.	*IBM Corp (stock)*				x								
Ex.	*(S) Keystone Fund*					x							
1	Citibank (Deposit Accounts) (J)									X			
2	US Bank NA - CD (formerly First Star) (DC)			X									
3	U.S. Savings Bonds (DC)		X										
4	Verizon - Common (DC)		X										
5	Bellsouth - Common (DC)		X										
6	Northwest Mutual Life Insurance (cash value) (S)			X									
7	Northwest Mutual Life Insurance (cash value)			X									
8	Senate Qualified Blind Trust (J and DC)									X			
9	AT&T Common (DC)	X											
10	Arkansas Public Employees Retirement System (S)		X										

BLOCK C
Type and Amount of Income

If "None (or less than $201)" is Checked, no other entry is needed in Block C for that item. This includes income received or accrued to the benefit of the individual.

Type of Income

#	S, DC, or J / Asset	Dividends	Rent	Interest	Capital Gains	Expected Investment Fund	Expected Trust	Qualified Blind Trust	Other (Specify Type)
Ex.	*IBM Corp (stock)*	x							*Example*
Ex.	*(S) Keystone Fund*					x			*Example*
1	Citibank (Deposit Accounts) (J)			X					
2	US Bank NA - CD (formerly First Star) (DC)			X					
3	U.S. Savings Bonds (DC)								
4	Verizon - Common (DC)	X							
5	Bellsouth - Common (DC)	X							
6	Northwest Mutual Life Insurance (cash value) (S)			X					
7	Northwest Mutual Life Insurance (cash value)			X					
8	Senate Qualified Blind Trust (J and DC)							X	
9	AT&T Common (DC)								
10	Arkansas Public Employees Retirement System (S)								

Amount of Income

#	S, DC, or J / Asset	None (ore less than $201)	$201 - $1,000	$1,001 - $2,500	$2,501 - $5,000	$5,001 - $15,000	$15,001 - $50,000	$50,001 - $100,000	$100,001 - $1,000,000	Over $1,000,000***	$1,000,001 - $5,000,000	Over $5,000,000	Actual Amount Required if "Other" Specified
Ex.	*IBM Corp (stock)*		x										*Example*
Ex.	*(S) Keystone Fund*				x								*Example*
1	Citibank (Deposit Accounts) (J)							X					
2	US Bank NA - CD (formerly First Star) (DC)		X										
3	U.S. Savings Bonds (DC)	X											
4	Verizon - Common (DC)		X										
5	Bellsouth - Common (DC)		X										
6	Northwest Mutual Life Insurance (cash value) (S)				X								
7	Northwest Mutual Life Insurance (cash value)				X								
8	Senate Qualified Blind Trust (J and DC)	X											Net Loss
9	AT&T Common (DC)	X											
10	Arkansas Public Employees Retirement System (S)	X											

Exhibit A

PART IIIA. PUBLICLY TRADED ASSETS AND UNEARNED INCOME SOURCES

Reporting Individual's Name ☞	HILLARY RODHAM CLINTON	Page Number ☞	8

BLOCK A
Identity of Publicly Traded Assets and Unearned Income Sources

Report the complete name of each publicly traded asset held by you, your spouse, or your dependent child, (See p.3, CONTENTS OF REPORTS Part B of Instructions) for production of income or investment which:

(1) had a value exceeding $1,000 at the close of the reporting period, and/or
(2) generated over $200 in "unearned" income during the reporting period.

Include on this PART IIIA a complete identification of each public bond, mutual fund, publicly traded partnership interest, excepted investment funds, bank accounts, excepted and qualified blind trusts, and publicly traded assets of a retirement plan.

BLOCK B
Valuation of Assets
At the close of reporting period.
If None, or less than $1,001, Check the first column

#	S, DC, or J	Block A	None (or less than $1,000)	$1,001 - $15,000	$15,001 - $50,000	$50,001 - $100,000	$100,001 - $250,000	$250,001 - $500,000	$500,001 – $1,000,000	Over $1,000,000***	$1,000,001 - $5,000,000	$5,000,001 - $25,000,000	$25,000,001 - $50,000,000	Over $50,000,000
Ex		*IBM Corp. (stock)*				x								
Ex		*(S) Keystone Fund*					x							
1		Lucent Technology - Common (DC)	☒											
2		State Street Corporation - Common (DC)		☒										
3		Riggs Bank of Washington, D.C.		☒										
4		Comcast Corp. (received in distribution from AT&T) (DC)		☒										
5														
6														
7														
8														
9														
10														
11														

BLOCK C
Type and Amount of Income
If "None (or less than $201)" is Checked, no other entry is needed in Block C for that item. This includes income received or accrued to the benefit of the individual.

#	Block A	Type of Income: Dividends	Rent	Interest	Capital Gains	Expected Investment Fund	Expected Trust	Qualified Blind Trust	Other (Specify Type)	Amount of Income: None (ore less than $201)	$201 - $1,000	$1,001 - $2,500	$2,501 - $5,000	$5,001 - $15,000	$15,001 - $50,000	$50,001 - $100,000	$100,001 - $1,000,000	Over $1,000,000***	$1,000,001 - $5,000,000	Over $5,000,000	Actual Amount Required if "Other" Specified
Ex	*IBM Corp. (stock)*	x							*Example*		x										*Example*
Ex	*(S) Keystone Fund*					x			*Example*				x								*Example*
1	Lucent Technology - Common (DC)									☒											
2	State Street Corporation - Common (DC)									☒											
3	Riggs Bank of Washington, D.C.									☒											
4	Comcast Corp. (received in distribution from AT&T) (DC)									☒											
5																					
6																					
7																					
8																					
9																					
10																					
11																					

PART VII. LIABILITIES

Reporting Individual's Name ☞ HILLARY RODHAM CLINTON | **Page Number** ☞ 9

Report liabilities over $10,000 owed by you, your spouse, or dependent child (See p.3 CONTENTS OF REPORTS Part B of Instructions), to any one creditor at any time during the reporting period. Check the highest amount owed during the reporting period. Exclude: (1) Mortgages on your personal residences unless rented; (2) loans secured by automobiles, household furniture or appliances; and (3) liabilities owed to certain relatives listed in Instructions. See Instructions for reporting revolving charge accounts.

		Name of Creditor	Address	Type of Liability	Date Incurred	Interest Rate	Term if Applicable	$10,001 - $15,000	$15,001 - $50,000	$50,001 - $100,000	$100,001 - $250,000	$250,001 - $500,000	$500,001 - $1,000,000	Over $1,000,000***	$1,000,001 - $5,000,000	$5,000,001 - $25,000,000	$25,000,001 - $50,000,000	Over $50,000,000
Ex.	S	*First District Bank*	*Wash., DC*	*Mortgage on undeveloped land*	*1981*	*13%*	*25yrs*			X		*E*	*x*	*a*	*m*	*p*	*l*	*E*
	DC or J	*(J) John Jones*	*Wash., DC*	*Promissory Note*	*1989*	*10%*	*On dmd*				X	*E*	*x*	*a*	*m*	*p*	*l*	*E*
1		Williams & Connolly - Washington, DC (S)		Legal Fees	1999 to 2002										X			
2		Skadden Arps - Washington, DC (S)		Legal Fees	1998								X					
3		Wright Lindsey & Jennings, Little Rock, AR (J)		Legal Fees	1998*						X							
4		Mayer Brown & Platt (S)		Legal Fees	1998						X							
5																		
6		* In 2002 WLJ advised that they had identified 1998 invoices that they had never provided to the Clintons.																
7																		
8																		
9																		
10																		
11																		
12																		

EXEMPTION TEST *(see instructions before marking box)*: If you omitted any liability because it meets the three-part test for exemption described in the Instructions, please check here. ☞ ☐

***This category applies only if the obligation was solely that of the spouse or dependent child. If the obligation was the filer's or a joint obligation with the spouse or dependent child, use the other categories as appropriate.

Exhibit A

PART IX. AGREEMENTS OR ARRANGEMENTS

Reporting Individual's Name ☞	HILLARY RODHAM CLINTON	Page Number ☞	10

Report your agreements or arrangements for future employment (including agreements with a publisher for writing a book or sale of other intellectual property), leaves of absence, continuation of payment by a former employer (including severance payments), or continuing participation in an employee benefit plan. See Instructions regarding the reporting of negotiations for any of these arrangements or benefits.

	Status and Terms of any Agreement or Arrangement	Parties	Date
Examples.	*Pursuant to partnership agreement, will receive lump sum payment of capital account & partnership share calculated on services performed through 11/0X and retained pension benefits (diversified, independently managed, fully funded, defined contribution plan)*	*Jones & Smith, Hometown, USA* *Example*	*1/83*
	Employment agreement with XYZ Co. to become Vice President of Government Relations. Terms of agreement include salary between $50,001-$100,000, signing bonus between $2,501-$5,000 and stock options	*XYZ Co., Bethesda, MD* *Example*	*1/03*
1	Publishing agreement regarding the literary work "It Takes A Village" (will receive royalty payments pursuant to usual and customary terms of the trade)	Simon & Shuster, Inc.	1/4/96
2	Publishing agreement for autobiographical literary work approved by Select Committee on Ethics (will receive royalty payments pursuant to usual and customary terms of the trade)	Simon & Shuster, Inc.	1/2/01
3	Publishing agreement regarding the work "Dear Socks, Dear Buddy" (royalty payments assigned to National Parks Foundation)	Simon & Shuster, Inc.	9/98
4	Charitable gift assignment regarding the work "Dear Socks, Dear Buddy" (royalty payments assigned to National Parks Foundation and paid directly by the publisher)	National Parks Foundation	9/98
5	Publishing agreement regarding the literary work "Invitation to the White House" (royalty payments assigned to the White House Historical Society)	Simon & Shuster, Inc.	12/99
6	Charitable gift assignment regarding the literary work "Invitation to the White House" (royalty payments assigned to the White House Historical Society and paid directly by the publisher)	White House Historical Society	12/99
7			
8			
9			
10			
11			
12			
13			

UNITED STATES SENATE FINANCIAL DISCLOSURE REPORT
FOR ANNUAL AND TERMINATION REPORTS

Last Name	First Name and Middle Initial	Annual Report Calendar Year Covered by Report	Senate Office / Agency in which Employed
CLINTON	HILLARY RODHAM	2003	U.S. SENATE
Senate Office Address (Number, Street, City, State, and ZIP Code)	Senate Office Telephone Number (Include Area Code)	Termination Report Termination Date (mm/dd/yy):	Prior Office / Agency in which Employed
476 RUSSELL OFFICE BUILDING, WASH. DC 20510	202-224-4451		

AFTER READING THE INSTRUCTIONS - ANSWER EACH OF THESE QUESTIONS AND ATTACH THE RELEVANT PART	YES	NO
Did any individual or organization make a donation to charity in lieu of paying you for a speech, appearance, or article in the reporting period? If Yes, Complete and Attach PART I.		X
Did you or your spouse have earned income (e.g., salaries or fees) or non-investment income of more than $200 from any reportable source in the reporting period? If Yes, Complete and Attach PART II.	X	
Did you, your spouse, or dependent child receive unearned or investment income of more than $200 in the reporting period or hold any reportable asset worth more than $1,000 at the end of the period? If Yes, Complete & Attach PART IIIA and/or IIIB.	X	
Did you, your spouse, or dependent child purchase, sell, or exchange any reportable asset worth more than $1,000 in the reporting period? If Yes, Complete and Attach PART IV.		X
Did you, your spouse, or dependent child receive any reportable gift in the reporting period (i.e., aggregating more than $285 and not otherwise exempt)? If Yes, Complete and Attach PART V.		X
Did you, your spouse, or dependent child receive any reportable travel or reimbursements for travel in the reporting period (i.e., worth more than $285 from one source)? If Yes, Complete and Attach PART VI.		X
Did you, your spouse, or dependent child have any reportable liability (more than $10,000) during the reporting period? If Yes, Complete and Attach PART VII.	X	
Did you hold any reportable positions on or before the date of filing in the current calendar year? If Yes, Complete and Attach PART VIII.		X
Do you have any reportable agreement or arrangement with an outside entity? If Yes, Complete and Attach PART IX.	X	
If this is your FIRST Report: Did you receive compensation of more than $5,000 from a single source in the two prior years? If Yes, Complete and Attach PART X.		

File this report and any amendments with the Secretary of the Senate, Office of Public Records, Room 232, Hart Senate Office Building, U.S. Senate, Washington, DC 20510. $200 Penalty for filing more than 30 days after due date.

This Financial Disclosure Statement is required by the Ethics in Government Act of 1978, as amended. The statement will be made available by the Office of the Secretary of the Senate to any requesting person upon written application and will be reviewed by the Select Committee on Ethics. Any individual who knowingly and willfully falsifies, or who knowingly and willfully fails to file this report may be subject to civil and criminal sanctions. (See 5 U.S.C. app. 6, 104, and 18 U.S.C. 1001.)

Certification	Signature of Reporting Individual	Date (Month, Day, Year)
I CERTIFY that the statements I have made on this form and all attached schedules are true, complete and correct to the best of my knowledge and belief.	Hillary Rodham Clinton	5-17-04

For Official Use Only - Do Not Write Below This Line

	Signature of Reviewing Official	Date (Month, Day, Year)
It is the Opinion of the reviewer that the statements made in this form are in compliance with Title I of the Ethics in Government Act		

FOR OFFICIAL USE ONLY
Do Not Write Below this Line

SECRETARY OF THE SENATE
04 MAY 17 PM 2:20

Exhibit A

PART II. EARNED AND NON-INVESTMENT INCOME

Reporting Individual's Name ☞ HILLARY RODHAM CLINTON | **Page Number** ☞ 2 a

Report the source (name and address), type, and amount of earned income to you from any spouse aggregating $200 or more during the reporting period. For your spouse, report the source (name and address) and type of earned income which aggregate $1,000 or more during the reporting period. No amount needs to be specified for your spouse. (See p.3, CONTENTS OF REPORTS Part B of Instructions.) Do not report income from employment by the U.S. Government for you or your spouse.

Individuals not covered by the Honoraria Ban:
For you and /or your spouse, report honoraria income received which aggregates $200 or more by exact amount, give the date of, and describe the activity (speech, appearance or article) generating such honoraria payment. Do not include payments in lieu of honoraria reported on Part I.

	Name of Income Source	Address (City, State)	Type of Income	Amount
Examples:	*JP Computers*	*Wash., DC* *Example*	*Salary* *Example*	*$15,000*
	MCI (Spouse)	*Arlington, VA* *Example*	*Salary* *Example*	*Over $1,000*
1	Hearst Magazines (Spouse)	Scottsdale, AZ	Speech 01/12/03	$125,000
2	Financial Innovations, Inc. (Spouse)	St. Lucia	Speech 01/18/03	$100,000
3	St. James Place (Spouse)	London, England	Speech 01/24/03	$175,000
4	Aventis (Spouse)	Hollywood, FL	Speech 01/29/03	$125,000
5	Caribbean Council for Global Studies (Spouse)	Isla Verde, PR	Speech 04/05/03	$125,000
6	Beth El Synagogue (Spouse)	St. Louis Park, MN	Speech 04/13/03	$125,000
7	EchoStar Satellite Corporation (Spouse)	Atlanta, GA	Speech 05/03/03	$100,000
8	Greenwood House (Spouse)	Trenton, NJ	Speech 05/18/03	$125,000
9	Fool Proof (Spouse)	Seattle, WA	Speech 09/16/03	$125,000
10	Banco ce Mexico (Spouse)	Mexico City, Mexico	Speech 10/09/03	$150,000
11	Verinvest S.C. on behalf of Mexico Business Summit (Spouse)	Veracruz, Mexico	Speech 10/13/03	$150,000
12	Council of Insurance Agents and Brokers (Spouse)	Greenbrier, WV	Speech 10/14/03	$125,000
13	A & E Television Networks (Spouse)	New York, NY	Speech 10/14/03	$125,000

PART II. EARNED AND NON-INVESTMENT INCOME

Reporting Individual's Name ☞	HILLARY RODHAM CLINTON	Page Number ☞	2 b

Report the source (name and address), type, and amount of earned income to you from any spouse aggregating $200 or more during the reporting period. For your spouse, report the source (name and address) and type of earned income which aggregate $1,000 or more during the reporting period. No amount needs to be specified for your spouse. (See p.3, CONTENTS OF REPORTS. Part B of Instructions.) Do not report income from employment by the U.S. Government for you or your spouse.

Individuals not covered by the Honoraria Ban:
For you and /or your spouse, report honoraria income received which aggregates $200 or more by exact amount, give the date of, and describe the activity (speech, appearance or article) generating such honoraria payment. Do not include payments in lieu of honoraria reported on Part I.

	Name of Income Source	Address (City, State)	Type of Income	Amount
Examples:	*JP Computers*	*Wash., DC* *Example*	*Salary* *Example*	*$15,000*
	MCI (Spouse)	*Arlington, VA* *Example*	*Salary* *Example*	*Over $1,000*
14	American Chamber of Commerce in Spain (Spouse)	Barcelona, Spain	Speech 10/20/03	$250,000
15	Diario de Noticias (Spouse)	Lisbon, Portugal	Speech 10/21/03	$250,000
16	Greater Washington Society of Association Executives (Spouse)	Washington, DC	Speech 10/27/03	$125,000
17	Antwerp Diamond High Council (Spouse)	Antwerp, Belgium	Speech 11/03/03	$200,000
18	dnmStrategies on behalf of Business Week's 7th Annual CEO Forum (Spouse)	Hong Kong, PRC	Speech 11/06/03	$200,000
19	Jiannanchun Group Co., LTD (Spouse)	Mianzhun, Sichuan, China	Speech 11/09/03	$250,000
20	Seoul Broadcasting System (Spouse)	Seoul, Korea	Speech 11/14/03	$250,000
21	Sakura Capital Management Company, Ltd. (Spouse) (speech was canceled, proceeds donated to the William J. Clinton Presidential Library Foundation on a tax neutral basis)	Tokyo, Japan	Speech Scheduled for 11/17/03	$500,000
22	Dentsu Inc. Chubu on behalf of Aichi Gakuin University (spouse)	Nisshin City, Japan	Speech 11/19/03	$250,000
23	Global Artists on behalf of Yamakawa Ryutsu System Co., Ltd. (Spouse)	Kyoto, Japan	Speech 11/19/03	$140,000

Exhibit A

PART II. EARNED AND NON-INVESTMENT INCOME

Reporting Individual's Name ☞	HILLARY RODHAM CLINTON	Page Number ☞	2 c

Report the source (name and address), type, and amount of earned income to you from any spouse aggregating $200 or more during the reporting period. For your spouse, report the source (name and address) and type of earned income which aggregate $1,000 or more during the reporting period. No amount needs to be specified for your spouse. (See p.3, CONTENTS OF REPORTS Part B of Instructions.) Do not report income from employment by the U.S. Government for you or your spouse.

Individuals not covered by the Honoraria Ban:
For you and /or your spouse, report honoraria income received which aggregates $200 or more by exact amount, give the date of, and describe the activity (speech, appearance or article) generating such honoraria payment. Do not include payments in lieu of honoraria reported on Part I.

	Name of Income Source	Address (City, State)	Type of Income	Amount
Examples:	*JP Computers*	*Wash., DC* *Example*	*Salary* *Example*	*$15,000*
	MC: (Spouse)	*Arlington, VA* *Example*	*Salary* *Example*	*Over $1,000*
24	Global Artists on behalf of Arita Co., Ltd (Spouse)	Fukuota, Japan	Speech 11/20/03	$ 140,000
25	MDM Investments Ltd. on behalf of Maz Concerts (Spouse)	Winnipeg, Manitoba, Canada	Speech 12/8/03	$ 125,000
26	Simon & Schuster, Inc. - Living History (book advance and royalties)	Parsippany, NJ	Book Royalties	$2,287,521
27	Simon & Schuster, Inc. - It Takes a Village (Senator Clinton donates the royalties from this book to charity)	Parsippany, NJ	Book Royalties	$ 1,238
28	Info USA, Inc. (Spouse)	Omaha, NE	Nonemployee Compensation	over $1,000
29	Yucaipa Global Opportunities Fund I, LLC (Spouse)	Los Angeles, CA	Guaranteed payments to partner	over $1,000

PART IIIA. PUBLICLY TRADED ASSETS AND UNEARNED INCOME SOURCES

Reporting Individual's Name ☞ HILLARY RODHAM CLINTON

Page Number ☞ 3

BLOCK A
Identity of Publicly Traded Assets and Unearned Income Sources

Report the complete name of each publicly traded asset held by you, your spouse, or your dependent child (See p.3, CONTENTS OF REPORTS Part B of Instructions) for production of income or investment which:

(1) had a value exceeding $1,000 at the close of the reporting period; and/or
(2) generated over $200 in "unearned" income during the reporting period.

Include on this PART IIIA a complete identification of each public bond, mutual fund, publicly traded partnership interest, excepted investment funds, bank accounts, excepted and qualified blind trusts, and publicly traded assets of a retirement plan.

BLOCK B
Valuation of Assets
At the close of reporting period.
If None, or less than $1,001, Check the first column.

S, DC or J	Block A	None (or less than ($1,001)	$1,001 - $15,000	$15,001 - $50,000	$50,001 - $100,000	$100,001 - $250,000	$250,001 - $500,000	$500,001 - $1,000,000	Over $1,000,000***	$1,000,001 - $5,000,000	$5,000,001 - $25,000,000	$25,000,001 - $50,000,000	Over $50,000,000
Example	*IBM Corp. (stock)*				X								
Example	*Keystone Fund*					X							
1	Citibank (Deposit Accounts) (J)									X			
2	Northwest Mutual Life Insurance (cash value)(S)			X									
3	Northwest Mutual Life Insurance (cash value)			X									
4	Senate Qualified Blind Trust (J)									X			
5	Arkansas Public Employees Retirement System (S)			X									
6	Riggs Bank of Washington, DC		X										
7													

BLOCK C
Type and Amount of Income
If "None (or less than $201)" is Checked, no other entry is needed in Block C for that item. This includes income received or accrued to the benefit of the individual.

Type of Income

S, DC or J	Block A	Dividends	Rent	Interest	Capital Gains	Excepted Investment Fund	Excepted Trust	Qualified Blind Trust	Other (Specify Type)
Example	*IBM Corp. (stock)*	X							*Example*
Example	*Keystone Fund*			X		X			*Example*
1	Citibank (Deposit Accounts) (J)			X					
2	Northwest Mutual Life Insurance (cash value)(S)			X					
3	Northwest Mutual Life Insurance (cash value)			X					
4	Senate Qualified Blind Trust (J)							X	
5	Arkansas Public Employees Retirement System (S)								
6	Riggs Bank of Washington, DC								
7									

Amount of Income

S, DC or J	Block A	None (or less than $201)	$201 - $1,000	$1,001 - $2,500	$2,501 - $5,000	$5,001 - $15,000	$15,001 - $50,000	$50,001 - $100,000	$100,001 - $1,000,000	Over $1,000,000**	$1,000,001 - $5,000,000	Over $5,000,000	Actual Amount Required if "other" Specified
Example	*IBM Corp. (stock)*		X										*Example*
Example	*Keystone Fund*				X								*Example*
1	Citibank (Deposit Accounts) (J)						X						
2	Northwest Mutual Life Insurance (cash value)(S)				X								
3	Northwest Mutual Life Insurance (cash value)				X								
4	Senate Qualified Blind Trust (J)								X				
5	Arkansas Public Employees Retirement System (S)	X											
6	Riggs Bank of Washington, DC	X											
7													

Exhibit A

PART VII. LIABILITIES

Reporting Individual's Name ☞ HILLARY RODHAM CLINTON | **Page Number** ☞ 4

Report liabilities over $10,000 owed by you, your spouse, or dependent child (See p.3 CONTENTS OF REPORTS Part B of Instructions), to any one creditor at any time during the reporting period. Check the highest amount owed during the reporting period. Exclude: (1) Mortgages on your personal residences unless rented; (2) loans secured by automobiles, household furniture or appliances; and (3) liabilities owed to certain relatives listed in Instructions. See Instructions for reporting revolving charge accounts.

	Name of Creditor	Address	Type of Liability	Date Incurred	Interest Rate	Term if Applicable	$10,001 - $15,000	$15,001 - $50,000	$50,001 - $100,000	$100,001 - $250,000	$250,001 - $500,000	$500,001 - $1,000,000	Over $1,000,000 ***	$1,000,001 - $5,000,000	$5,000,001 - $25,000,000	$25,000,001 - $50,000,000	Over $50,000,000
S DC or J	Ex-ample First District Bank	Wash., DC	Mortgage on undeveloped land	1981	13%	25yrs			X		E	x	a	m	p	l	e
	John Jones	Wash., DC	Promissory Note	1989	10%	on dmd				X	E	x	a	m	p	l	e
1	Williams & Connolly (S)*	Wash., DC	Legal Fees	2000 to 2002										X			
2	Wright Lindsey & Jennings (J)*	Little Rock, AR	Legal Fees	1998						X							
3	Skadden Arps (S)	Wash., DC	Legal Fees	1998								X					
4																	
5																	
6																	
7																	
	* These obligations were paid in full by December 31, 2003																

PART IX. AGREEMENTS OR ARRANGEMENTS

Reporting Individual's Name	HILLARY RODHAM CLINTON	Page Number	5

Report your agreements or arrangements for future employment (including agreements with a publisher for writing a book or sale of other intellectual property), leaves of absence, continuation of payment by a former employer (including severance payments), or continuing participation in an employee benefit plan. See Instructions regarding the reporting of negotiations for any of these arrangements or benefits.

	Status and Terms of any Agreement or Arrangement	Parties	Date
Example:	*Pursuant to partnership agreement, will receive lump sum payment of capital account & partnership share calculated on services performed through 11/0X and retained pension benefits (diversified, independently managed, fully funded, defined contribution plan)*	*Jones & Smith, Hometown, USA* *Example*	*1/83*
	Employment agreement with XYZ Co. to become Vice President of Government Relations Terms of agreement include salary between $50,001-$100,000, signing bonus between $2,501-$5,000 and stock options.	*XYZ Co., Bethesda, MD* *Example*	*1/83*
1	Publishing agreement regarding the literary work "It Takes A Village" (will receive royalty payments pursuant to usual and customary terms of the trade)	Simon & Schuster, Inc.	01/04/96
2	Publishing agreement regarding the literary work "Living History" approved by Select Committee on Ethics (will receive royalty payments pursuant to usual and customary terms of the trade)	Simon & Schuster, Inc.	01/02/01
3	Publishing agreement regarding the work "Dear Socks, Dear Buddy" (royalty payments assigned to National Parks Foundation)	Simon & Schuster, Inc.	09/98
4	Charitable gift assignment regarding the work "Dear Socks, Dear Buddy" (royalty payments assigned to National Parks Foundation and paid directly by the publisher)	National Parks Foundation	09/98
5	Publishing agreement regarding the literary work "Invitation to the White House" (royalty payments assigned to the White House Historical Association)	Simon & Schuster, Inc.	12/99
6	Charitable gift assignment regarding the literary work "Invitation to the White House" (royalty payments assigned to the White House Historical Association and paid directly by the publisher)	White House Historical Society	12/99
7			
8			
9			
10			
11			
12			
13			
14			

Exhibit A

UNITED STATES SENATE FINANCIAL DISCLOSURE REPORT FOR ANNUAL AND TERMINATION REPORTS

Last Name	First Name and Middle Initial	Annual Report Calendar Year Covered by Report	Senate Office / Agency in which Employed
CLINTON	HILLARY RODHAM	2004	U.S SENATE
Senate Office Address (Number, Street, City, State, and ZIP Code)	**Senate Office Telephone Number (Include Area Code)**	**Termination Report Termination Date (mm/dd/yy):**	**Prior Office / Agency in which Employed**
476 RUSSELL OFFICE BUILDING, WASH. DC 20510	202-224-4451		

AFTER READING THE INSTRUCTIONS - ANSWER EACH OF THESE QUESTIONS AND ATTACH THE RELEVANT PART	YES	NO
Did any individual or organization make a donation to charity in lieu of paying you for a speech, appearance, or article in the reporting period? If Yes, Complete and Attach PART I.		X
Did you or your spouse have earned income (e.g., salaries or fees) or non-investment income of more than $200 from any reportable source in the reporting period? If Yes, Complete and Attach PART II.	X	
Did you, your spouse, or dependent child receive unearned or investment income of more than $200 in the reporting period or hold any reportable asset worth more than $1,000 at the end of the period? If Yes, Complete & Attach PART IIIA and/or IIIB.	X	
Did you, your spouse, or dependent child purchase, sell, or exchange any reportable asset worth more than $1,000 in the reporting period? If Yes, Complete and Attach PART IV.		X
Did you, your spouse, or dependent child receive any reportable gift in the reporting period (i.e., aggregating more than $305 and not otherwise exempt)? If Yes, Complete and Attach PART V.		X
Did you, your spouse, or dependent child receive any reportable travel or reimbursements for travel in the reporting period (i.e., worth more than $305 from one source)? If Yes, Complete and Attach PART VI.	X	
Did you, your spouse, or dependent child have any reportable liability (more than $10,000) during the reporting period? If Yes, Complete and Attach PART VII.		X
Did you hold any reportable positions on or before the date of filing in the current calendar year? If Yes, Complete and Attach PART VIII.		X
Do you have any reportable agreement or arrangement with an outside entity? If Yes, Complete and Attach PART IX.	X	
If this is your FIRST Report: Did you receive compensation of more than $5,000 from a single source in the two prior years? If Yes, Complete and Attach PART X.		

Each question must be answered and the appropriate PART attached for each "YES" response.

File this report and any amendments with the Secretary of the Senate, Office of Public Records, Room 232, Hart Senate Office Building, U.S. Senate, Washington, DC 20510. $200 Penalty for filing more than 30 days after due date.

This Financial Disclosure Statement is required by the Ethics in Government Act of 1978, as amended. The statement will be made available by the Office of the Secretary of the Senate to any requesting person upon written application and will be reviewed by the Select Committee on Ethics. Any individual who knowingly and willfully falsifies, or who knowingly and willfully fails to file this report may be subject to civil and criminal sanctions. (See 5 U.S.C. app. 6, 104, and 18 U.S.C. 1001.)

Certification	Signature of Reporting Individual	Date (Month, Day, Year)
I CERTIFY that the statements I have made on this form and all attached schedules are true, complete and correct to the best of my knowledge and belief.	Hillary Rodham Clinton	5/16/05
For Official Use Only - Do Not Write Below This Line		
It is the Opinion of the reviewer that the statements made in this form are in compliance with Title I of the Ethics in Government Act.	Signature of Reviewing Official	Date (Month, Day, Year)

FOR OFFICIAL USE ONLY
Do Not Write Below this Line

05 MAY 16 PM 3:3
SECRETARY OF THE SENATE

PART II. EARNED AND NON-INVESTMENT INCOME

Reporting Individual's Name ☞	HILLARY RODHAM CLINTON	Page Number ☞	2

Report the source (name and address), type, and amount of earned income to you from any source aggregating $200 or more during the reporting period. For your spouse, report the source (name and address) and type of earned income which aggregate $1,000 or more during the reporting period. No amount needs to be specified for your spouse. (See p.3, CONTENTS OF REPORTS, Part B of Instructions.) Do not report income from employment by the U.S. Government for you or your spouse.

Individuals not covered by the Honoraria Ban:
For you and /or your spouse, report honoraria income received which aggregates $200 or more by exact amount, give the date of, and describe the activity (speech, appearance or article) generating such honoraria payment. Do not include payments in lieu of honoraria reported on Part I.

	Name of Income Source	Address (City, State)	Type of Income	Amount
Examples:	*JP Computers*	*Wash., DC* *Example*	*Salary* *Example*	*$15,000*
	MCI (Spouse)	*Arlington, VA* *Example*	*Salary* *Example*	*Over $1,000*
1	Fantasma (Spouse)	Sunrise, FL	Speech 01/25/04	$ 125,000
2	Citigroup (Spouse)	Paris, France	Speech 03/12/04	$ 250,000
3	Hon. Frank McKenna's Annual Business Networking Event (Spouse)	Wallace, Nova Scotia	Speech 05/05/04	$ 125,000
4	Urban Land Institute (Spouse)	New York, NY	Speech 11/05/04	$ 125,000
5	The Star Forum (Spouse)	Cherry Hill, NJ	Speech 11/10/04	$ 125,000
6	Goldman Sachs (Spouse)	New York, NY	Speech 12/03/04	$ 125,000
7	Simon & Schuster, Inc. - Living History	Parsippany, NJ	Book Royalties	$ 2,376,716
8	Simon & Schuster, Inc. - It Takes A Village - (Senator Clinton donates the royalties from this book to charity)	Parsippany, NJ	Book Royalties	$ 10,012
9	Random House (Spouse)	New York, NY	Book Royalties	over $1,000
10	Info USA (Spouse)	Omaha, NE	Nonemployee Compensation	over $1,000
11	Yucaipa Global Oppurtunities Fund I, LLC (Spouse)	Los Angeles, CA	Guaranteed payments to partner	over $1,000
12				
13				

Exhibit A

PART IIIA. PUBLICLY TRADED ASSETS AND UNEARNED INCOME SOURCES

Reporting Individual's Name ☞	HILLARY RODHAM CLINTON	Page Number ☞	3A

BLOCK A — **Identity of Publicly Traded Assets and Unearned Income Sources**

Report the complete name of each publicly traded asset held by you, your spouse, or your dependent child, (See p 3, CONTENTS OF REPORTS Part B of Instructions) for production of income or investment which:

(1) had a value exceeding $1,000 at the close of the reporting period; and/or
(2) generated over $200 in "unearned" income during the reporting period.

Include on this PART IIIA a complete identification of each public bond, mutual fund, publicly traded partnership interest, excepted investment funds, bank accounts, excepted and qualified blind trusts, and publicly traded assets of a retirement plan.

BLOCK B — **Valuation of Assets**
At the close of reporting period.
If None, or less than $1,001, Check the first column.

BLOCK C — **Type and Amount of Income**
If "None (or less than $201)" is Checked, no other entry is needed in Block C for that item. This includes income received or accrued to the benefit of the individual.

Block B — Valuation of Assets:

S, DC or J	Asset	None (or less than $1,001)	$1,001 - $15,000	$15,001 - $50,000	$50,001 - $100,000	$100,001 - $250,000	$250,001 - $500,000	$500,001 - $1,000,000	Over $1,000,000***	$1,000,001 - $5,000,000	$5,000,001 - $25,000,000	$25,000,001 - $50,000,000	Over $50,000,000
Example	IBM Corp. (stock)				X								
Example	Keystone Fund					X							
1	Citibank (Deposit Accounts) (J)										X		
2	Northwestern Mutual Life Insurance (cash value)(S)			X									
3	Northwestern Mutual Life Insurance (cash value)			X									

Block C — Type of Income:

S, DC or J	Asset	Dividends	Rent	Interest	Capital Gains	Excepted Investment Fund	Excepted Trust	Qualified Blind Trust	Other (Specify Type)
Example	IBM Corp. (stock)	X							Example
Example	Keystone Fund			X		X			Example
1	Citibank (Deposit Accounts) (J)			X					
2	Northwestern Mutual Life Insurance (cash value)(S)			X					
3	Northwestern Mutual Life Insurance (cash value)			X					

Block C — Amount of Income:

S, DC or J	Asset	None (or less than $201)	$201 - $1,000	$1,001 - $2,500	$2,501 - $5,000	$5,001 - $15,000	$15,001 - $50,000	$50,001 - $100,000	$100,001 - $1,000,000	Over $1,000,000***	$1,000,001 - $5,000,000	Over $5,000,000	Actual Amount Required if "other" Specified
Example	IBM Corp. (stock)		X										Example
Example	Keystone Fund	X											Example
1	Citibank (Deposit Accounts) (J)							X					
2	Northwestern Mutual Life Insurance (cash value)(S)					X							
3	Northwestern Mutual Life Insurance (cash value)					X							

PART IIIA. PUBLICLY TRADED ASSETS AND UNEARNED INCOME SOURCES

Reporting Individual's Name ☞ HILLARY RODHAM CLINTON | **Page Number** ☞ 3B

BLOCK A — Identity of Publicly Traded Assets and Unearned Income Sources

Report the complete name of each publicly traded asset held by you, your spouse, or your dependent child, (See p.3, CONTENTS OF REPORTS Part B of Instructions) for production of income or investment which:

(1) had a value exceeding $1,000 at the close of the reporting period, and/or
(2) generated over $200 in "unearned" income during the reporting period.

Include on this PART IIIA a complete identification of each public bond, mutual fund, publicly traded partnership interest, excepted investment funds, bank accounts, excepted and qualified blind trusts, and publicly traded assets of a retirement plan

BLOCK B — Valuation of Assets
At the close of reporting period.
If None, or less than $1,001, Check the first column

BLOCK C — Type and Amount of Income
If "None (or less than $201)" is Checked, no other entry is needed in Block C for that item. This includes income received or accrued to the benefit of the individual.

#	Block A	B: None (or less than $1,001)	B: $1,001 - $15,000	B: $15,001 - $50,000	B: $50,001 - $100,000	B: $100,001 - $250,000	B: $250,001 - $500,000	B: $500,001 - $1,000,000	B: Over $1,000,000***	B: $1,000,001 - $5,000,000	B: $5,000,001 - $25,000,000	B: $25,000,001 - $50,000,000	B: Over $50,000,000	Type of Income: Dividends	Rent	Interest	Capital Gains	Excepted Investment Fund	Excepted Trust	Qualified Blind Trust	Other (Specify Type)	Amount of Income: None (or less than $201)	$201 - $1,000	$1,001 - $2,500	$2,501 - $5,000	$5,001 - $15,000	$15,001 - $50,000	$50,001 - $100,000	$100,001 - $1,000,000	Over $1,000,000***	$1,000,001 - $5,000,000	Over $5,000,000	Actual Amount Required if "other" Specified
S, DC or J Example	IBM Corp. (stock)				X									X							Example		X										Example
Example	Keystone Fund					X										X		X			Example	X											Example
4	Senate Qualified Blind Trust (J)										X									X									X				
5	Riggs Bank of Washington, D.C.	X																				X											
6	Arkansas Public Employees Retirement System (S)			X												X							X										
7																																	
8																																	

Exhibit A

PART VI. REIMBURSEMENTS

Reporting Individual's Name ☞		Page Number ☞	4

Report necessary travel related expenses from each source aggregating more than $305 in value during the reporting period received by you, your spouse and/or dependent child in connection with your provision of services at a speaking engagement, fact-finding event, or other event (personal campaign, or otherwise). Disclosure is required regardless of whether those expenses were **reimbursed** to the individual or **paid directly** by the sponsoring organization. A description of the itinerary, including date(s) and the nature of expenses is required. If you are reimbursed for more than one trip from the same sponsor (and the trips added together are worth more than $305), then you must report each trip individually, even if the reimbursement for each separate trip does not equal more than $305. Report Gifts of travel in Part V.

Exclude: Travel related expenses provided by federal, state, D.C., and local governments; or by a foreign government; reimbursements from campaign funds which are reported to the FEC; reimbursements to a spouse or dependent child totally independent of his or her relationship to you; and reimbursements reported to the Office of Public Records pursuant to Senate Rule 35. For further information, see Instructions.

	Name of Source	Address of Source	Dates and Brief Description
Example:	*All States Company*	*Maintown, TX* Example	*Roundtrip air travel from Washington, D.C. to Maintown, TX and lunch for self and spouse for speaking engagement: May 1-3,200X* Example
1	The Panetta Institute	Seaside, CA	Lodging expenses for speech made in Seaside, California on June 28, 2004
2			
3			
4			
5			
6			
7			
8			
9			
10			
11			
12			

PART IX. AGREEMENTS OR ARRANGEMENTS

Reporting Individual's Name	HILLARY RODHAM CLINTON	Page Number	5

Report your agreements or arrangements for future employment (including agreements with a publisher for writing a book or sale of other intellectual property), leaves of absence, continuation of payment by a former employer (including severance payments), or continuing participation in an employee benefit plan. See Instructions regarding the reporting of negotiations for any of these arrangements or benefits.

	Status and Terms of any Agreement or Arrangement	Parties	Date
Example:	*Pursuant to partnership agreement, will receive lump sum payment of capital account & partnership share calculated on services performed through 11/9X and retained pension benefits (diversified, independently managed, fully funded, defined contribution plan)*	*Jones & Smith, Hometown, USA* *Example*	*1/83*
Example:	*Employment agreement with XYZ Co. to become Vice President of Government Relations. Terms of agreement include salary between $50,001-$100,000, signing bonus between $2,501-$5,000 and stock options*	*XYZ Co., Bethesda, MD* *Example*	*1/0X*
1	Publishing agreement regarding the literary work "It Takes a Village" (will receive royalty payments pursuant to usual and customary terms of the trade)	Simon & Schuster, Inc.	01/04/96
2	Publishing agreement regarding the literary work "Living History" approved by Select Committee on Ethics (will receive royalty payments pursuant to usual and customary terms of the trade)	Simon & Schuster, Inc.	01/02/01
3	Publishing agreement regarding the work "Dear Socks, Dear Buddy" (royalty payments assigned to National Parks Foundation)	Simon & Schuster, Inc.	09/98
4	Charitable gift assignment regarding the work "Dear Socks, Dear Buddy" (royalty payments assigned to National Parks Foundation and paid directly by the publisher)	National Parks Foundation	09/98
5	Publishing agreement regarding the literary work "Invitation to the White House" (royalty payments assigned to the White House Historical Society)	Simon & Schuster, Inc.	12/99
6	Charitable gift assignment regarding the literary work "Invitation to the White House (royalty payments assigned to the White House Historical Society and paid directly by the publisher)	White House Historical Society	12/99
7			
8			
9			
10			
11			
12			
13			
14			

Exhibit A

00000230323

UNITED STATES SENATE FINANCIAL DISCLOSURE REPORT FOR ANNUAL AND TERMINATION REPORTS

Last Name	First Name and Middle Initial	Annual Report Calendar Year Covered by Report:	Senate Office / Agency in Which Employed
CLINTON	HILLARY RODHAM	2005	U.S. SENATE
Senate Office Address (Number, Street, City, State, and ZIP Code)	**Senate Office Telephone Number (include Area Code)**	**Termination Report Termination Date (mm/dd/yy):**	**Prior Office / Agency in Which Employed**
476 RUSSELL OFFICE BLDG. WASHINGTON, DC 20510	202-224-4451		

AFTER READING THE INSTRUCTIONS - ANSWER EACH OF THESE QUESTIONS AND ATTACH THE RELEVANT PART

Question	YES	NO
Did any individual or organization make a donation to charity in lieu of paying you for a speech, appearance, or article in the reporting period? If Yes, Complete and Attach PART I.		X
Did you or your spouse have earned income (e.g., salaries or fees) or non-investment income of more than $200 from any reportable source in the reporting period? If Yes, Complete and Attach PART II.	X	
Did you, your spouse, or dependent child receive unearned or investment income of more than $200 in the reporting period or hold any reportable asset worth more than $1,000 at the end of the period? If Yes, Complete & Attach PART IIIA and/or IIIB.	X	
Did you, your spouse, or dependent child purchase, sell, or exchange any reportable asset worth more than $1,000 in the reporting period? If Yes, Complete and Attach PART IV.		X
Did you, your spouse, or dependent child receive any reportable gift in the reporting period (i.e., aggregating more than $305 and not otherwise exempt)? If Yes, Complete and Attach PART V.		X
Did you, your spouse, or dependent child receive any reportable travel or reimbursements for travel in the reporting period (i.e., worth more than $305 from one source)? If Yes, Complete and Attach PART VI.		X
Did you, your spouse, or dependent child have any reportable liability (more than $10,000) during the reporting period? If Yes, Complete and Attach PART VII.		X
Did you hold any reportable positions on or before the date of filing in the current calendar year? If Yes, Complete and Attach PART VIII.		X
Do you have any reportable agreement or arrangement with an outside entity? If Yes, Complete and Attach PART IX.	X	
If this is your FIRST Report: Did you receive compensation of more than $5,000 from a single source in the two prior years? If Yes, Complete and Attach PART X.		

Each question must be answered and the appropriate PART attached for each "YES" response.

File this report and any amendments with the Secretary of the Senate, Office of Public Records, Room 232, Hart Senate Office Building, U.S. Senate, Washington, DC 20510. $200 Penalty for filing more than 30 days after due date.

This Financial Disclosure Statement is required by the Ethics in Government Act of 1978, as amended. The statement will be made available by the Office of the Secretary of the Senate to any requesting person upon written application and will be reviewed by the Select Committee on Ethics. Any individual who knowingly and willfully falsifies, or who knowingly and willfully fails to file this report may be subject to civil and criminal sanctions. (See 5 U.S.C. app. 6, 104, and 18 U.S.C. 1001.)

FOR OFFICIAL USE ONLY
Do Not Write Below this Line

Certification	Signature of Reporting Individual	Date (Month, Day, Year)
I CERTIFY that the statements I have made on this form and all attached schedules are true, complete and correct to the best of my knowledge and belief.	Hillary Rodham Clinton	May 12, 2006

For Official Use Only - Do Not Write Below This Line

	Signature of Reviewing Official	Date (Month, Day, Year)
It is the Opinion of the reviewer that the statements made in this form are in compliance with Title I of the Ethics in Government Act		

MAY 15 PM 2:41

8

00000230324

Reporting Individual's Name

PART II. EARNED AND NON-INVESTMENT INCOME

Page Number 2

Report the source (name and address), type, and amount of earned income to you from any source aggregating $200 or more during the reporting period. For your spouse, report the source (name and address) and type of earned income which aggregate $1,000 or more during the reporting period. No amount needs to be specified for your spouse. (See p.3, CONTENTS OF REPORTS Part B of Instructions.) Do not report income from employment by the U.S. Government for you or your spouse.

Individuals not covered by the Honoraria Ban:
For you and /or your spouse, report honoraria income received which aggregates $200 or more by exact amount, give the date of, and describe the activity (speech, appearance or article) generating such honoraria payment. Do not include payments in lieu of honoraria reported on Part I.

	Name of Income Source	Address (City, State)	Type of Income	Amount
Example:	*JP Computers*	*Wash., DC* *Example*	*Salary* *Example*	*$15,000*
	MCI (Spouse)	*Arlington, VA* *Example*	*Salary* *Example*	*Over $1,000*
1	Serono International (Spouse)	Paradise Island, The Bahamas	Speech 02/03/05	$150,000
2	Jewish Federation Council of Greater L.A. (Spouse)	Los Angeles, CA	Speech 02/16/05	$125,000
3	CLSA (Spouse)	Hong Kong, PRC	Speech 02/22/05	$100 000
4	Savage/Rothenberg Productions (Spouse)	Los Angeles, CA	Speech 03/02/05	$125,000
5	Savage/Rothenberg Productions (Spouse)	Los Angeles, CA	Speech 03/03/05	$125,000
6	Association of Southern California Defense Counsel (Spouse)	Los Angeles, CA	Speech 03/04/05	$125,000
7	Goldman Sachs (Spouse)	Kiawah Island, SC	Speech 04/20/05	$125,000
8	Global Strategic Ventures (Spouse)	New York, NY	Speech 04/26/05	$150,000
9	Deutsche Bank (Spouse)	Baltimore, MD	Speech 05/04/05	$150,000
10	Lancaster Chamber of Commerce (Spouse)	Lancaster, PA	Speech 05/04/05	$150,000
11	National Multi-Housing Council (Spouse)	New York, NY	Speech 05/10/05	$150,000
12	KMD (Spouse)	Copenhagen, Denmark	Speech 05/17/05	$250,000
13	Griwa Consulting GMBH (Spouse)	Berne, Switzerland	Speech 05/18/05	$250,000
14	American Academy of Achievement (Spouse)	New York, NY	Speech 06/01/05	$150,000

Exhibit A

00000230325

Reporting Individual's Name HILLARY RODHAM CLINTON	PART II. EARNED AND NON-INVESTMENT INCOME	Page Number 3

Report the source (name and address), type, and amount of earned income to you from any source aggregating $200 or more during the reporting period. For your spouse, report the source (name and address) and type of earned income which aggregate $1,000 or more during the reporting period. No amount needs to be specified for your spouse. (See p.3, CONTENTS OF REPORTS Part B of Instructions.) Do not report income from employment by the U.S. Government for you or your spouse.

Individuals not covered by the Honoraria Ban:
For you and /or your spouse, report honoraria income received which aggregates $200 or more by exact amount, give the date of, and describe the activity (speech, appearance or article) generating such honoraria payment. Do not include payments in lieu of honoraria reported on Part I.

	Name of Income Source	Address (City, State)	Type of Income	Amount
Example	*JP Computers*	*Wash., DC* *Example*	*Salary* *Example*	*$15,000*
Example	*MCI (Spouse)*	*Arlington VA* *Example*	*Salary* *Example*	*Over $1,000*
1	Goldman Sachs (Spouse)	Paris, France	Speech 06/06/06	$250,000
2	Congregation Beth-El Zedeck (Spouse)	Indianapolis, IN	Speech 06/08/05	$150,000
3	America's Health Insurance Plans (Spouse)	Las Vegas, NV	Speech 06/10/05	$150,000
4	Goldman Sachs (Spouse)	Greensboro, GA	Speech 06/13/05	$150,000
5	Gold Service International (Spouse)	Mexico City, Mexico	Speech 06/21/05	$200,000
6	Gold Service International (Spouse)	Bogota, Columbia	Speech 06/22/05	$200,000
7	Gold Service International (Spouse)	Sao Paulo, Brazil	Speech 06/23/05	$200,000
8	Gold Service International (Spouse)	Sao Paulo, Brazil	Speech 06/24/05	$200,000
9	Blex S.L. (Spouse)	Canary Islands, Spain	Speech 07/24/05	$350,000
10	Carnegie Abbey Club (Spouse)	Portsmouth, RI	Speech 08/11/05	$150,000
11	Deutsche Bank (Spouse)	New York, NY	Speech 08/11/05	$150,000
12	HSM Italia (Spouse)	Video Conference from New York	Speech 09/20/05	$125,000
13	Young President's Organization (Spouse)	New York, NY	Speech 09/20/05	$150,000
14	Leading Minds (Spouse)	Copenhagen, Denmark	Speech 10/03/05	$125,000

00000230326

Reporting Individual's Name		Page Number
HILLARY RODHAM CLINTON	**PART II. EARNED AND NON-INVESTMENT INCOME**	4

Report the source (name and address), type, and amount of earned income to you from any source aggregating $200 or more during the reporting period. For your spouse, report the source (name and address) and type of earned income which aggregate $1,000 or more during the reporting period. No amount needs to be specified for your spouse. (See p.3, CONTENTS OF REPORTS Part B of Instructions.) Do not report income from employment by the U.S. Government for you or your spouse.

Individuals not covered by the Honoraria Ban:
For you and /or your spouse, report honoraria income received which aggregates $200 or more by exact amount, give the date of, and describe the activity (speech, appearance or article) generating such honoraria payment. Do not include payments in lieu of honoraria reported on Part I.

	Name of Income Source	Address (City, State)	Type of Income	Amount
Example	*JP Computers*	*Wash., DC* *Example*	*Salary* *Example*	*$15,000*
	MCI (Spouse)	*Arlington, VA* *Example*	*Salary* *Example*	*Over $1,000*
1	Adam Smith Conferences (Spouse)	Moscow, Russia	Speech 10/12/05	$125,000
2	tinePublic, Inc. (Spouse)	London, Ontario, Canada	Speech 10/17/05	$125,000
3	International Centre for Business Information (Spouse)	Video Conference from Toronto, Canada	Speech 10/18/05	$125,000
4	The Power Within (Spouse)	Toronto, Canada	Speech 10/18/05	$350,000
5	The Power Within (Spouse)	Calgary, Canada	Speech 10/19/05	$300,000
6	Leading Minds (Spouse)	Sydney, Australia	Speech 10/27/05	$125,000
7	Jewish Federation of Metropolitan Chicago (Spouse)	Chicago, IL	Speech 11/07/05	$150,000
8	YPO Windy City Chapter (Spouse)	Chicago, IL	Speech 11/07/05	$100,000
9	Jewish Federation of Metropolitan Chicago (Spouse)	Chicago, IL	Speech 11/08/05	$150,000
10	Golden Tree Asset Management (Spouse)	New York, NY	Speech 11/09/05	$150,000
11	Macklowe Properties on behalf of State of Israel Bonds Development Corporation (Spouse)	New York, NY	Speech 11/10/05	$250,000
12	Global Business Enterprises (Spouse)	Abu Dhabi	Speech 11/15/05	$300,000
13	Leading Minds (Spouse)	Dubai, UAE	Speech 11/28/05	$125,000
14	Hubert Burda Media GmbH (Spouse)	Munich, Germany	Speech 12/01/05	$300,000

Exhibit A

00000230327

Reporting Individual's Name: HILLARY RODHAM CLINTON

PART II. EARNED AND NON-INVESTMENT INCOME

Page Number: 5

Report the source (name and address), type, and amount of earned income to you from any source aggregating $200 or more during the reporting period. For your spouse, report the source (name and address) and type of earned income which aggregate $1,000 or more during the reporting period. No amount needs to be specified for your spouse. (See p.3, CONTENTS OF REPORTS Part B of Instructions.) Do not report income from employment by the U.S. Government for you or your spouse.

Individuals not covered by the Honoraria Ban:
For you and /or your spouse, report honoraria income received which aggregates $200 or more by exact amount, give the date of, and describe the activity (speech, appearance or article) generating such honoraria payment. Do not include payments in lieu of honoraria reported on Part I.

	Name of Income Source	Address (City, State)	Type of Income	Amount
Example:	*JP Computers*	*Wash., DC* *Example*	*Salary* *Example*	*$15,000*
	MCI (Spouse)	*Arlington, VA* *Example*	*Salary* *Example*	*Over $1,000*
1	Leading Minds (Spouse)	Munich, Germany	Speech scheduled for 12/13/05	$125,000
2	Simon & Schuster Inc. - Living History	Parsippany, NJ	Book Royalties	$872,891
3	Simon & Schuster Inc. - It Takes a Village (Senator Clinton donates the royalties from this book to charity)	Parsippany, NJ	Book Royalties	$4,465
4	Random House (Spouse)	New York, NY	Book Royalties	over $1,000
5	Info USA (Spouse)	Omaha, NE	Nonemployee Compensation	over $1,000
6	Yucaipa Global Opportunities Fund I, LLC (Spouse)	Los Angeles, CA	Guaranteed payments to partner	over $1,000
7				
8				
9				
10				
11				
12				
13				
14				

00000230328

Reporting Individual's Name: HILLARY RODHAM CLINTON

PART IIIA. PUBLICLY TRADED ASSETS AND UNEARNED INCOME SOURCES

Page Number: 6

BLOCK A — Identity of Publicly Traded Assets And Unearned Income Sources

Report the complete name of each publicly traded asset held by you, your spouse, or your dependent child. *(See p.3, CONTENTS OF REPORTS Part B of Instructions)* for production of income or investment which
(1) had a value exceeding $1,000 at the close of the reporting period; and/or
(2) generated over $200 in "unearned" income during the reporting period.
Include on this PART IIIA a complete identification of each public bond, mutual fund, publicly traded partnership interest, excepted investment funds, bank accounts, excepted and qualified blind trusts, and publicly traded assets of a retirement plan.

BLOCK B — Valuation of Assets

At the close of reporting period. If None, or less than $1,001, Check the first column

BLOCK C — Type and Amount of Income

If "None (or less than $201)" is Checked, no other entry is needed in Block C for that item. This includes income received or accrued to the benefit of the individual.

#	Identity (Block A)	None (or less than $1,001)	$1,001 - $15,000	$15,001 - $50,000	$50,001 - $100,000	$100,001 - $250,000	$250,001 - $500,000	$500,001 – $1,000,000	Over $1,000,000***	$1,000,001 - $5,000,000	$5,000,001 - $25,000,000	$25,000,001 - $50,000,000	Over $50,000,000	Dividends	Rent	Interest	Capital Gains	Excepted Investment Fund	Excepted Trust	Qualified Blind Trust	Other (Specify Type)	None (or less than $201)	$201 - $1,000	$1,001 - $2,500	$2,501 - $5,000	$5,001 - $15,000	$15,001 - $50,000	$50,001 - $100,000	$100,001 - $1,000,000	Over $1,000,000***	$1,000,001 - $5,000,000	Over $5,000,000	Actual Amount Required if "Other" Specified
Example: S, DC, or J	*IBM Corp. (stock)*				X									X							*Example*		X										*Example*
	(S) Keystone Fund					X										X		X			*Example*	X											*Example*
1	Citibank (Deposit Accounts) (J)										X					X													X				
2	Northwestern Mutual Life Insurance (cash value) (S)			X												X										X							
3	Northwestern Mutual Life Insurance (cash value)			X												X										X							
4	Senate Qualified Blind Trust (J)										X									X									X				
5	Arkansas Public Employees Retirement System (S)			X												X							X										
6	National Life Insurance Company (cash value) (S)				X											X						X											
7																																	
8																																	
9																																	
10																																	

EXEMPTION TEST *(see instructions before marking box)* If you omitted any asset because it meets the three-part test for exemption described in the instructions, please check box to the right ☐

*** This category applies only if the asset is/was held independently by the spouse or dependent child. If the asset is/was either held by the filer or jointly held, use the other categories of value, as appropriate.

Exhibit A

00000230329

Reporting Individual's Name

PART VII. LIABILITIES

Page Number 7

Report liabilities over $10,000 owed by you, your spouse, or dependent child (See p.3 CONTENTS OF REPORTS Part B of Instructions), to any one creditor at any time during the reporting period. Check the highest amount owed during the reporting period. Exclude: (1) Mortgages on your personal residences unless rented; (2) loans secured by automobiles, household furniture or appliances; and (3) liabilities owed to certain relatives listed in Instructions. See Instructions for reporting revolving charge accounts.

	Name of Creditor	Address	Type of Liability	Date Incurred	Interest Rate	Term if Applicable	Category of Amount of Value (x): $10,001 - $15,000	$15,001 - $50,000	$50,001 - $100,000	$100,001 - $250,000	$250,001 - $500,000	$500,001 - $1,000,000	Over $1,000,000***	$1,000,001 - $5,000,000	$5,000,001 - $25,000,000	$25,000,001 - $50,000,000	Over $50,000,000
Example. S, DC, or J	*First District Bank*	*Wash., DC*	*Mortgage on undeveloped land*	*1991*	*13%*	*25yrs.*			X		E	X	A	M	P	L	E
	(J) John Jones	*Wash., DC*	*Promissory Note*	*1999*	*10%*	*On dmd*				X	E	X	A	M	P	L	E
1	Citigroup	New York, NY	Credit Card (monthly balance - paid)	2005		Revolving Ac		X									
2																	
3																	
4																	
5																	
6																	
7																	
8																	
9																	
10																	
11																	
12																	

EXEMPTION TEST *(see instructions before marking box)*: If you omitted any asset because it meets the three-part test for exemption described in the instructions, please check box to the right. ☐

*** This category applies only if the asset is/was held independently by the spouse or dependent child. If the asset is/was either held by the filer or jointly held, use the other categories of value, as appropriate.

00000230330
Reporting Individual's Name

PART IX. AGREEMENTS OR ARRANGEMENTS

Page Number 8

Report your agreements or arrangements for future employment (including agreements with a publisher for writing a book or sale of other intellectual property), leaves of absence, continuation of payment by a former employer (including severance payments), or continuing participation in an employee benefit plan. See Instructions regarding the reporting of negotiations for any of these arrangements or benefits.

	Status and Terms of any Agreement or Arrangement	Parties		Date
Example	*Pursuant to partnership agreement, will receive lump sum payment of capital account & partnership share calculated on services performed through 11/0X and retained pension benefits (diversified, independently managed, fully funded, defined contribution plan)*	*Jones & Smith, Hometown, USA*	**Example**	*1 / 83*
	Employment agreement with XYZ Co. to become Vice President of Government Relations. Terms of agreement include salary between $50,001-$100,000, signing bonus between $2,501-$5,000 and stock options	*XYZ Co., Bethesda, MD*	**Example**	*1 / 0X*
1	Publishing agreement regarding the literary work "It Takes a Village" (will receive royalty payments pursuant to usual and customary terms of the trade)	Simon & Schuster, Inc.		01/04/96
2	Publishing agreement regarding the literary work "Living History" approved by Select Committee on Ethics (will receive royalty payments pursuant to usual and customary terms of the trade)	Simon & Schuster, Inc.		01/02/01
3	Publishing agreement regarding the work "Dear Socks, Dear Buddy" (royalty payments assigned to the National Parks Foundation)	Simon & Schuster, Inc.		09/98
4	Charitable gift assignment regarding the work "Dear Socks, Dear Buddy" (royalty payments assigned to National Parks Foundation and paid directly by the publisher)	National Parks Foundation		09/98
5	Publishing agreement regarding the literary work "Invitation to the White House" (royalty payments assigned to the White House Historical Society)	Simon & Schuster, Inc.		12/99
6	Charitable gift assignment regarding the literary work "Invitation to the White House" (royalty payments assigned to the White House Historical Society and paid directly by the publisher)	White House Historical Society		12/99
7				
8				
9				
10				
11				
12				
13				
14				

EXHIBIT B

Bill Clinton's Foreign Money

Foreign entities that have paid former president Bill Clinton—money that is now accessible by Senator Clinton, and thus her campaign.

3/12/01	Decision Makers Interaction; Maastricht, Netherlands	$150,000
3/13/01	Media Control GmbH; Baden Baden, Hausanschrift, Germany	$250,000
3/14/01	Borsen Executive Club; Copenhagen, Denmark	$150,000
5/10/01	CLSA Ltd.; Hong Kong, PRC	$250,000
5/14/01	Dinamo Norge; Lysaker, Norway	$150,000
5/15/01	The Talar Forum; Stockholm, Sweden	$183,333
5/16/01	Wirstchafts Blatt; Vienna, Austria	$183,333
5/17/01	Puls Biznesu; Warsaw, Poland	$183,333
5/18/01	Fundacion Rafael Del Pino; Madrid, Spain	$250,000
5/21/01	Independent News and Media; Dublin, Ireland	$150,000
5/26/01	The Sunday Times Hay Festival; Wales, U.K.	$150,000
6/5/01	Paris Golf & Country Club; Paris, France	$150,000
6/8/01	Yorshire International Business Convention; Yorkshire, England	$200,000
6/25/01	Canadian Society for Yad Vashem; Toronto, Canada	$125,000
7/7/01	The McCarthy Group; London, England	$200,000
7/10/01	The Varsavsky Foundation; Madrid, Spain	$175,000
7/11/01	Valor Economics S.A.; Sao Paulo, Brazil	$150,000
8/21/01	MIKI Corporation; Tokyo, Japan	$150,000
8/22/01	MIKI Corporation; Tokyo, Japan	$150,000
8/23/01	MIKI Corporation; Tokyo, Japan	$150,000

Exhibit B

8/27/01	Fundacao Armando Alvares Penteado; Sao Paulo, Brazil	$250,000
9/8/01	Markson Sparks on behalf of Morehead Children's Hospital; Sydney, Australia	$150,000
9/9/01	Markson Sparkson behalf of the Labor Council of New South Wales; Sydney, Australia	$150,000
9/10/01	J.T. Campbell & Co.; Melbourne, Australia	$150,000
10/22/01	Colonial Life Ins. Co. Ltd.; Trinidad and Tobago, West Indies	$200,000
10/25/01	Comitato per il Congresso Nazionale della Pubblicita; Milan, Italy	$350,000
10/29/01	Seeliger Y Conde; Barcelona, Spain	$200,000
11/8/01	Renaissance Calgary; Calgary, Canada	$125,000
11/9/01	Pinpoint Knowledge Management, the Portables; Richmond, Canada	$125,000
11/14/01	Galeries Lafayette-Monoprix; Paris, France	$250,000
12/10/01	Jewish National Fund; Glasgow, Scotland	$133,334
12/11/01	Jewish National Fund; Manchester, England	$133,333
12/12/01	Jewish National Fund; London, England	$133,333
12/13/01	The London School of Economics and Political Science; London, England	$28,100
12/14/01	British Broadcasting Corporation; London, England	$75,000
12/16/01	Scherer Consulting Group and Jorg Lohr Training; Freising, Germany	$150,000
1/17/02	The Dabbagh Group on behalf of Stars; Dubai, United Arab Emirates	$300,000
1/18/02	Future Generation Foundation (The Geel Al-Mostaqbal Association); Cairo, Egypt	$175,000
1/20/02	The Dabbagh Group on behalf of the Jeddah Economic Forum; Jeddah, Saudi Arabia	$175,000
1/21/02	Ness Technologies, Inc.; Tel Aviv, Israel	$150,000
2/18/02	ORT Montreal; Montreal, Canada	$125,000

2/22/02	Australian Council for the Promotion of Peaceful Reunification of China; Sydney, Australia	$300,000
2/23/02	Markson Sparks on behalf of Princess Margaret Children's Hospital; Perth, Australia	$125,000
2/25/02	Markson Sparks on behalf of The Women and Children's Hospital; Adelaide, Australia	$125,000
2/26/02	Australian Information Industry Association; Adelaide, Australia	$250,000
2/27/02	Markson Sparks on behalf of The Microsurgery Foundation; Melbourne, Australia	$125,000
3/1/02	Markson Sparks on behalf of The Royal Children's Hospital Foundation; Brisbane, Australia	$125,000
3/2/02	Markson Sparks on behalf of The Prince of Wales Medical Research Institute; Sydney, Australia	$125,000
3/16/02	Maruri Communication Group; Guayaquil, Ecuador	$200,000
3/18/02	Listin Diario; LaRomana, Dominican Republic	$250,000
4/5/02	Personal Dynamics on behalf of Provente.com; Montreal, Canada	$125,000
4/13/02	EPC International on behalf of Workshop Ischgl-Club of the Alps; Ischgl, Austria	$245,000
5/21/02	Global Artists on behalf of Nihon University; Tokyo, Japan	$200,000
5/22/02	CLSA Ltd.; Hong Kong, PRC	$250,000
5/23/02	DNM Strategies on behalf of JingJi Real Estate Development Group; Shenzhen, PRC	$200,000
5/24/02	Success Resources Pte Ltd.; Singapore	$250,000
5/27/02	BMW Group of New Zealand; Auckland, New Zealand	$137,500
6/6/02	Protocol Resource and Operation Devices; Dublin, Ireland	$200,000
6/10/02	Aripaeva Kirjastus; Tallinn, Estonia	$150,000
6/11/02	The American University in Dubai; Dubai, United Arab Emirates	$150,000

Exhibit B

7/6/02	Nordstom International APS on behalf of World Celebrity Golf; Stockholm, Sweden	$300,000
7/6/02	Ahmet San Productions on behalf of TUSAID; Istanbul, Turkey	$250,000
7/29/02	Toronto Hadassah-WIZO; Toronto, Canada	$125,000
10/4/02	The German Union of Small and Medium-Sized Companies; Munich, Germany	$100,000
10/05/02	Media Control GmbH; Baden Baden, Germany	$100,000
11/4/02	London Drugs; Mississauga, Canada	$125,000
11/19/02	Mito City Political Research Group; Mito City, Japan	$400,000
11/21/02	Global Artists; Tokyo, Japan	$100,000
12/2/02	Value Grupo Financiero; Monterrey, Mexico	$175,000
12/7/02	National Society for the Prevention of Cruelty to Children; Lancashire, England	$100,000
12/13/02	GBD Group; Rotterdam, Netherlands	$125,000
12/14/02	United Israel Appeal of Geneva; Geneva, Switzerland	$150,000
12/15/02	RDM Group; Rotterdam, Netherlands	$250,000
1/18/03	Financial Innovations, Inc.; St. Lucia, West Indies	$100,000
1/24/03	St. James Place; London, England	$175,000
4/5/03	Carribbean Council for Global Studies; Isla Verde, Puerto Rico	$125,000
10/9/03	Banco de Mexico; Mexico City, Mexico	$150,000
10/9/03	Verinvest S.C. on behalf of Mexico Business Summit; Veracruz, Mexico	$150,000
10/20/03	American Chamber of Commerce in Spain; Barcelona, Spain	$250,000
10/21/03	Diario de Noticias; Lisbon, Portugal	$250,000
11/03/03	Antwerp Diamond High Council; Antwerp, Belgium	$200,000

11/9/03	Jiannanchun Group Co. Ltd.; Mianzhun, PRC	$250,000
11/14/03	Seoul Broadcasting System; Seoul, South Korea	$250,000
11/19/03	Dentsu, Inc. on behalf of Aichi Gakuin University; Nisshin City, Japan	$250,000
11/19/03	Global Artists on behalf of Yamakawa Ryutsu System Co., Ltd.; Kyoto, Japan	$140,000
11/20/03	Global Artists on behalf of Arita Co., Ltd.; Fukuota, Japan	$140,000
12/9/03	MDM Investments on behalf of Maz Concerts; Winnipeg, Canada	$125,000
5/5/04	Hon. Frank McKenna's Annual Business Networking Event; Wallace, Canada	$125,000
2/3/05	Serono International; Paradise Islands, The Bahamas	$150,000
2/22/05	CLSA; Hong Kong, PRC	$100,000
5/4/05	Deutsche Bank; Baltimore, Maryland	$150,000
5/17/05	KMD; Copenhagen, Denmark	$250,000
5/18/05	Griwa Consulting GMBH; Berne, Switzerland	$250,000
6/21/05	Gold Service International; Mexico City, Mexico	$200,000
6/22/05	Gold Service International; Bogota, Columbia	$200,000
6/23/05	Gold Service International; Sao Paulo, Brazil	$200,000
6/24/05	Gold Service International; Sao Paulo, Brazil	$200,000
7/24/05	Blex S.L.; Canary Islands, Spain	$350,000
9/20/05	HSM Italia; Video Conference from New York	$125,000
10/3/05	Leading Minds; Copenhagen, Denmark	$125,000
10/12/05	Adam Smith Conferences; Moscow, Russia	$125,000
10/17/05	tinePublic, Inc.; London, Canada	$125,000
10/18/05	International Centre for Business Information; Video Conference from Toronto, Canada	$125,000
10/18/05	The Power Within; Toronto, Canada	$350,000
10/19/05	The Power Within; Toronto, Canada	$300,000

Exhibit B

10/27/05	Leading Minds; Sydney, Australia	$125,000
11/15/05	Global Business Enterprises; Abu Dhabi, United Arab Emirates	$300,000
11/28/05	Leading Minds; Dubai, United Arab Emirates	$125,000
12/1/05	Hubert Burda Media GmbH; Munich, Germany	$300,000
12/13/05	Leading Minds; Munich, Germany	$125,000

EXHIBIT 

Letter from Hillary Clinton to Peter Paul

HILLARY RODHAM CLINTON

August 18, 2000

Mr. Peter Paul
23586 Parksouth Street
Calabasas, California 91302

Dear Peter:

Thank you so very much for hosting Saturday night's tribute to the President and for everything you did to make it the great occasion that it was. We will remember it always.

With gratitude for your friendship and warm regards, I remain

Sincerely yours,

Hillary

Hillary Rodham Clinton

Thanks so much

450 Seventh Avenue, Suite 804 New York, NY 10123 Tel (212) 239-2000 Fax (212) 563-4259 www.hillary2000.org

Paid for by the Hillary Rodham Clinton for U.S. Senate Committee, Inc.
Contributions are not Tax Deductible for Federal Income Tax Purposes

EXHIBIT

Indictment of David Rosen, Chairman of Hillary's Finance Committee

UNITED STATES DISTRICT COURT

FOR THE CENTRAL DISTRICT OF CALIFORNIA

June 2002 Grand Jury

UNITED STATES OF AMERICA, Plaintiff, v. DAVID F. ROSEN, Defendant.	CR 03-1219 I N D I C T M E N T [18 U.S.C. § 1001: False Statements; 18 U.S.C. § 2 Causing an Act to be Done and Aiding and Abetting]

The Grand Jury charges:

[18 U.S.C. §§ 1001 and 2]

INTRODUCTORY ALLEGATIONS

At all times material to this indictment:

1. Defendant DAVID F. ROSEN was the National Finance Director for the 2000 United States Senate campaign of a candidate for the United States Senate ("Senator A"), and an experienced political fundraiser who had been associated with several other campaigns for federal office.

2. As part of the election campaign, a joint fundraising committee was established ("the Joint Committee" or "the JFC") under the Federal Election Campaign Act of 1971 ("FECA"), 2 U.S.C. § 431(4),

and organized under regulations promulgated by the Federal Election Commission ("FEC"). The JFC consisted of three participants: (a) Senator A's campaign committee; (b) a national senatorial party committee; and (c) a state party committee.

3. The JFC was legally permitted to raise both "hard money" and "soft money." Funds raised and spent to influence the election of a particular candidate to federal office were known as "hard money" or "federal funds," which were subject to individual contribution limits and prohibitions against corporate contributions and expenditures. In contrast, "soft money" or "non-federal funds" were funds raised for purposes other than to influence the nomination or election of federal candidates and were not subject to FECA's individual contribution limits and FECA's prohibitions on corporate contributions and expenditures. The federal regulations governing joint fundraising committees were designed to prevent such committees from circumventing FECA's restrictions on the sources of and dollar limits on hard money.

4. The JFC also accepted "in-kind" contributions -- contributions in the form of goods or services provided for free or at below-market prices, and contributions occurring when a person or corporate entity pays a bill for fundraising or other expenses.

5. The FEC was an independent regulatory agency whose mission was to administer and enforce FECA -- the statute that governs the financing of federal elections. The duties of the FEC were to facilitate and insure the disclosure of campaign finance information required by law to be publicly disclosed and to enforce the provisions of the law including limits and prohibitions on contributions. The FEC also reviewed and audited submissions from joint fundraising committees to insure compliance with the law.

2

6. The JFC was required to prepare and file financial disclosure reports with the FEC on a quarterly basis. Among other things, these reports were to include the total amount of all funds received and all disbursements made by the JFC in connection with joint fundraising activities, as well as the source and total amount of contributions received from prohibited sources, such as corporations, including any in-kind contributions. These forms required that the information provided by the JFC be truthful, complete and accurate. Once filed, the FEC by law made these forms available to the public. Additionally, the JFC was required to maintain documents related to contributions, donations and expenditures for inspection by the FEC.

7. Defendant DAVID ROSEN, as the National Finance Director for Senator A's 2000 fundraising efforts, played a leading role in raising money for the campaign. Defendant ROSEN's responsibilities included soliciting and collecting donations for the campaign and the JFC; assisting in planning fundraising events; working with donors who underwrote event costs and who provided "in-kind" contributions; coordinating with event planners and producers who helped create and put on events; reviewing invoices and bills associated with fundraising events; and working directly with vendors who provided goods and services.

8. Defendant DAVID ROSEN's duties also included an obligation to accurately report the source and amount of contributions received, and expenses incurred, from fundraising events to the JFC's FEC compliance officer in Washington D.C., who was responsible for preparing and filing the JFC's reports with the FEC.

9. On or about July 11, 2000, defendant DAVID ROSEN, a wealthy

3

contributor ("C-1") and officials from Senator A's campaign discussed putting together a fundraiser to benefit Senator A's United States Senate campaign -- a Hollywood tribute complete with an "all-star concert" and dinner. C-1 pledged to underwrite the costs of this event. C-1 and another contributor ("C-2") agreed to host this fundraising event ("the Gala" or "the Hollywood Gala").

10. From in or about July 2000, up to and including in or about August 2000, defendant DAVID ROSEN worked out of C-1's media company's corporate offices in Los Angeles, California, which also served as the main planning office for the Hollywood Gala. Defendant ROSEN was responsible for all fundraising, planning, costs, and expenses for the Gala, and worked closely with producers and coordinators responsible for planning virtually every aspect of the Gala.

11. As part of this planning, in or about July and August 2000, defendant DAVID ROSEN was aware of the increasing costs of planning and throwing the Gala, which ultimately exceeded $1.2 million, including over $600,000 for the concert portion of the event. Between in or about July 2000, up to and including in or about October 2000, C-1 paid more than $1.1 million to produce the Hollywood Gala. C-1 used several corporate entities controlled by him ("C-1's corporate entities") to make these payments, payments which should have been disclosed as in-kind contributions or donations to the FEC.

12. On or about August 12, 2000, approximately 1,200 people attended the concert portion of the Gala. Tickets to the concert cost $1,000 each. Following the concert, approximately 350 people attended a sit-down dinner. Tickets for both the concert and dinner were $25,000 per couple.

13. In or about August 2000 through October 2000, following the

Gala, defendant DAVID ROSEN provided the JFC's compliance officer with information about the costs of the event, in-kind contributions and donations received for the purpose of preparing the JFC's third-quarter filing with the FEC. Defendant ROSEN understated to the compliance officer the costs and approximately $1.1 million in in-kind contributions and donations made by C-1.

14. Among other things, the compliance officer requested documentation supporting the costs of the concert-portion of the event. In response, defendant DAVID ROSEN instructed a member of the Hollywood Gala planning team to obtain a fictitious invoice in the amount of $200,000 for the concert production costs of the Hollywood Gala, even though defendant ROSEN well knew the concert production costs were substantially greater than $200,000. Acting on defendant ROSEN's instructions, a member of the Hollywood Gala planning team obtained such a fictitious invoice in the amount of $200,000 and provided it to defendant ROSEN.

15. In or about August and September 2000, defendant DAVID ROSEN faxed receipts and invoices for goods and services provided at the Gala from Los Angeles to the JFC's FEC compliance officer in Washington, D.C., including the fictitious $200,000 invoice. In providing the costs to the JFC's FEC compliance officer, defendant DAVID ROSEN withheld certain true costs of the Gala, including costs associated with the production of the concert, printing costs and other goods and services provided by vendors, as well as in-kind contributions and donations.

16. In or about October 2000, defendant DAVID ROSEN provided a summary of costs, in-kind contributions and donations associated with the Gala to the JFC's FEC compliance officer, knowing that the

5

compliance officer would use this information to prepare mandatory FEC filings. In addition to this written summary, defendant ROSEN also provided the compliance officer with additional financial information about the Gala by telephone and by facsimile.

17. In or about October 2000, after receiving the written summary and other information provided by defendant DAVID ROSEN and others, the JFC's compliance officer raised questions with defendant ROSEN via telephone about some of the in-kind contributions and Gala expenses provided by defendant ROSEN. Defendant ROSEN informed the JFC's compliance officer over the telephone that these numbers were accurate.

18. On or about October 15, 2000, the compliance officer submitted the JFC's Third Quarterly Report of receipts and disbursements with the FEC, which covered the time period of July 1, 2000, through September 30, 2000. On Schedule H-3 of Form 3X, the JFC reported to the FEC that it had only received $366,564.69 in in-kind contributions in connection with the Hollywood Gala, which was designated as Event 39, when in fact the JFC had received approximately $1.1 million in in-kind contributions and donations.

19. On or about January 30, 2001, as required by the FEC, the JFC filed an amended report and disclosed additional expenses for the Gala. On Schedule H-3 of this amended filing, the JFC reported to the FEC a total of $401,419 in-kind contributions and donations.

20. On or about May 2, 2001, the FEC sent a letter to the Treasurer of the JFC requesting additional information from the JFC regarding the transfer of funds from the hard money account to the soft money account in connection with the Gala. On or about May 7, 2001, the Treasurer of the JFC responded by letter to the FEC and

6

stated that the JFC had properly allocated funds from the hard money to the soft money accounts.

21. On or about July 30, 2001, the Treasurer of the JFC submitted another letter to the FEC in response to the FEC's inquiry regarding the Gala. In this letter, the Treasurer stated that the JFC's accounting of in-kind contributions was accurate and that for the Gala, the JFC reported nonfederal in-kind contributions and donations in the amount of $401,419.03. The Treasurer of the JFC sent these letters in reliance on information provided by defendant DAVID ROSEN.

22. The Grand Jury incorporates by reference and re-alleges these introductory allegations into each count of this Indictment.

COUNT ONE

[18 U.S.C. §§ 1001 and 2]

On or about October 15, 2000, in the Central District of California and elsewhere, defendant DAVID ROSEN, in a matter within the jurisdiction of the executive branch of the Government of the United States, that is, the Federal Election Commission, did knowingly and willfully cause to be made a materially false, fictitious and fraudulent statement and representation, namely, defendant DAVID ROSEN caused compliance officers with the JFC to file a report with the FEC dated on or about October 15, 2000, specifically Schedule H-3 of Form 3X, falsely declaring that the JFC only received $366,564.69 in in-kind contributions from Event 39, the designation for the Hollywood Gala, when in fact, as defendant DAVID ROSEN then well knew, the JFC received substantially in excess of that amount in connection with that event.

7

Exhibit D

COUNT TWO

[18 U.S.C. §§ 1001 and 2]

On or about January 30, 2001, in the Central District of California and elsewhere, defendant DAVID ROSEN, in a matter within the jurisdiction of the executive branch of the Government of the United States, that is, the Federal Election Commission, did knowingly and willfully cause to be made a materially false, fictitious and fraudulent statement and representation, namely, defendant DAVID ROSEN caused compliance officers with the JFC to file an amended report with the FEC dated on or about January 30, 2001, specifically, Schedule H-3 of Form 3X, falsely declaring that the JFC only received $401,419.03 in in-kind contributions from Event 39, the designation for the Hollywood Gala, when in fact, as defendant DAVID ROSEN then well knew, the JFC received substantially in excess of that amount in connection with that event.

COUNT THREE

[18 U.S.C. § 1001 and 2]

On or about July 30, 2001, in the Central District of California and elsewhere, defendant DAVID ROSEN, in a matter within the jurisdiction of the executive branch of the Government of the United States, that is, the Federal Election Commission, did knowingly and willfully cause to be made a materially false, fictitious and fraudulent statement and representation, namely, defendant DAVID ROSEN caused compliance officers with the JFC to send to the FEC a July 30, 2001 letter that falsely stated that the JFC had raised only $401,419.03 in in-kind contributions from Event 39, the designation for the Hollywood Gala, when in fact, as defendant DAVID ROSEN well knew, the JFC received substantially in excess of that amount in connection with that event.

COUNT FOUR

[18 U.S.C. §§ 1001 and 2]

In or about August and September 2000, in the Central District of California and elsewhere, defendant DAVID ROSEN, in a matter within the jurisdiction of the executive branch of the Government of the United States, that is, the Federal Election Commission, did knowingly and willfully cause to be made and used a false writing and document knowing that writing and document contained a materially false, fictitious and fraudulent statement and entry, namely defendant DAVID ROSEN caused individuals involved with the production of the Hollywood Gala to create a fictitious invoice for $200,000, and provided this fictitious invoice to JFC compliance officers as alleged support for expenses incurred during the Gala, knowing that JFC compliance officers would rely on this document in preparing the JFC's

9

official FEC filings and that the document would be available for inspection and relied upon by FEC officials conducting an audit or review of the JFC's fundraising activities.

A TRUE BILL

Foreperson

NOEL L. HILLMAN
Chief, Public Integrity Section

Joshua G. Berman
Trial Attorney
Public Integrity Section
Criminal Division
United States Department of Justice

10

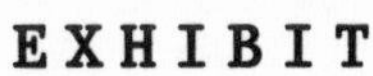

EXHIBIT E

Hillary's Campaign Committee Settlement with the Federal Election Commission (FEC)

FEDERAL ELECTION COMMISSION
WASHINGTON, D C 20463

DEC 2 9 2005

Marc E. Elias, Esq.
Brian G. Svoboda, Esq.
Perkins Coie LLP
607 Fourteenth Street, N.W.
Washington, D.C. 20005-2011

Lyn Utrecht, Esq.
James Lamb, Esq.
Ryan, Phillips, Utrecht & MacKinnon
1133 Connecticut Ave., N.W., Suite 300
Washington, D.C. 20036

RE: MUR 5225
New York Senate 2000 and
Andrew Grossman, in his official capacity as treasurer

Dear Ms. Utrecht and Messrs. Elias, Svoboda and Lamb:

On December 13, 2005, the Federal Election Commission accepted the signed conciliation agreement and civil penalty submitted on your client's behalf in settlement of a violation of 2 U.S.C. § 434(b), a provision of the Federal Election Campaign Act of 1971, as amended, and 11 C.F.R. § 102.17(c)(8)(i)(A). Accordingly, the file has been closed in this matter.

Documents related to the case will be placed on the public record within 30 days. *See* Statement of Policy Regarding Disclosure of Closed Enforcement and Related Files, 68 Fed. Reg. 70,426 (Dec. 18, 2003). Information derived in connection with any conciliation attempt will not become public without the written consent of the respondent and the Commission. *See* 2 U.S.C. § 437g(a)(4)(B).

Exhibit E

Counsel for New York Senate 2000 and Andrew Grossman, as treasurer
MUR 5225
Page 2

Enclosed you will find a copy of the fully executed conciliation agreement for your files. Please note that the civil penalty is due within 30 days of the conciliation agreement's effective date. If you have any questions, please contact me at (202) 694-1650.

Sincerely,

Thomas J. Andersen

Thomas J. Andersen
Attorney

Enclosure
Conciliation Agreement

BEFORE THE FEDERAL ELECTION COMMISSION

In the Matter of)
)
New York Senate 2000 and) MUR 5225
Andrew Grossman, in his official capacity)
as treasurer)

CONCILIATION AGREEMENT

This matter was initiated by a signed, sworn, and notarized complaint dated August 3, 2001. An investigation was conducted, and the Federal Election Commission ("Commission") found probable cause to believe that New York Senate 2000 and Andrew Grossman, in his official capacity as treasurer, violated 2 U.S.C. § 434(b) and 11 C.F.R. § 102.17(c)(8)(i)(A).

NOW THEREFORE, the Commission and the Respondents, having duly entered into conciliation pursuant to 2 U.S.C. § 437g(a)(4)(A)(i), do hereby agree as follows:

I. The Commission has jurisdiction over the Respondents and the subject matter of this proceeding.

II. Respondents have had a reasonable opportunity to demonstrate that no action should be taken in this matter.

III. Respondents enter voluntarily into this agreement with the Commission.

IV. The pertinent facts in this matter are as follows:

Parties

1. New York Senate 2000 is registered with the Commission as a joint fundraising committee, and is a political committee within the meaning of 2 U.S.C. § 431(4). In 1999 and 2000, New York Senate 2000 served as a joint fundraising representative for participants that included Hillary Rodham Clinton for U.S. Senate Committee, Inc., the Democratic Senatorial Campaign Committee and the New York State Democratic Committee.

2. Andrew Grossman is the current treasurer of New York Senate 2000, and has served as treasurer since its creation in 1999.

Applicable Law

3. The Federal Election Campaign Act of 1971, as amended ("the Act"), requires political committees to disclose contributions and disbursements pursuant to 2 U.S.C. § 434(b). The Commission's regulations require political committees to report in-kind contributions as both contributions and expenditures. 11 C.F.R. § 104.13(a).

4. Joint fundraising committees are responsible for collecting contributions, paying fundraising costs, distributing the proceeds, maintaining records and properly disclosing contributions and expenses. 11 C.F.R. § 102.17(b) and (c). Joint fundraising representatives such as New York Senate 2000 must report all funds received and all disbursements made in the reporting period in which they are received and made, respectively. 11 C.F.R. § 102.17(c)(8). The fundraising representative shall report the total amount of non-federal contributions received during the reporting period as a memo entry. 11 C.F.R. 102.17(c)(8)(i)(A).

Facts

5. On August 12, 2000, New York Senate 2000 sponsored a fundraising event in Brentwood, California designated in New York Senate 2000's disclosure reports as "Event 39."

6. New York Senate 2000 reported total Event 39 costs of $519,077 for calendar year 2000, of which $401,419 consisted of in-kind contributions, and total direct proceeds (i.e., not counting in-kind contributions) of $1,072,015, which included $363,465 in federal funds and $708,550 in non-federal funds.

7. The Commission determined that certain costs associated with Event 39 were not disclosed by New York Senate 2000, as summarized below:

DESCRIPTION	REPORTED	UNREPORTED
Dinner and Reception In-kinds	$153,863	$109,067
Concert (minus $100,000 included in reported Direct Expenses of $117,658)	$200,000	$395,154
Travel and Lodging In-kinds		$92,135
Printing In-kinds	$12,702	$125,539
Other In-kinds reported	$34,854	
Direct Expenses reported	$117,658	
Subtotals	$519,077	$721,895

Total Event Costs: $1,240,972

V. The Commission found probable cause to believe that New York Senate 2000 did not disclose all of the Event 39 costs in accordance with the Act and the Commission's regulations. Respondents contend that they implemented and enforced reasonable processes to collect and report information regarding event expenses. However, in order to settle this matter, Respondents will not further contest the Commission's probable cause findings that it failed to report $721,895 in in-kind contributions, in violation of 2 U.S.C. § 434(b) and 11 C.F.R. § 102.17(c)(8)(i)(A).

Settlement Requirements

VI. 1. Respondents will pay a civil penalty to the Federal Election Commission in the amount of Thirty-Five Thousand Dollars ($35,000) pursuant to 2 U.S.C. § 437g(a)(5)(A).

2. Respondents will amend New York Senate 2000's disclosure report to reflect the unreported $721,895 in in-kind contributions. Respondents shall include in the amended report information as provided or confirmed by the Commission. The amended report shall be filed within 30 days of receipt of such information or 30 days from the date this agreement becomes effective, whichever is later. The Commission agrees that New York Senate 2000 may

thereafter terminate, in accordance with the applicable provisions of the Act and Commission regulations.

Other Provisions

VII. The Commission, on request of anyone filing a complaint under 2 U.S.C. § 437g(a)(1) concerning the matters at issue herein or on its own motion, may review compliance with this agreement. If the Commission believes that this agreement or any requirement thereof has been violated, it may institute a civil action for relief in the United States District Court for the District of Columbia.

VIII. This agreement, unless violated, shall serve as a complete bar to any further action against New York Senate 2000 and its current and former joint fundraising participants, agents, employees and officers for acts arising out of, or relating to New York Senate 2000, Event 39 and all fundraising events held by New York Senate 2000 between September 16, 1999 through November 7, 2000. *See* 2 U.S.C. § 437g(a)(4), (5).

IX. This agreement shall become effective as of the date that all parties hereto have executed same and the Commission has approved the entire agreement.

X. Respondents shall have no more than 30 days from the date this agreement becomes effective to comply with and implement the requirements contained in this agreement and to so notify the Commission.

MUR 5225
New York Senate 2000
Conciliation Agreement

5

XI. This Conciliation Agreement constitutes the entire agreement between the partie: on the matters raised herein, and no other statement, promise, or agreement, either written or oral, made by either party or by agents of either party, that is not contained in this written agreement shall be enforceable

FOR THE COMMISSION:

Lawrence H. Norton
General Counsel

BY: [signature] 12/29/05

Rhonda J. Vosdingh
Associate General Counsel
for Enforcement

Date

FOR THE RESPONDENT:

[signature] 12/12/5

Andrew Grossman
Treasurer

Date

and organized under regulations promulgated by the Federal Election Commission ("FEC"). The JFC consisted of three participants: (a) Senator A's campaign committee; (b) a national senatorial party committee; and (c) a state party committee.

3. The JFC was legally permitted to raise both "hard money" and "soft money." Funds raised and spent to influence the election of a particular candidate to federal office were known as "hard money" or "federal funds," which were subject to individual contribution limits and prohibitions against corporate contributions and expenditures. In contrast, "soft money" or "non-federal funds" were funds raised for purposes other than to influence the nomination or election of federal candidates and were not subject to FECA's individual contribution limits and FECA's prohibitions on corporate contributions and expenditures. The federal regulations governing joint fundraising committees were designed to prevent such committees from circumventing FECA's restrictions on the sources of and dollar limits on hard money.

4. The JFC also accepted "in-kind" contributions -- contributions in the form of goods or services provided for free or at below-market prices, and contributions occurring when a person or corporate entity pays a bill for fundraising or other expenses.

5. The FEC was an independent regulatory agency whose mission was to administer and enforce FECA -- the statute that governs the financing of federal elections. The duties of the FEC were to facilitate and insure the disclosure of campaign finance information required by law to be publicly disclosed and to enforce the provisions of the law including limits and prohibitions on contributions. The FEC also reviewed and audited submissions from joint fundraising committees to insure compliance with the law.

2

EXHIBIT 

Hillary Clinton's Statement to the FEC on Alleged Fundraising Irregularities

DAVID E. KENDALL (Admitted *Pro Hac Vice*)
CHRISTIAN A. WEIDEMAN (State Bar No. 226339)
WILLIAMS & CONNOLLY LLP
725 Twelfth Street, N.W.
Washington, D.C. 20005
Telephone: (202) 434-5000
Facsimile: (202) 434-5029

Attorneys for Defendant
HILLARY RODHAM CLINTON

SUPERIOR COURT OF THE STATE OF CALIFORNIA

COUNTY OF LOS ANGELES

CENTRAL DISTRICT

PETER F. PAUL, Plaintiff, vs. WILLIAM JEFFERSON CLINTON, HILLARY RODHAM CLINTON, HILLARY RODHAM CLINTON FOR U.S. SENATE COMMITTEE, INC., NEW YORK SENATE 2000, DAVID ROSEN, GARY SMITH, JAMES LEVIN, AND AARON TONKEN, Defendants.	CASE NO. BC 304174 [Assigned to Hon. Aurelio N. Munoz] **DECLARATION OF HILLARY RODHAM CLINTON** Date: April 7, 2006 Time: 8:30 A.M. Dept. 47 Original Complaint Filed: October 14, 2003 First Amended Cplt. Filed: February 27, 2004 Discovery Cut-Off: None Trial Date: None

I, Hillary Rodham Clinton, declare and state:

1. I am a defendant in the matter entitled, *Peter F. Paul v. William Jefferson Clinton, et al.*, Case No. BC 304174. I make this declaration in support of the Reply Memorandum in Support of Motion by Hillary Rodham Clinton and Hillary Rodham Clinton for U.S. Senate Committee, Inc. to Strike Counts Five and Fourteen of Plaintiff's First Amended Complaint and in Opposition to Plaintiff's Motion for Limited Discovery and Continuance of Defendants' Anti-SLAPP Motion. I have firsthand knowledge of the facts stated herein, and could and would testify competently thereto if called as a witness in this case.

DECLARATION OF HILLARY RODHAM CLINTON

Exhibit F

2. I remember meeting Mr. Peter F. Paul sometime in early 2000. I understood him to be a top executive of Stan Lee Media, Inc.

3. I remember attending a fundraising luncheon in early summer of 2000 at Spago, a restaurant in Los Angeles, California, followed by a fundraising event at the home of Ms. Cynthia Gershman. I remember Mr. Paul attending both events and I remember speaking with him at one or perhaps both of these events. I do not remember any of the statements I may have made to Mr. Paul during one or perhaps both of these events. However, I have no recollection whatsoever of discussing any arrangement with him whereby he would support my campaign for the United States Senate in exchange for anything from me or then-President Clinton, and I do not believe that I made any such statements because I believe I would remember such a discussion if it had occurred. I also have no recollection whatsoever of talking with him about any future business arrangement of any kind between him and then-President Clinton, and I do not believe that I made any such statements because I believe I would remember such a discussion if it had occurred.

4. In the summer of 2000, I knew Mr. Gary Smith and believed his work to be professional and of very high quality. I remember that he was asked to produce a fundraising event for my Senate campaign, which was held on August 12, 2000. However, I do not recall being involved in any way in the negotiations concerning Mr. Smith's fees for that event.

5. I remember attending a fundraising event on the evening of August 12, 2000 at the home of Mr. Ken Roberts in Los Angeles, California, and a brunch the next day at the home of Ms. Barbra Streisand and Mr. James Brolin. I remember Mr. Paul attending the August 12th event but have no memory of him at the second event. I may have spoken with him but I do not remember any of the statements I may have made to Mr. Paul. However, I have no recollection whatsoever of discussing any arrangement with him whereby he would support my campaign for the United States Senate in exchange for anything from me or then-President Clinton, and I do not believe that I made any such statements because I believe I would remember such a discussion if it had occurred. I also have no recollection whatsoever of talking with him about any future business arrangement of any kind between him and then-President Clinton, and I do not believe

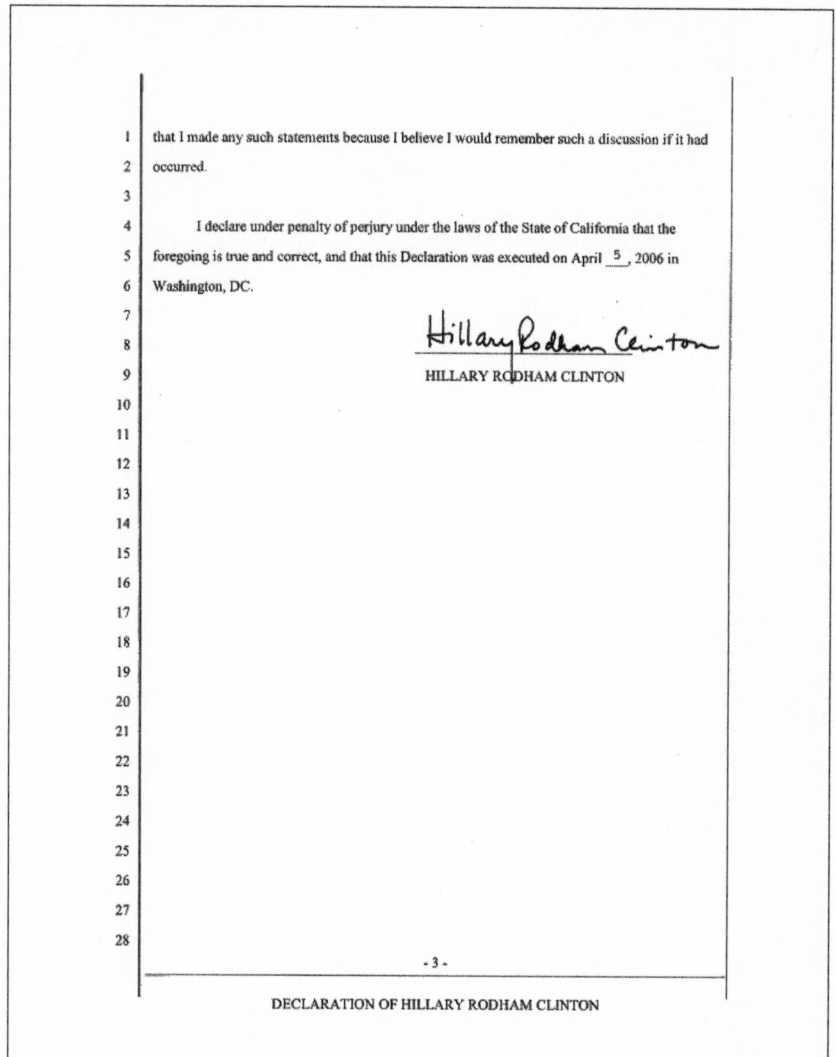

that I made any such statements because I believe I would remember such a discussion if it had occurred.

I declare under penalty of perjury under the laws of the State of California that the foregoing is true and correct, and that this Declaration was executed on April 5, 2006 in Washington, DC.

Hillary Rodham Clinton

HILLARY RODHAM CLINTON

- 3 -

DECLARATION OF HILLARY RODHAM CLINTON

EXHIBIT G

FEC Notice to Friends of Hillary 2006

FEDERAL ELECTION COMMISSION
WASHINGTON, D.C. 20463

RQ-2

April 4, 2006

John F. X. Mannion, Treasurer
Friends of Hillary
1717 K Street Northwest, Suite 309A
Washington, DC 20036

Response Due Date:
May 4, 2006

Identification Number: C00358895

Reference: Year End Report (10/1/05 - 12/31/05)

Dear Mr. Mannion:

This letter is prompted by the Commission's preliminary review of the report(s) referenced above. This notice requests information essential to full public disclosure of your federal election campaign finances. **An adequate response must be received at the Senate Public Records Office by the response date noted above.** An itemization of the information needed follows:

> -Schedule A of your report discloses one or more contributions that appear to exceed the limits set forth in the Act (see attached). You should examine all of your contributions to check for additional excessive contributions. The Committee's procedures for processing contributions should also be reviewed.
>
> An individual or a political committee other than an authorized committee or a qualified multi-candidate committee may not make a contribution to a candidate for federal office in excess of $2,100 per election. An authorized committee may not make a contribution to a candidate for federal office in excess of $2,000 per election. A qualified multi-candidate committee and all affiliated committees may not make a contribution(s) to a candidate for federal office in excess of $5,000 per election. The term "contribution" includes any gift, subscription, loan, advance, or deposit of money or anything of value made by any person for the purpose of influencing any election for federal office. (2 U.S.C. § 441a(a) and (f); 11 CFR §§ 110.1(b), (e) and (k), and 102.13(c))
>
> If any apparently excessive contribution in question was incompletely or incorrectly reported, you must amend your original report with clarifying information.

Friends of Hillary
Page 2 of 4

The Commission notes your request for the redesignation and/or reattribution of all of these contributions. Please be reminded that all refunds, redesignations and reattributions must be made within sixty (60) days of receipt of the contribution. To date, one or more of the apparent excessive contributions have not been refunded, redesignated, or reattributed.

For reattributions, the funds can be retained if within sixty (60) days of receipt the excessive amount was properly reattributed to another person. An excessive contribution is considered properly reattributed if (1) the contributors provide the committee with written documentation, signed by each contributor, authorizing a reattribution and indicating the amount of the contribution to be attributed to each contributor, or (2) the committee reattributes, by presumption, the excessive portion of the contribution if the contribution was made on a written instrument from a joint account and was signed by only one of the account holders. In this case, the treasurer must notify the contributors in writing within 60 days of receiving the contribution that the committee intends to reattribute the excessive portion and must give the contributor who signed the check an opportunity to request a refund. (11 CFR § 110.1(k)(3)(ii)(B))

For redesignations, the funds can be retained if within sixty (60) days of receipt, the excessive amount was properly designated for a different election. An excessive contribution is considered properly redesignated if (1) the committee obtains signed written documentation from the contributor(s) authorizing the redesignation of the contribution for another election, provided that the new designation does not exceed the limitations on contributions made with respect to that election, or (2) the committee redesignates, by presumption, the excessive portion of the contribution for another election provided that the new designation does not exceed the limitations on contributions made with respect to that election. In this case, the treasurer must notify the contributor of the redesignation in writing within 60 days of the treasurer's receipt of the contribution. The notification must give the contributor an opportunity to request a refund. (11 CFR § 110.1(b)(5)(ii)(B)) A contribution can only be redesignated to a previous election to the extent that the contribution does not exceed the committee's net debts outstanding for that election. (11 CFR § 110.1(b)(3)(i))

If the foregoing conditions for reattributions or redesignations are not met within 60 days of receipt, the excessive amount must be refunded. (11 CFR § 103.3(b)(1))

Friends of Hillary
Page 3 of 4

Schedule B of the report covering the period in which they are made. Redesignations and reattributions are reported as memo entries on Schedule A of the report covering the period in which the authorization for the redesignation and/or reattribution is received. (11 CFR § 104.8(d)(2), (3) and (4))

The acceptance of excessive contributions is a serious problem. Again, the committee's procedures for processing contributions should be examined and corrected in order to avoid this problem. Although the Commission may take further legal action, prompt action by you to refund or redesignate and/or reattribute of the excessive amount will be taken into consideration.

-A review of your itemized receipts indicates a discrepancy in your aggregate election cycle-to-date totals. The reported aggregate totals on your report should include all contributions from an individual or committee given in the election cycle. Please review your procedures for compliance with this requirement and amend your report(s) as necessary. (11 CFR §104.3(a)(3))

Please note you will not receive an additional notice from the Commission on this matter. Adequate responses received on or before this date will be taken into consideration in determining whether audit action will be initiated. **Requests for extensions of time in which to respond will not be considered.** Failure to provide an adequate response by this date may result in an audit of the committee. Failure to comply with the provisions of the Act may also result in an enforcement action against the committee. Any response submitted by your committee will be placed on the public record and will be considered by the Commission prior to taking enforcement action.

A written response or an amendment to your original report(s) correcting the above problems should be filed with the Senate Public Records Office. Please contact the Senate Public Records Office at (202) 224-0322 for instructions on how and where to file an amendment. If you should have any questions regarding this matter or wish to verify the adequacy of your response, please contact me on our toll-free number (800) 424-9530 (at the prompt press 5 to reach the Reports Analysis Division) or my local number (202) 694-1168.

Sincerely,

Michelle Lee Grant

Michelle Lee Grant
Senior Campaign Finance Analyst
Reports Analysis Division

495

Exhibit G

Excessive and/or Prohibited Contributions
Friends of Hillary (C00358895)
Year End Report (10/1/05-12/31/05)

P = Primary Election
G = General Election

CONTRIBUTOR NAME		DATE	AMOUNT	ELECTION
Adler	Sara	1/24/05	$1,000.00	P2006
Adler	Sara	12/14/05	$2,000.00	P2006
Beckwith	Robert	3/6/03	$500.00	P2006
Beckwith	Robert	1/14/04	$500.00	P2006
Beckwith	Robert	2/22/05	$1,000.00	P2006
Beckwith	Robert	7/20/05	$1,000.00	P2006
Beckwith	Robert	8/2/05	($1,000.00)	P2006
Beckwith	Robert	12/30/05	$500.00	P2006
Bregman	Davis	9/30/03	$500.00	G2006
Bregman	Davis	12/26/03	$1,000.00	G2006
Bregman	Davis	12/10/05	$51.00	G2006
Bregman	Davis	12/14/05	$1,000.00	G2006
Cherry	Myron	3/24/03	$1,000.00	P2006
Cherry	Myron M.	12/3/05	$1,000.00	P2006
Constantinople	Anthony	12/9/05	$3,690.00	G2006
Creel	Debbie	1/31/04	$2,000.00	P2006
Creel	Deborah	10/29/05	$100.00	P2006
Creel	Deborah	10/29/05	$2,000.00	P2006
Dubin	Glenn	12/1/05	$3,100.00	G2006
Effron	Craig W.	5/10/04	$500.00	G2006
Effron	Craig W.	12/11/01	$1,900.00	G2006
Epstein	Randi	9/27/05	$2,100.00	G2006
Epstein	Randi	11/15/05	$1,000.00	G2006
Flora	Michael	12/5/05	$2,200.00	G2006

Page 1 of 4

FEC Notice to Friends of Hillary 2006

Excessive and/or Prohibited Contributions
Friends of Hillary (C00358895)
Year End Report (10/1/05-12/31/05)

P = Primary Election
G = General Election

CONTRIBUTOR NAME		DATE	AMOUNT	ELECTION
Galbally	Elizabeth M.	6/20/05	$2,100.00	P2006
Galbally	Elizabeth M.	12/29/05	$2,100.00	P2006
Gardy	Mark C.	12/7/05	$2,900.00	G2006
Gelber	Brian	12/19/05	$3,900.00	G2006
Huang	Sze-Jing	11/7/05	$2,100.00	G2006
Huang	Sze-Jing	11/7/05	$4,200.00	G2006
Jacobs	Joseph	11/25/05	$2,400.00	G2006
Jakes	Peter	6/6/05	$900.00	G2006
Jakes	Peter	12/6/05	$2,500.00	G2006
Jawad	Tariq	11/4/05	$2,200.00	G2006
Kayne	Suzanne L.	12/21/04	$1,000.00	G2006
Kayne	Suzanne L.	12/5/05	$2,400.00	G2006
Layton	Barbara Ann	8/6/05	$150.00	G2006
Layton	Barbara Ann	12/13/05	$3,000.00	G2006
Lennon	Karen	3/21/03	$2,000.00	P2006
Lennon	Karen	11/10/05	$210.00	P2006
Lennon	Karen	12/7/05	$40.00	P2006
Lichtenstein	Dorothy	11/17/05	$4,100.00	G2006
Lyons	James	1/14/04	$500.00	P2006
Lyons	James	2/24/05	$1,000.00	P2006
Lyons	James	10/17/05	$1,000.00	P2006
Marcuss	Stanley J.	7/28/04	$1,000.00	P2006

Page 2 of 4

Exhibit G

Excessive and/or Prohibited Contributions
Friends of Hillary (C00358895)
Year End Report (10/1/05-12/31/05)

P = Primary Election
G = General Election

CONTRIBUTOR NAME		DATE	AMOUNT	ELECTION
Marcuss	Stanley	12/28/05	$1,200.00	P2006
Mattin	Helen	1/14/04	$1,000.00	P2006
Mattin	Helen	6/23/04	$1,000.00	P2006
Mattin	Helen	12/30/05	$500.00	P2006
McIlroy	Hayden	11/25/03	$1,000.00	P2006
McIlroy	Hayden	12/9/04	$1,000.00	P2006
McIlroy	Hayden	12/29/05	$250.00	P2006
Milstein	Edward	10/17/02	$1,000.00	G2006
Milstein	Edward	11/29/05	$2,900.00	G2006
Moore	William H.	4/15/05	$300.00	G2006
Moore	William H.	12/12/05	$2,000.00	G2006
Murphy	Arthur J.	4/15/05	$2,100.00	P2006
Murphy	Arthur	12/3/05	$1,000.00	P2006
O'Dwyer	Brian	8/5/04	$1,000.00	G2006
O'Dwyer	Brian	12/2/05	$4,100.00	G2006
Otterstein	Sven A.	3/6/03	$200.00	P2006
Otterstein	Sven A.	9/22/03	$200.00	P2006
Otterstein	Sven A.	2/25/04	$250.00	P2006
Otterstein	Sven A.	3/5/04	$250.00	P2006
Otterstein	Sven A.	3/29/04	$250.00	P2006
Otterstein	Sven A.	4/22/04	$200.00	P2006
Otterstein	Sven A.	5/11/04	$200.00	P2006
Otterstein	Sven A.	8/11/04	$250.00	P2006
Otterstein	Sven A.	9/29/04	$100.00	P2006
Otterstein	Sven A.	12/7/05	$350.00	P2006
Otterstein	Sven A.	12/30/05	$500.00	P2006

Excessive and/or Prohibited Contributions
Friends of Hillary (C00358895)
Year End Report (10/1/05-12/31/05)

P = Primary Election
G = General Election

CONTRIBUTOR NAME		DATE	AMOUNT	ELECTION
Schupf	Sara	3/5/04	$1,500.00	G2006
Schupf	Sara	5/25/05	$400.00	G2006
Schupf	Sara	12/27/05	$1,000.00	G2006
Smith	Richard A	12/12/05	$2,200.00	P2006
Starr	Kenneth	4/10/05	$900.00	G2006
Starr	Kenneth	11/29/05	$4,000.00	G2006
Steiner	David S.	9/12/05	$1,900.00	G2006
Steiner	David S.	12/12/05	$2,200.00	G2006
Steiner	Sylvia L.	12/12/05	$3,100.00	G2006
Stringer	Howard	7/8/05	$1,000.00	P2006
Stringer	Howard	12/9/04	$1,000.00	P2006
Stringer	Howard	12/30/05	$2,000.00	P2006
Thypin	Marylin	4/27/04	$2,000.00	P2006
Thypin	Marylin	12/9/05	$500.00	P2006
Wagner	Marsha	11/15/05	$3,100.00	G2006
Yerman	Frederick W.	6/24/04	$1,000.00	P2006
Yerman	Frederick W.	9/8/05	$1,000.00	P2006
Yerman	Frederick W.	12/5/05	$1,100.00	P2006
Yerman	Frederick W.	12/5/05	$2,100.00	G2006
Yerman	Frederick W.	12/13/05	$100.00	G2006

Page 4 of 4

EXHIBIT H

Where Hillary Gets Her Money: Political Action Committee Donations to Friends of Hillary

2002 Cycle

Merrill Lynch — Securities & Investment	$6,000
National Education Association — Public Sector Unions	$6,000
Amalgamated Transit Union — Transportation Unions	$5,000
Communication Workers of America — Industrial Unions	$5,000
International Brotherhood of Electrical Workers — Industrial Unions	$5,000
Kmart Corp. — Retail Sales	$5,000
Office & Professional Employees Union — Misc. Unions	$5,000
Rhode Island PAC — Leadership PACs	$5,000
Sheet Metal Workers Union — Building Trade Unions	$5,000
General Electric — Misc. Energy	$3,500
Ironworkers Union — Building Trade Unions	$3,000
MWH Americas — Environmental Service/Equipment	$2,500
Policy Group — Securities & Investment	$2,464
BAE Systems North America — Defense Aerospace	$2,000
BellSouth Corp. — Telephone Utilities	$2,000
Citigroup Inc. — Commercial Banks	$2,000

Exhibit H

Donor / Industry	Amount
Constellation Brands Beer, Wine & Liquor	$2,000
Entergy Corp. Electric Utilities	$2,000
International Longshoremen's Assn. Transportation Unions	$2,000
KeySpan Energy Electric Utilities	$2,000
Transport Workers Unions Transportation Unions	$2,000
United Steel Workers of America Industrial Unions	$2,000
Washington Group International General Contractors	$2,000
Magazine Publishers of America Printing & Publishing	$1,500
Ocean Spray Cranberries Crop Production and Basic Processing	$1,500
Air Line Pilots Assn. Transportation Unions	$1,000
American Health Care Assn. Hospitals/Nursing Homes	$1,000
American Federation of Teachers Public Sector Unions	$1,000
American Maritime Officers Transportation Unions	$1,000
American Resort Development Assn. Real Estate	$1,000
American Speech-Language Hearing Assn. Health Professionals	$1,000
American Veterinary Medical Association Agricultural Services/Products	$1,000
Boilermakers Union Industrial Unions	$1,000
Cablevision Systems TV/Movies/Music	$1,000
Chicago Board Options Exchange Securities & Investment	$1,000
Duke Energy Electric Utilities	$1,000

Farm Credit Council Agricultural Services/Products	$1,000
FleetBoston Financial Commercial Bank	$1,000
General Motors Automotive	$1,000
Greenberg, Traurig et al. Lawyers/Law Firms	$1,000
Johnson & Johnson Pharmaceuticals/Health Products	$1,000
Kamber Group Lobbyists	$1,000
Petroleum Marketers Assn. Oil & Gas	$1,000
Piper Rudnick LLP Lawyers/Law Firms	$1,000
Professionals in Advertising PAC Business Services	$1,000
Marine Engineers Beneficial Assn./Dst. 1 Transportation Unions	$1,000
Nat'l. Assn. of Alcoholism/Drug Abuse Coun. Health Professionals	$1,000
National Court Reporters Assn. Business Services	$1,000
National Funeral Directors Assn. Misc. Services	$1,000
National Grid USA Electric Utilities	$1,000
New York State Electric & Gas Electric Utilities	$1,000
Nike Inc. Misc. Manufacturing and Distrb.	$1,000
NorPAC Pro-Israel	$1,000
Northpoint Technology Telecom Services and Equipment	$1,000
Radiology Advocacy Alliance Health Professionals	$1,000
Schroeder for Congress Cmte. Candidate Committees	$1,000

Seafarers International Union
Transportation Unions $1,000

Transportation Communications Union
Transportation Unions $1,000

United Auto Workers
Industrial Unions $1,000

United Mine Workers
Industrial Unions $1,000

Union of Needletrades Employees
Industrial Unions $1,000

Winston & Strawn
Lawyers/Law Firms $1,000

Cassidy & Assoc.
Lobbyists $652

Boat Owners Assn. of the US
Misc. Transport $500

Holland & Knight
Lawyers/Law Firms $500

Human Rights Campaign
Human Rights $500

National Assn. of Air Traffic Specialists
Transportation Unions $500

National Assn. of Water Companies
Misc. Energy $500

National Treasury Employees Union
Public Sector Unions $500

Preston, Gates et al.
Lawyers/Law Firms $500

Refined Sugars Inc.
Crop Production & Basic Processing $500

Reed Elsevier Inc.
Printing & Publishing $500

American Occupational Therapy Assn.
Health Professionals $250

Armenian American PAC
Human Rights $250

Bank of America
Commercial Banks $250

Bracewell & Patterson
Lawyers/Law Firms $250

2004 Cycle

Bricklayers Union
Building Trade Unions $10,000

Corning Inc.
Telecom Services & Equipment $10,000

E*TRADE Financial Group
Securities & Investment $10,000

Metropolitan Life Insurance
Insurance..$10,000

New York Mercantile Exchange
Securities & Investment $10,000

New Jersey United
Leadership PAC $10,000

Office & Professional Employees Union
MISC. Unions $10,000

Searchlight Leadership Fund
Leadership PAC $10,000

Cablevision Systems
TV/Music/Movies $9,000

Citigroup Inc.
Commercial Banks $6,000

Continuum Health Partners
Hospitals/Nursing Homes $5,750

Piper Rudnick LLP
Lawyers/Law Firms $5,750

Amalgamated Transit Union
Transportation Unions...$5,000

American Resort Development Assn.
Real Estate $5,000

American Society of Anesthesiologists
Health Professionals...$5,000

Carpenters & Joiners Union
Building Trade Unions $5,000

Communications Workers of America
Industrial Unions $5,000

Fulbright & Jaworski
Lawyers/Law Firms $5,000

Exhibit H

Intl. Brotherhood of Electrical Workers Industrial Unions	$5,000
KidsPAC Leadership PAC	$5,000
Laborers Union Building Trade Unions	$5,000
Painters & Allied Trades Union Building Trade Unions	$5,000
Prudential Financial Insurance	$5,000
Rhode Island PAC Leadership PAC	$5,000
Sheet Metal Workers Union Builders Trade Union	$5,000
Teaching Hospital Education PAC Hospitals/Nursing Homes	$5,000
Time Warner TV/Music/Movies	$5,000
American Hospital Assn. Hospitals/Nursing Homes	$4,750
American Federation of Teachers Public Sector Unions	$4,500
Irish-Americans for a Democratic Victory Democratic/Liberal	$4,500
Consolidated Edison of New York Electric Utilities	$4,072
Jobs, Opportunities & Education PAC Leadership PAC	$4,000
Cmte. to Reelect Ed Towns Candidate Committees	$4,000
Verizon Communications Telephone Utilities	$4,000
New York Life Insurance Insurance	$3,500
Plumbers/Pipefitters Union Local 773 Building Trade Unions	$3,500
Bank of America Commercial Banks	$3,000
Directors Guild of America MISC. Unions	$3,000

Greenberg, Traurig et al. — Lawyers/Law Firms	$3,000
SBC Communications — Telephone Utilities	$3,000
Agri-Mark Inc. — Dairy	$2,500
American Maritime Officers — Transportations Unions	$2,500
BellSouth Corp. — Telephone Utilities	$2,500
Bond Market Assn. — Securities & Investment	$2,500
Buchanan Ingersoll — Lawyers/Law Firms	$2,500
CHRIS PAC — Leadership PAC	$2,500
Coca-Cola Enterprises — Food & Beverage	$2,500
Johnson & Johnson — Pharmaceuticals/Health Products	$2,500
National Multi Housing Council — Real Estate	$2,500
Northrup Grumman — Defense Aerospace	$2,500
O'Melveny & Myers — Lawyers/Law Firms	$2,500
Oldcastle Materials — Building Materials & Equipment	$2,500
Petroleum Marketers Assn. — Oil & Gas	$2,500
Plumbers/Pipefitters Union — Building Trade Unions	$2,500
Sugar Cane Growers Co-op of Florida — Crop Production & Basic Processing	$2,500
Transport Workers Union — Transportation Unions	$2,500
American Express — Insurance	$2,000
AT&T — Telephone Utilities	$2,000

Assn. of Trial Lawyers of America
Lawyers/Law Firms $2,000

Boilermakers Union
Industrial Unions $2,000

Caremark RX
Pharmaceuticals/Health Products....................$2,000

Cingular Wireless
Telecom Services & Equipment $2,000

Cmte. to Elect Gary Ackerman
Candidate Committees $2,000

Coca-Cola Co.
Food & Beverage....................$2,000

Crowley for Congress
Candidate Committees $2,000

Dykeme Gossett
Lawyers/Law Firms $2,000

Feingold Senate Cmte.
Candidate Committees $2,000

Friends of Barbara Boxer
Candidate Committees $2,000

Friends of Carl Levin
Candidate Committees $2,000

Friends of Carolyn McCarthy
Candidate Committees $2,000

Friends of Max Cleland for Senate Cmte.
Candidate Committees $2,000

Friends of Rahm Emanuel
Candidate Committees $2,000

General Electric
Defense Aerospace $2,000

Green Worlds Coalition Fund
Environment....................$2,000

Himman Straub
Lawyers/Law Firms $1,000

International Assn. of Fire Fighters
Public Sector Unions $2,000

Ironworkers Union
Building Trade Unions $2,000

Jazz PAC
Democratic/Liberal $2,000

Kerry for Senate Cmte.
Candidate Committees $2,000

KeyCorp.
Commercial Banks $2,000

Leahy for US Senator Cmte.
Candidate Committees $2,000

Mason Tenders District Council of NY
Building Trade Unions $2,000

McNulty for Congress
Candidate Committees $2,000

National Assn. of Postmasters
Public Sector Unions $2,000

National Assn. of Spine Specialists
Health Professionals $2,000

Leadership in the New Century
Leadership PAC $2,000

Rush Holt for Congress
Candidate Committees $2,000

Service Employees International Union
MISC. Unions $2,000

Steve Israel for Congress
Candidate Committees $2,000

Sprint Corp.
Telephone Utilities $2,000

Ted Strickland for Congress
Candidate Committees $2,000

Tim Bishop for Congress
Candidate Committees $2,000

Van Hollen for Congress
Candidate Committees $2,000

Vinson & Elkins
Lawyers/Law Firms $2,000

Washington Group International
General Contractors $2,000

Morgan Stanley
Securities & Investment $1,500

Northrup Grumman
Misc. Defense $1,500

US Central Credit Union
Credit Unions $1,500

American Health Care Assn.
Hospitals/Nursing Homes $1,000

Arent, Fox et al.
Lawyers/Law Firms $1,000

Armenian American PAC
Leadership PAC $1,000

Blue Cross & Blue Shield
Insurance $1,000

Boswell for Congress
Candidate Committees $1,000

Bridgestone Americas
Chemical & Related Manufacturing $1,000

Cellular Telecom & Internet Assn.
Telecom Services & Equipment $1,000

Cosmetic, Toiletry & Fragrance Assn.
Misc. Manufacturing & Distb. $1,000

Chicago Board Options Exchange
Securities & Investment $1,000

Daimler/Chrysler
Automotive $1,000

Dewey Ballantine LLP
Lawyers/Law Firms $1,000

Farm Credit Council
Agricultural Services/Products $1,000

Hollings for Senate
Candidate Committees $1,000

Holland & Knight
Lawyers/Law Firms $1,000

Hill & Knowlton
Lobbyists $1,000

International Council Cruise Lines
Sea Transport $1,000

Int'l. Longshoremen's/Warehousemen's
Transportation Unions $1,000

Investment Co. Institute
Securities & Investment $1,000

Italian American Dem. Leadership Council
Democratic/Liberal $1,000

Karen McCarthy for Congress
Candidate Committees $1,000

National Assn. of Realtors
Real Estate $1,000

National Leadership PAC
Leadership PAC $1,000

National Jewish Democratic Council
Leadership PAC $1,000

National Treasury Employees Union
Public Sector Unions $1,000

Nat'l. Cmte. to Preserve Social Security
MISC. Issues $1,000

NARAL New York
Abortion Policy/Pro-Choice $1,000

New York Building Congress PAC
General Contractors...$1,000

O'Neill & Assoc.
Lawyers/Law Firms $1,000

Operating Engineers Local 68
Building Trade Unions $1,000

Our Common Values PAC
Leadership PAC $1,000

People for the American Way
Democratic/Liberal $1,000

Planned Parenthood
Abortion Policy/Pro-Choice $1,000

Pfizer Inc.
Pharmaceuticals/Health Products....................................$1,000

Qaulocomm Inc.
Telecom Services & Equipment $1,000

Real Estate Roundtable
Real Estate $1,000

Serono Inc.
Pharmaceuticals/Health Products....................................$1,000

Skadden, Arps
Lawyers/Law Firms $1,000

Sonnenschein, Nath & Rosenthal
Lawyers/Law Firms $1,000

Tim Ryan for Congress
Candidate Committees $1,000

Thelen, Reid & Priest
Lawyers/Law Firms $1,000

Tom James Co
Beer, Wine & Liquor $1,000

United Transportation Union
Transportation Unions $1,000

Virginia Leadership PAC
Leadership PAC $1,000

Vocational PAC
Education $1,000

Walt Disney Co.
TV/Music/Movies $1,000

Welch Allyn Inc.
Pharmaceuticals/Health Products $1,000

Williams & Jensen
Lawyers/Law Firms $1,000

Exxon Mobil
Oil & Gas $750

NARAL Pro-Choice America
Abortion Policy/Pro-Choice $750

Sidley, Austin et al.
Lawyers/Law Firms $750

Empire State Democratic Initiative Corp.
Democratic/Liberal $597

American Fedn. of School Admins.
Public Sector Unions $500

Barnes & Thornburg
Lawyers/Law Firms $500

LaSalle Bank
Commercial Banks $500

Operating Engineers Local 106
Building Trade Unions $500

Richard E. Neal for Congress Cmte.
Candidate Committees $500

Greenworth Financial
Insurance $150

2006 Cycle
(based on data released by the FEC on Monday, March 13, 2006)

Contributor	Amount
AFSCME Public Sector Union	$10,000
Barrack, Rodos & Bacine Lawyers/Law Firms	$10,000
Brotherhood of Locomotive Engineers Transportation Unions	$10,000
Limited Brands Retail Centers	$10,000
Machinists/Aerospace Workers Union Industrial Unions	$10,000
National Assn. of Letter Carriers Public Sector Union	$10,000
Prairie PAC Leaderships PACs	$10,000
International Assn. of Fire Fighters Public Sector Union	$8,000
United Transportation Union Transportation Union	$9,000
American International Group Insurance	$7,000
Express Scripts Health Services/HMOs	$7,000
National Rural Letter Carriers Association Public Sector Union	$7,000
Service Employees International Union Misc. Union	$6,750
Americans United in Support of Democracy Pro-Israel	$6,500
New York Life Insurance Insurance	$6,500
Northrup Grumman Misc. Defense	$6,000
American Podiatric Medical Assn. Health Professionals	$5,500
Nixon Peabody LLP Lawyers/Law Firms	$5500
Joint Action Cmte. for Political Affairs Pro-Israel	$5,118

Affiliated Computer Services
Computers/Internet $5,000

AFLAC Inc.
Insurance $5,000

AFL-CIO
MISC. Union $5,000

Altria
Tobacco $5,000

American Association of Nurse Anesthetists
Health Professionals $5,000

American Federation of Gov't. Employees
Public Sector Union $5,000

American Postal Workers Union
Public Sector Union $5,000

American Society of Anesthesiologists
Health Professionals $5,000

Anheuser-Busch
Beer, Wine & Liquor $5,000

Assn. of Trial Lawyers of America
Lawyers/Law Firms $5,000

Boilermakers Union
Industrial Unions $5,000

CHRIS PAC
Leaderships PACs $5,000

Cisco Systems
Computers/Internet $5,000

Cmte. for a Democratic Majority
Leaderships PACs $5,000

Constellation Brands
Beer, Wine & Liquor $5,000

Credit Union National Association
Credit Unions $5,000

DASHPAC
Leaderships PACs $5,000

Federal Express
Air Transport $5,000

Eastman Kodak
Misc. Manufacturing & Distributing $5,000

General Motors
Automotive $5,000

Goldman Sachs
Securities & Investment $5,000

Hoffman-La Roche
Pharmaceuticals/Health Products..$5,000

Iranian-American PAC
Foreign & Defense Policy $5,000

Ironworkers Union
Building Trade Unions $5,000

MOPAC
Pro-Israel $5,000

National Association of Home Builders
Construction Services $5,000

National Action Cmte.
Pro-Israel $5,000

National PAC
Pro-Israel $5,000

New York Bankers Association
Commercial Banks $5,000

New York Stock Exchange
Securities & Investment $5,000

King & Spaulding
Lawyers/Law Firms $5,000

Lockheed Martin
Defense Aerospace $5,000

Lockridge, Grindal et al.
Lawyers/Law Firms $5,000

Painters & Allied Trades Union
Building Trade Unions $5,000

Pfizer Inc.
Pharmaceuticals/Health Products..$5,000

Seafarers International Union
Transportation Union $5,000

Teaching Hospital Education PAC
Hospitals/Nursing Homes $5,000

Time Warner
TV/Movies/Music $5,000

Wolf, Block et al.
Lawyers/Law Firms $5,000

Arnold & Porter
Lawyers/Law Firms $4,987

American Federation of Teachers Public Sector Union	$4,500
American Psychiatric Assn. Health Professionals	$4,500
BellSouth Corp. Telephone Utilities	$4,500
United Parcel Service Air Transport	$4,500
AT&T Telephone Utilities	$4,000
BAE Systems North America Defense Aerospace	$4,000
Boeing Co. Defense Aerospace	$4,000
Brotherhood of Railroad Signalmen Transportation Unions	$4,000
Irish Americans for a Democratic Victory Democratic/Liberal	$4,000
KeySpan Energy Electric Utilities	$4,000
National Venture Capital Association Securities & Investment	$4,000
Verizon Communications Telephone Utilities	$4,000
Torricelli for US Senate Candidate Committees	$4,000
Hope Fund Leaderships PACs	$4,200
Keeping America's Promise Leaderships PACs	$4,200
Human Rights Campaign Human Rights	$3,500
Ernst & Young Accounting	$3,500
Morgan Stanley Securities & Investment	$3,500
National Association of Postmasters Public Sector Union	$3,500
National Associations of Federal Credit Credit Unions	$3,500

Skadden, Arps Lawyers/Law Firms	$3,500
Assurant Inc. Insurance	$3,000
Caremark RX Pharmaceuticals/Health Products	$3,000
Carpenters & Joiners Union Building Trade Unions	$3,000
General Electric Defense Aerospace	$3,000
Health Net Inc. Health Services/HMOs	$3,000
Investment Co. Institute Securities & Investment	$3,000
Laborers Union Building Trade Unions	$3,000
Nat'l. Assn./Insurance & Financial Advisors Insurance	$3,000
National Association of Realtors Real Estate	$3,000
National Committee to Preserve Social Security MISC. Issues	$3,000
Preston Gates et al. Lawyers/Law Firms	$3,000
Sprint Nextel Telecom Services & Equipment	$3,000
Washington Group International General Contractors	$3,000
American Optometric Assn. Health Professionals	$2,500
Coca-Cola Co. Food & Beverage	$2,500
Coca-Cola Enterprises Food & Beverage	$2,500
Fannie Mae Real Estate	$2,500
International Longshoremen's Assn. Transportation Unions	$2,500
M-PAC Leaderships PACs	$2,500

National Air Traffic Controllers Assn.
Transportation Union $2,500

National Education Association
Public Sector Union $2,500

National Treasury Employees Union
Public Sector Union $2,500

Operating Engineers Local 487
Building Trade Unions $2,500

PepsiCo. Inc.
Food Processing & Sales $2,500

Welch Allyn Inc.
Pharmaceuticals/Health Products $2,500

Patton Boggs LLP
Lawyers/Law Firms $2,438

Unite Here
Misc. Union $2,420

Nadler for Congress
Candidate Committees $2,200

Democrats for America's Future
Democratic/Liberal $2,100

NARAL New York
Abortion Policy/Pro-Choice $2,100

Ruben Hinojosa for Congress
Candidate Committees $2,100

Asbestos Workers Union
Building Trade Unions $2,000

American Veterinary Medical Assn.
Agricultural Services/Products $2,000

Alston & Bird
Lawyers/Law Firms $2,000

American Occupational Therapy Assn.
Health Professionals $2,000

Baker Botts LLP
Lawyers/Law Firms $2,000

Bond Market Association
Securities & Investment $2,000

Cash American International
Finance/Credit Companies $2,000

City PAC
Pro-Israel $2,000

Collegiate Funding Services LLC	
Finance/Credit Companies	$2,000
Comcast Corp.	
TV/Movies/Music	$2,000
CSX Corporation	
Railroads	$2,000
CVS Corp.	
Retail Sales	$2,000
HSBC North America	
Finance/Credit Companies	$2,000
International Council of Shopping Centers	
Retail Centers	$2,000
Intermagnetics General Corp.	
Misc. Manufacturing & Distributing	$2,000
International Longshoremen's Warehousemen's Union	
Transportation Union	$2,000
EDO Corp.	
Defense Electronics	$2,000
Edison Schools	
Education	$2,000
Farm Credit Council	
Agricultural Services/Products	$2,000
Federation of American Hospitals	
Hospitals/Nursing Homes	$2,000
Friends of Patrick Kennedy '98	
Candidate Committees	$2,000
Friends of Senator Carl Levin	
Candidate Committees	$2,000
FMR Corp.	
Securities & Investment	$2,000
Group Health Inc.	
Health Services/HMOs	$2,000
Intel Corp.	
Computers/Internet	$2,000
ITT Industries	
Electronics MFG & Services	$2,000
L-3 Communications	
Defense Electronics	$2,000
Magazine Publishers of America	
Printing & Publishing	$2,000

Marine Engineers Beneficial Assn./District 1
Transportation Union $2,000

Mortgage Bankers Assn. of America
Real Estate $2,000

National Assn. of Postal Supervisors
Public Sector Union $2,000

National Grid USA
Electric Utilities $2,000

National Electrical Contractors Assn.
Special Trade Contractors $2,000

National Elevator Construction Union
Building Trade Unions $2,000

New York Hospital Association
Hospitals/Nursing Homes $2,000

O'Melveny & Myers
Lawyers/Law Firms $2,000

Pharmaceutical Care Management Assn.
Human Rights $2,000

Plumbers/Pipefitters Union Local 1
Building Trade Unions $2,000

Quest Diagnostics
Health Services/HMOs $2,000

Raytheon Co.
Defense Electronics $2,000

Robins, Kaplan et al.
Lawyers/Law Firms $2100

Rochester Higher Education & Research
Education $2,000

STV Engineers
Construction Services $2,000

Technologies
Defense Electronics $2,000

Ted Strickland for Congress
Candidate Committees $2,000

Transportation Communications Union
Transportation Union $2,000

Transport Workers Union
Transportation Union $2,000

Troutman Sanders
Lawyers/Law Firms $2,000

Ullico Inc.
Insurance $2,000

United Health Group
Health Services/HMOs $2,000

US Steel
Steel Production $2,000

Verizon Wireless
Telecom Services & Equipment $2,000

Viacom
TV/Movies/Music $2,000

Vinson & Elkins
Lawyers/Law Firms $2,000

New York Building Congress PAC
General Contractors $1,840

Continuum Health Partners
Hospitals/Nursing Homes $1,800

DLA Piper Rudnick et al.
Lawyers/Law Firms $1,750

Mckennea, Long 7& Aldridge
Lawyers/Law Firms $1,750

Technet
Computers/Internet $1,687

Agri-Mark Inc.
Dairy $1,500

American Hospital Association
Hospitals/Nursing Homes $1,500

American Maritime Officers
Transportation Unions $1,500

DuPont Co.
Chemical & Related Manufacturing $1,500

Dykema Gosset
Lawyers/Law Firms $1,500

Microsoft Corp.
Computers/Internet $1,500

Par Technology
Defense Electronics $1,500

Professional Airways Systems Specialists
Transportation Union $1,500

T-Mobile USA
Telecom Services & Equipment $1,500

Exhibit H

Donor / Industry	Amount
Universal Music Group — TV/Movies/Music	$1,500
Entergy Corp. — Electric Utilities	$1,420
Parsons Brinckerhoff — Construction Services	$1,420
Accenture — Business Services	$1,000
AFL-CIO Bldg/Construction Trades Dept — Building Trade Unions	$1,000
Albert H Halff Association — Construction Services	$1,000
American Dental Assn. — Health Professionals	$1,000
American Federation of Musicians — MISC. Union	$1,000
American Gaming Association — Gambling	$1,000
Americans for Good Government — Pro-Israel	$1,000
American Express — Insurance	$1,000
America's Health Insurance Plans — Insurance	$1,000
American Road & Transport Builders Assn. — General Contractors	$1,000
American Staffing Association — Business Services	$1,000
American Watch Association — Misc. Manufacturing & Distributing	$1,000
Arent, Fox et al. — Lawyers/Law Firms	$1,000
Armenian American PAC — Human Rights	$1,000
ASCAP — TV/Movies/Music	$1,000
Assn. for the Advancement of Psychology — Health Professionals	$1,000
Bank America — Commercial Banks	$1,000

Bank One Corp.
Commercial Banks $1,000

Bikes Belong Coalition
MISC. Issues $1,000

Blue Cross & Blue Shield
Insurance $1,000

Blue Cross & Blue Shield of Calif.
Insurance $1,000

Brian Higgins for Congress
Candidate Committees $1,000

Bridgestone Americas
Chemical & Related Manufacturing $1,000

Californian PAC
Pro-Israel $1,000

Calpone Corp.
Electric Utilities $1,000

Career College Association
Education $1,000

Cellular Telecom & Internet Assn.
Telecom Services & Equipment $1,000

Cigna Corp.
Insurance $1,000

Collier Shannon Scott
Lobbyists $1,000

Cummins Inc.
Misc. Manufacturing & Distributing $1,000

Dickstein, Shapiro & Morin
Lawyers/Law Firms $1,000

Directors Guild of America
MISC. Union $1,000

Distilled Spirits Council
Beer, Wine & Liquor $1,000

Duke Energy
Electric Utilities $1,000

Freddie Mac
Real Estate $1,000

Gap Inc.
Retail Sales $1,000

Gannet, Fleming et al.
Construction Services $1,000

Heineken USA
Beer, Wine & Liquor....................$1,000

Hoeffel for Senate Committee
Candidate Committees....................$1,000

Hogan & Hartson
Lawyers/Law Firms....................$1,000

Invacare Corp.
Pharmaceuticals/Health Products....................$1,000

Jim Turner for Congress Committee
Candidate Committees....................$1,000

Jenner & Block
Lawyers/Law Firms....................$1,000

KPMG LLP
Accounting....................$1,000

LaFarge North Americas
Waste Management....................$1,000

Langevin for Congress
Candidate Committees....................$1,000

Liberty Mutual Insurance
Insurance....................$1,000

Major League Baseball Commissioners Office
Recreation/Live Entertain....................$1,000

Managed Funds Association
Securities & Investment....................$1,000

Manton for Congress
Candidate Committees....................$1,000

McGuire, Woods et al.
Lawyers/Law Firms....................$1,000

Medco Health Solutions
Health Services/HMOs....................$1,000

Medtronic Inc.
Pharmaceuticals/Health Products....................$1,000

MWH Americas
Environmental Svcs./Easter....................$1,000

Moran for Congress
Candidate Committees....................$1,000

National Association Real Estate Investment Trusts
Real Estate....................$1,000

National Cable & Telecommunications Assn.
TV/Movies/Music....................$1,000

National Community Action Foundation
Non-Profit Institutions $1,000

National Farmers Union
Agricultural Services/Products $1,000

National Milk Producers Federation
Dairy $1,000

National Organization for Women
Women's Issues..$1,000

National Structured Settlements Trade Assn.
Insurance..$1,000

Nelson, Mullin et al.
Lawyers/Law Firms $1,000

New Century Financial Corp.
Real Estate $1,000

Northwestern Mutual Life
Insurance..$1,000

Oldcastle Materials
Building Materials & Equipment $1,000

Operating Engineers Local 17
Building Trade Unions $1,000

Operating Engineers Local 138
Building Trade Unions $1,000

Parsons Corp.
Construction Services $1,000

Philips Electronics North America
Electronics MFG & Services $1,000

Pitney Bowes Inc.
Misc. Manufacturing & Distributing $1,000

Pride Mobility Products
Pharmaceuticals/Health Products..$1,000

Principal Life Insurance
Insurance..$1,000

Real Estate Roundtable
Real Estate $1,000

Reed Smith LLP
Lawyers/Law Firms $1,000

Retails, Wholesale & Dept Store Union
MISC. Union..$1,000

Rocky Mountain PAC
Leaderships PACs $1,000

Exhibit H

Sandler, Travis & Rosenberg Lawyers/Law Firms	$1,000
Sempra Energy Electric Utilities	$1,000
Sodexho Inc. Food & Beverage	$1,000
Sony Pictures Entertainment TV/Movies/Music	$1,000
Steamfitters Local 638 Building Trade Unions	$1,000
Textron Inc. Defense Aerospace	$1,000
Van Ness Feldmen Lawyers/Law Firms	$1,000
Wexler& Walker Public Policy Association Lobbyists	$1,000
Winston & Strawn Lawyers/Law Firms	$1,000
XM Satellite Radio TV/Movies/Music	$1,000
Dairylea Cooperative Dairy	$500
Federal Managers Association Public Sector Union	$500
Glass Molders Pottery Plastic Workers Industrial Unions	$500
Greenberg, Traurig et al. Lawyers/Law Firms	$500
Mechanical Technology Inc. Defense Electronics	$500
Nat'l Assn. of Alcoholism/Drug Abuse Counsel Health Professionals	$500
Paul, Hastings et al. Lawyers/Law Firms	$500
Pepper Hamilton LLP Lawyers/Law Firms	$500
Qorvis Communications Business Services	$500
Sonnenschein, Nath & Rosenthal Lawyers/Law Firms	$500

John Evans for Senate Committee Candidate Committees	$300
Cmte. to Re-Elect Loretta Sanchez Candidate Committees	$210
Bryan Cave LLP Lawyers/Law Firms	$200
Exxon Mobil Oil & Gas	$200
Ms President PAC Women's Issues	$100
Power Mobility Coalition Pharmaceuticals/Health Products	$100

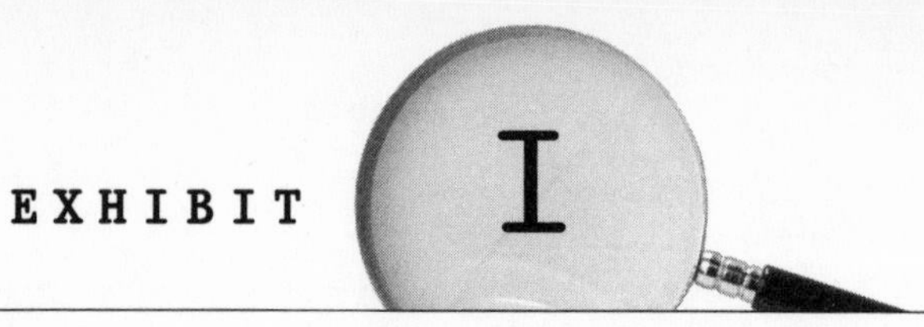

Hillary's Influence: HILLPAC Contributions to Political Campaigns

Sen. Clinton's Political Action Committee, HILLPAC, has contributed to the campaigns of the following candidates, all of whom are Democrats:

2002 CYCLE
CONTRIBUTIONS TO SENATE CANDIDATES

Candidate	Amount
Baucus, Max (MT)	$10,000
Blinken, Alan John (ID)	$5,000
Bowles, Erskine (NC)	$5,000
Boxer, Barbara (CA)	$10,000
Bradbury, Bill (OR)	$10,000
Carnahan, Jean (MO)	$10,000
Cleland, Max (GA)	$10,000
Clement, Bob (TN)	$10,000
Durbin, Dick (IL)	$10,000
Harkin, Tom (IA)	$10,000
Johnson, Tim (SD)	$10,000
Kirk, Ron (TX)	$5,000
Landrieu, Mary (LA)	$5,000
Lautenberg, Frank (NJ)	$5,000
Levin, Carl (MI)	$10,000
Mondale, Walter (MN)	$5,000
Parker, Susan (AL)	$5,000
Pingree, Chellie (ME)	$5,000
Pryor, Mark (AR)	$10,000
Reed, Jack (RI)	$10,000
Rockefeller, Jay (WV)	$10,000
Sanders, Alex (SC)	$5,000
Shaheen, Jeanne (NH)	$10,000
Strickland, Tom (CO)	$10,000
Torricelli, Robert (NJ)	$10,000
Tristani, Gloria (NM)	$5,000

Walters, David Lee (OK) $15,000
Weinberg, Lois Combs (KY) $10,000
Wellstone, Paul (MN) $10,000

CONTRIBUTIONS TO HOUSE CANDIDATES

Ackerman, Gary (NY)..$5,000
Baird, Brian (WA)..$10,000
Baldwin, Tammy (WI)..$10,000
Bean, Melissa (IL)..$5,000
Bell, Chris (TX) $5,000
Berkley, Shelley (NV)..$10,000
Bishop, Timothy (NY) $10,000
Boswell, Leonard (IA)..$10,000
Carden, Timothy (NJ)..$5,000
Cardoza, Dennis (CA)..$5,000
Carson, Julia (OH)..$10,000
Chapman, Ron (TX)..$5,000
Clark, Martha Fuller (NH) $10,000
Conway, Jack (KY) $10,000
Cordova, George Adam (AZ)..$5,000
Courtney, Joe (CT) $10,000
Crowley, Joseph (NY) $5,000
Cuellar, Henry (TX)..$5,000
Davis, Lincoln (TN)..$5000
Edwards, Chet (TX)..$10,000
Emanuel, Rahm (IL)..$5,000
Engel, Eliot L. (NY)..$5,000
Evans, Lane (IL)..$6,000
Feeley, Mike (CO) $5,000
Fink, David Howard (MI) $10,000
Hathorn, Michael Carl (AR)..$5,000
Herrera, Dario (NV) $10,000
Herseth, Stephanie (SD) $5,000
Hill, Baron (IN) $10,000
Hinchey, Maurice (NY) $5,000

Hoeffel, Joseph (PA)	$5,000
Holden, Tim (PA)	$5,000
Holt, Rush (NJ)	$10,000
Hooley, Darlene (OR)	$5,000
Hutchinson, Ann (IA)	$10,000
Inslee, Jay (WA)	$5,000
Israel, Steve (NY)	$10,000
Jacobs, Harry (FL)	$5,000
Kanjorski, Paul E. (PA)	$5,000
Kelley, Kevin (MI)	$5,000
Kouri, Chris (NC)	$5,000
Larsen, Rick (WA)	$10,000
Lowey, Nita (NY)	$5,000
Lucas, Louise (VA)	$1000
Luther, Bill (MN)	$10,000
Maloney, Carolyn B. (NY)	$5,000
Maloney, Jim (CT)	$10,000
Marlinga, Carl J. (MI)	$10,000
Marshall, Jim (GA)	$5,000
Matsunaka, Stan (CO)	$5,000
Mattsson, Arne (NY)	$5,000
McCarthy, Carolyn (NY)	$5,000
McCollum, Betty (MN)	$5,000
McNulty, Michael R. (NY)	$5,000
Meeks, Gregory W. (NY)	$5,000
Michaud, Mike (ME)	$5,000
Miller, Brad (NC)	$5,000
Moore, Dennis (KS)	$10,000
Moran, Jim (VA)	$5,000
Nadler, Jerrold (NY)	$5,000
Nolla, Carlos J. (KS)	$5,000
Norris, John (IA)	$10,000
O'Brien, Edward J. (PA)	$5,000
Owens, Major R. (NY)	$5,000
Phelps, David (IL)	$10,000
Rangel, Charles B. (NY)	$5,000

Roberts, Carol A (FL) $10,000
Romero, Richard M (NM) $5,000
Ross, Mike (AR) 10,000
Ruppersberger, Dutch (MD) $5,000
Ryan, Tim (OH) $5,000
Sanchez, Linda (CA) $5,000
Schneider, Jan (FL) $5,000
Serrano, Jose E (NY) $5,000
Shows, Ronnie (MS) $10,000
Slaughter, Louise M (NY) $5,000
Smith, John Arthur (NM) $5,000
Strickland, Ted (OH) $5,000
Sumers, Anne (NJ) $5,000
Swett, Katrina (NH) $10,000
Thomas, Julie (IA) $10,000
Thompson, Jill Long (IN) $10,000
Thurman, Karen L (FL) $5,000
Towns, Edolphus (NY) $5,000
Turnham, Joe (AL) $5,000
Van Hollen, Chris (MD) $5,000
Velazquez, Nydia M (NY) $5,000
Walker, Charles "Champ" Jr (GA) $5,000
Weiner, Anthony D (NY) $5,000
Wofford, Dan (PA) $5,000

2004 CYCLE
CONTRIBUTIONS TO SENATE CANDIDATES

Bayh, Evan (IN) $10,000
Breaux, John (LA) $5,000
Carson, Brad R (OK) $5,000
Castor, Betty (FL) $10,000
Daschle, Tom (SD) $10,000
Dodd, Chris (CT) $10,000
Dorgan, Byron L (ND) $10,000
Farmer, Nancy (MO) $10,000

Feingold, Russell D (WI)	$10,000
Fingerhut, Eric D (OH)	$5,000
Hoeffel, Joseph M (PA)	$10,000
Inouye, Daniel K (HI)	$10,000
Knowles, Tony (AK)	$5,000
Lincoln, Blanche (AR)	$10,000
Majette, Denise L (GA)	$5,000
Mikulski, Barbara A (MD)	$10,000
Mongiardo, Daniel (KY)	$10,000
Murray, Patty (WA)	$10,000
Obama, Barack (IL)	$10,000
Reid, Harry (NV)	$10,000
Salazar, Ken (CO)	$10,000
Schumer, Charles E (NY)	$10,000
Wyden, Ron (OR)	$10,000

CONTRIBUTIONS TO HOUSE CANDIDATES

Barbaro, Frank (NY)	$5,000
Barend, Samara (NY)	$5,000
Bean, Melissa (IL)	$5,000
Bishop, Timothy H (NY)	$10,000
Boswell, Leonard L (IA)	$5,000
Carnahan, Russ (MO)	$2,500
Cleaver, Emanuel (MO)	$5,000
Davis, Lincoln (TN)	$5,000
Edwards, Chet (TX)	$5,000
Frost, Martin (TX)	$5,000
Higgins, Brian M (NY)	$5,000
Hill, Baron (IN)	$5,000
Lampson, Nick (TX)	$5,000
McCarthy, Carolyn (NY)	$10,000
Michaud, Mike (ME)	$5,000
Moore, Dennis (KS)	$5,000
Romero, Richard M (NM)	$5,000
Sandlin, Max (TX)	$5,000

Schneider, Jan (FL) $5,000
Stenholm, Charles (TX) $5,000

2006 CYCLE (AS OF MARCH 16, 2006)
CONTRIBUTIONS TO SENATE CANDIDATES

Akaka, Daniel (HI) $5,000
Byrd, Robert (WV) $10,000
Carper, Tom (DE) $5,000
Casey, Bob (PA) $10,000
Feinstein, Dianne (CA) $5,000
Kennedy, Edward (MA) $5,000
Lieberman, Joe (CT) $5,000
Nelson, Bill (FL) $5,000
Pederson, Jim (AZ) $5,000
Stabenow, Debbie (MI) $5,000

CONTRIBUTIONS TO HOUSE CANDIDATES

Matsui, Doris (CA) $5,000

EXHIBIT J

Hillary's Endorsement of a Secret White House Database for the Democratic National Committee

THE WHITE HOUSE

WASHINGTON

CONFIDENTIAL

MEMORANDUM TO: Harold Ickes
Bruce Lindsey

cc: The First Lady

FROM: Marsha Scott

DATE: June 28, 1994

SUBJECT: Recommendation for Design of New Database

This sounds promising. Please advise. HRC

As you know, over the past year I and my staff have had extensive interaction with Percy's people and their system in Arkadelphia. We spent two days in Arkadelphia working with their people to learn their operation and software capabilities. Our technicians have worked regularly with their designers. In order to obtain lists for various functions and projects, I have requested from the PeopleBase system, many different types of information with varying time frames for turnaround time. (If you need specifics, I will be glad to provide the documentation). My overall impression is that while he has made some improvements, Percy's system and staff cannot adequately meet our quality or response demands and should not be considered for future use.

Currently in the White House we are preparing, as you know, to implement a new database system starting August 1. While that system is modeled after the PeopleBase software, it has major differences. The main differences are ease of use, function flexibility and correction capabilities. By the first of the year we should have any flaws identified and corrected and the majority of the White House using the new system. We will then have a year to fully train and familiarize our folks to its' many possibilities and uses. If they like it, as they seem to now, they will use it. The PeopleBase system was not used during the campaign because it was not user friendly. For the most part, only people from the Governor's staff used it. While I feel the new system far surpasses PeopleBase as a useful tool, it will be technically compatible with PeopleBase.

My team and I are also engaged in conversations with the DNC about the new system they are proposing. We have asked that their system be modeled after whatever system we decide to use outside the White House. I need you to make very clear to them that their system must be technologically compatible, if not the same, as whatever system we decide to use for political purposes later on. These discussions are currently in progress and a clear direction from you to the DNC will eliminate much unnecessary wrangling.

M 32438

Exhibit J

The time to act is now. Cloning or duplicating database systems is not difficult if carefully planned by a good design team. We have proven that it can also be done relatively quickly and inexpensively. Therefore, I suggest that instead of continuing with an old outdated system (PeopleBase) that does not meet our current demands, let my team work with the DNC to help them design a system that will meet our needs and technical specifications. We can show them what to do and then clone another system for our specific uses later on. Any information stored with PeopleBase could then be dumped into the new system and made available, when deemed necessary, to the DNC or other entities we choose to work with for political purposes.

The time to make these decisions is now while we have the opportunity to coordinate the various projects. Please let me know your thoughts as soon as possible. In the meantime I am proceeding as if this is the plan.

M 32439

EXHIBIT K

Hillary's Letter to Constituents on Iraq Policy

November 29, 2005

Dear Friend,

The war in Iraq is on the minds of many of you who have written or who have called my office asking questions and expressing frustration. When the President addresses the nation tomorrow on the war, the American people want and deserve to know how we got there, why we are still there, how we have executed the war and what we should do now. In short, the President must explain his plan for the war in Iraq.

There are no quick and easy solutions to the long and drawn out conflict this Administration triggered that consumes a billion dollars a week, involves 150,000 American troops, and has cost thousands of American lives.

I do not believe that we should allow this to be an open-ended commitment without limits or end. Nor do I believe that we can or should pull out of Iraq immediately. I believe we are at a critical point with the December 15th elections that should, if successful, allow us to start bringing home our troops in the coming year, while leaving behind a smaller contingent in safer areas with greater intelligence and quick strike capabilities. This will advance our interests, help fight terrorism and protect the interests of the Iraqi people.

In October 2002, I voted for the resolution to authorize the Administration to use force in Iraq. I voted for it on the basis of the evidence presented by the Administration, assurances they gave that they would first seek to resolve the issue of weapons of mass destruction peacefully through United Nations sponsored inspections, and the argument that the resolution was needed because Saddam Hussein never did anything to comply with his obligations that he was not forced to do.

Their assurances turned out to be empty ones, as the Administration refused repeated requests from the U.N. inspectors to finish their work. And the "evidence" of weapons of mass destruction and links to al Qaeda turned out to be false.

Based on the information that we have today, Congress never would have been asked to give the President authority to use force against Iraq. And if Congress had been asked, based on what we know now, we never would have agreed, given the lack of a long-term plan, paltry international support, the proven absence of weapons of mass destruction, and the reallocation of troops and resources that might have been used in Afghanistan to eliminate Bin Laden and al Qaeda, and fully uproot the Taliban.

Before I voted in 2002, the Administration publicly and privately assured me that they intended to use their authority to build international support in order to get the U.N. weapons inspectors back into Iraq, as articulated by the President in his Cincinnati speech on October 7th, 2002. As I said in my October 2002 floor statement, I took "the President at his word that he will try hard to pass a U.N. resolution and will seek to avoid war, if at all possible."

Instead, the Bush Administration short-circuited the U.N. inspectors — the last line of defense against the possibility that our intelligence was false. The Administration also abandoned securing a larger international coalition, alienating many of those who had joined us in Afghanistan.

From the start of the war, I have been clear that I believed that the Administration did not have an adequate plan for what lay ahead.

I take responsibility for my vote, and I, along with a majority of Americans, expect the President and his Administration to take responsibility for the false assurances, faulty evidence and mismanagement of the war.

Given years of assurances that the war was nearly over and that the insurgents were in their "last throes," this Administration was either not being honest with the American people or did not know what was going on in Iraq.

As a member of the Armed Services Committee, I heard General Eric Shinseki, the Army Chief of Staff, tell us that it would take several hundred thousand troops to stabilize Iraq. He was subsequently mocked and marginalized by the Bush Administration.

In October 2003, I said "In the last year, however, I have been first perplexed, then surprised, then amazed, and even outraged and always frustrated by the implementation of the authority given the President by this Congress" and "Time and time again, the Administration has had the opportunity to level with the American people. Unfortunately, they haven't been willing to do that."

I have continually raised doubts about the President's claims, lack of planning and execution of the war, while standing firmly in support of our troops.

After my first trip to Iraq in November 2003, I returned troubled by the policies of the Administration and faulted the President for failing to level with the American public. At the Council on Foreign

Relations, I chided the President for failing to bring in enough international partners to quell the insurgency.

I spoke out often at the Armed Services Committee to Administration officials pointing out that the estimates they provided about the war, its length and cost lacked even basic credibility.

And I challenged Secretary Rumsfeld more than once that he had no benchmarks to measure actual progress which would lead us to believe we had a strategy that was working.

Last month, I signed a letter with Senate Minority Leader Harry Reid and dozens of other Democratic Senators voicing strong concerns that, without a solid plan, Iraq could become what it was not before the war: a haven for radical Islamist terrorists determined to attack America, our allies and our interests. The letter asked the Administration "to immediately provide a strategy for success in order to prevent this outcome."

Just a few weeks ago, I joined a bipartisan majority in the United States Senate in voting for an amendment to the Defense Authorization bill calling upon the President and his Administration to provide answers and a plan for the war.

It is time for the President to stop serving up platitudes and present us with a plan for finishing this war with success and honor—not a rigid timetable that terrorists can exploit, but a public plan for winning and concluding the war. And it is past time for the President, Vice President, or anyone else associated with them to stop impugning the patriotism of their critics.

Criticism of this Administration's policies should not in any way be confused with softness against terrorists, inadequate support for democracy or lack of patriotism. I am grateful to the men and women of our armed forces and have been honored to meet them twice in Iraq. They honor our country every day with their courage, selfless dedication, and success in battle. I am also grateful to the thousands of unknown men and women in our security forces and around the world who have been fighting the larger war against terrorism, finding terrorists' cells, arresting them and working to prevent future attacks. And I applaud the brave people who have been risking their lives every day to bring democracy and peace to Afghanistan and Iraq.

I recently returned from visiting Israel and Jordan, seeing first hand the tragedy of spreading terrorism. As a New York Senator, I believe New York has a special bond with the victims of such terrorism, and we understand both the need to fight terrorism and the need for a clear plan in Iraq so that we can focus our resources in the right ways to prevent it from again reaching our shores.

America has a big job to do now. We must set reasonable goals to finish what we started and successfully turn over Iraqi security to Iraqis. We must deny terrorists the prize they are now seeking in Iraq. We must repair the damage done to our reputation. We must reform our intelligence system so we never go to war on false premises again. We must repair the breach with the Muslim world. And we must continue to fight terrorism wherever it exists.

Like all Americans, I hope the Iraqi elections are a true expression of democracy, one that is committed to majority rule, minority rights, women's rights, and the basic rule of law. I hope these elections will finally put the Iraqi people on the road to real security and independence.

If these elections succeed, we should be able to start drawing down our troops, but we should also plan to continue to help secure the country and the region with a smaller footprint on an as-needed basis. I call on the President both for such a plan and for a full and honest accounting of the failures of intelligence — something we owe not only to those killed and wounded and their families, but to all Americans.

We have to continue the fight against terrorism and make sure we apply America's best values and effective strategies in making our world and country a better and safer place. We have to do what is right and smart in the war against terrorists and pursuit of democracy and security. That means repudiating torture which undermines America's values. That means reforming intelligence and its use by decision makers. That means rejecting the Administration's doctrine of preemptive war and their preference to going it alone rather than building real international support.

I know when America leads with its values and fearlessly faces the facts, we make the best decisions. That is what is missing at the highest levels of our government, and what we desperately need now— answers to the questions about Iraq that only the President can provide. I hope he will level with the American people and provide us those answers in his Annapolis speech and give us the plan that has been sorely lacking.

Sincerely yours,

Hillary Rodham Clinton

EXHIBIT L

How Hillary Voted

Congressional Weekly said in April 2006 that "Since taking office, she [Clinton] has sided with her fellow Democrats more than 95 percent of the time in Senate roll call votes. Her voting, in other words, has been much less moderate than the public persona she has worked hard to cultivate."

Former Clinton aide Dick Morris was more critical in his book *Condi vs. Hillary*. After examining Clinton's Senate record, Morris wrote... "There is nothing in her [Clinton's] voting record that a preprogrammed machine could not have done as well. In neither her record of passed legislation nor her voted is there the slightest reflection of the effective senator she promised New Yorkers she would be."

Below is a sampling of ratings Clinton has received from various interest groups.

ABORTION

Year	NARAL Pro-Choice America	National Right to Life
2001	100%	0%
2002	100	0
2003	100	0
2004	100	0
2005	100	0

BUDGET, SPENDING, AND TAXES

Year	Americans for Tax Reform	National Taxpayers Union	Citizens Against Government Waste
2001	5%	3%	0%
2002	5	17	6
2003	5	21	N/A
2004	10	11	8
2005	5	9	17%

Exhibit L

BUSINESS AND CONSUMERS

Year	National Federation of Independent Business	U.S. Chamber of Commerce
2001	17%	43%
2002	25	45
2003	0	35
2004	0	50
2005	14%	35

CONSERVATIVE/LIBERAL

Year	American Conservative Union	Eagle Forum	U.S. Public Interest Research Group	National Committee for an Effective Congress	Americans for Democratic Action
2001	12%	9%	85%	98%	95%
2002	10	2	81	95	95
2003	10	5	95	95	95
2004	0	20	100	N/A	95
2005	12	25	91	95	100

EDUCATION

Year	National Education Association
2001	100%
2002	100
2003	82
2004	85
2005	100

CIVIL LIBERTIES

Year	American Civil Liberties Union
2001–02	60%
2003–04	78
2005–06	71

ENVIRONMENTAL ISSUES

Year	League of Conservation Voters	Defenders of Wildlife Action Fund
2001–02	88%	N/A
2003–04	92	90%
2005–06	95	100

FAMILY AND CHILDREN'S ISSUES

Year	Concerned Women for America	Family Research Council	Children's Defense Fund
2001–02	29%	N/A	100%
2003–04	7	14%	100
2005–06	11	N/A	100

GUN ISSUES

Year	Gun Owners of America	Brady Campaign to Prevent Gun Violence
2001–02	F-	100%
2003–04	F-	100
2005–06	F-	N/A

IMMIGRATION

Year	Federation for American Immigration Reform
2004	0%
2005	0

Exhibit 1

LABOR

Year	American Federation of State, County & Municipal Employees	Service Employees International Unions	AFL-CIO
2001	100%	100%	N/A
2002	100	100	92
2003	100	100	85
2004	100	100	100
2005	N/A	100	93

NOTES

#1 – The Foreign Cash File

1. Investigation of Illegal or Improper Activities in Connection with 1996 Federal Election Campaigns. Final Report of the Committee on Governmental Affairs. Senate Report 105-167 105th Congress 2nd Session March 10, 1998.
2. Ibid.
3. Marc Lacey, "House Subpoenas Torrance Businessman," *Los Angeles Times*, November 8, 1997.
4. This section is adapted from: Amanda Carpenter, "Bill Clinton Hauls in Foreign Cash," *Human Events*, May 6, 2006.
5. Editorial, "Striking It Rich in Japan," *New York Times*, October 26, 1989.
6. Financial disclosure forms, Exhibit B.
7. Mike Croder, "Taiwanese Protestors Criticize Clinton for Speaking at Conference Promoting Chinese Reunification," Associated Press Worldstream, February 22, 2002.
8. Transcript, "Remarks by President Bush at Tsinghua University," PR Newswire, February 22, 2002.
9. Adapted from: Amanda Carpenter, "Democrat Blasts Clinton's Foreign Honoraria as Unseemly," *Human Events*, May 16, 2006.
10. http://www.clintonglobalinitiative.org.
11. Adapted from: Amanda Carpenter, "Communist CEO Gave Bill Clinton $200,000," *Human Events*, June 2, 2006.

12. "Bill and Bono Jam With Investors," PR Newswire, May 23, 2002.
13. Stan Lehman, "Bill Clinton in Brazil Says Rich Nations Should Pardon Debt," Associated Press Worldstream, June 23, 2005.
14. Adapted from: Amanda Carpenter, "Bill Clinton Pushes 'Peace Park' in Korean Demilitarized Zone," *Human Events*, July 3, 2006.
15. "In Mexico, ex-U.S. President Clinton Calls for Migration Reform, Says Wife Hasn't Decided to Run Yet," Associated Press Worldstream, June 21, 2005.
16. http://www.clintonglobalinitiative.org.

#2 – The Campaign Cash File

1. MUR 5225 General Counsel's Brief, Federal Election Commission, July 5, 2005.
2. Author interview with Peter Paul, 2006.
3. "The Cuban Coffee Caper," *Time*, February 12, 1979.
4. Author interview with Peter Paul, 2006.
5. Barbara Olson, *The Final Days: The Last, Desperate Abuses of Power in the Clinton White House* (Washington, D.C.: Regnery, 2001), 52–53.
6. MUR 5225 General Counsel's Brief.
7. Dick Morris, "How Hill Gained," *New York Post*, April 25, 2005.
8. MUR 5225 General Counsel's Brief.
9. Byron York, "Hillary Clinton and the Sweatshop Tycoon of Saipan," *The Hill*, March 16, 2006.
10. Mike McIntire, "Rubbing Shoulders With Trouble, and Presidents," *New York Times*, May 7, 2006.
11. Beth Fouhy, "Wal-Mart Controversy Pits Clinton's Political Ambition Against Her Past," Associated Press, March 8, 2006.
12. Michael McAuliff, "Feds Nip Hil Over $6M Haul," *New York Daily News*, April 8, 2006.
13. Deborah Orin, "Hill's Filthy Lucre: Holds On to 27G from ImClone Sam," *New York Post*, August 9, 2002.
14. Deborah Orin, "Hill Retreating from Dirty ImClone Dollars," *New York Post*, August 10, 2002.
15. Bob Port, "Clinton, Lazio Smash Money Records," *New York Daily News*, December 31, 2000.
16. http://www.opensecrets.org.
17. "Clinton Keeps Raising Money, Giuliani Account Keeps Quiet," Associated Press, March 21, 2006.

18. Michael McAuliff, "Name Game Bags Hil at Least 340G. Rents Donor Lists for Cash," *New York Daily News*, April 30, 2006.
19. Ian Bishop, "Hill's Expan$ion Turned D.C. Home Into Fund-Raise Pad," *New York Post*, September 6, 2005.
20. Adapted from: Amanda Carpenter, "How Hillary Courted Corning, Inc.," *Human Events*, July 31, 2006.
21. James B. Flaws, "Clinton Has Done a Lot for Southern Tier," *Buffalo News*, March 24, 2003.
22. http://clinton.senate.gov. Press releases, June 16, 2005; August 9, 2005; February 6, 2006; June 29, 2006.

#3 – The Economics File

1. Beth Fouhy, "San Francisco Rolls Out Red Carpet for the Clintons," Associated Press, June 28, 2004.
2. "Hillary Calls for Estate Tax Break for Farmers" White House Bulletin, April 26, 2000.
3. Remarks by Senator Hillary Clinton at the Campaign for America's Future "Take Back America 2006" Conference, June 13, 2006.
4. Statement of Senator Hillary Rodham Clinton on Estate Tax Vote, June 8, 2006.
5. Remarks at a Democratic fundraiser, April 28, 2003. Shown on *Hardball*, May 1, 2003.
6. Congressional Record, "Congressional Budget for the U.S. Government for Fiscal Year 2004." March 20, 2003. 108th Congress, 1st session.
7. "Sen. Clinton Sees U.S. Economic Collapse," UPI, January 24, 2005.
8. Larry Eichel, "Clinton: Government Lets Down Hispanics," *Philadelphia Inquirer*, July 19, 2005.
9. Rex Nutting, "Fourth-Quarter GDP Revised Up To 1.7%," MarketWatch, March 30, 2006.
10. *Larry King Live*, June 21, 2006.
11. Joel Kirkland, "Clinton Pushes Oil and Gas Industry to Finance Alternatives; IPAA Calls Plan Unrealistic," *Inside FERC*, May 29, 2006.
12. Press Release, "Senator Clinton's Rhetoric Doesn't Match Her Record," Office of Senator James Inhofe, May 23, 2006.
13. Terence P. Jeffrey, "Enviro-Elitist Poses as Gas-Pump Populist," *Human Events*, September 19, 2005.
14. Dan Balz, "Oil Firms Turn Katrina into Profits, Clinton Says; N.Y. Senator Criticizes Lack of National Leadership, Freedom from Imports," *Washington Post*, September 3, 2005.

#4 – The Porkbarrel File

1. Statement of Roy A. Bernardi, assistant secretary for community planning and development, U.S. Department of Housing and Urban Development, before the U.S. House of Representatives Committee on Financial Services Subcommittee on Housing and Community Opportunity, March 14, 2002.
2. "Report: Buffalo Misspent Federal Aid for 30 Years," Associated Press State & Local Wire, November 14, 2004.
3. Press release, "Sen. Schumer: Meat Axe Slashes Federal Budget, Cuts Core Out of Big Apple," *US Fed News*, February 7, 2005.
4. Roger Dupuis II, "Popular Grants Targeted by Bush," *Ithaca Journal*, February 15, 2005.

#5 – The Healthcare File

1. Hillary Rodham Clinton, *It Takes a Village and Other Lessons Children Teach Us* (New York: Simon & Schuster, 1996), 336.
2. Congressional Record, S8419, June 24, 2003.
3. Congressional Record, S8529, June 25, 2003.
4. Press release, "First Federal Money for 9/11 Health Treatment Announced: New Federal Plan to Distribute $75 Million for 9/11 Injured Responders," http://.clinton.senate.gov, March 8, 2006.
5. Press release, "NY Reps Continue to Push for $125 Million for Injured 9/11 Responders," http://clinton.senate.gov, November 10, 2005.
6. Robin Toner and Anne E. Kornblut, "Wounds Salved, Clinton Returns to Health Care," *New York Times*, June 10, 2006.

#6 – The Families File

1. Terence P. Jeffrey, "Here's a Job for Hillary," *Human Events*, February 18, 2000.
2. Bob Fois, "On Gay Marriage, Covering Clinton and Common Sense," *News Copy*, New York, June 7, 2006.
3. Frankie Edozien, "Gay-Rights Honcho $hows Big Chill for Hill," *New York Post*, February 22, 2006.
4. Deepti Hajela, "New York Sen. Clinton Says Gay Marriage Not a Main Concern," Associated Press, June 5, 2006.
5. Glenn Thrush, "Clinton Raps Vouchers," *Newsday*, February 22, 2006.

6. Hillary Rodham Clinton, *It Takes a Village and Other Lessons Children Teach Us* (New York: Simon & Schuster, 1996), 336.
7. Congressional Record, 109th Congress, S 35, January 25, 2006.
8. Press release, "Statement of Senator Hillary Rodham Clinton on the Nominations of John Ashcroft and Gale Norton," http://clinton.senate.gov, January 29, 2001.
9. Patrick D. Healy, "Senator Clinton Assails Bush and G.O.P at a Campaign Fund-Raiser," *New York Times*, June 6, 2005.
10. Press release, "Statement of Senator Hillary Rodham Clinton on the Nominations of John Ashcroft and Gale Norton," http://clinton.senate.gov, January 29, 2001.
11. Press release, "Statement of Senator Hillary Rodham Clinton on the Nomination of John Roberts to be Chief Justice of the United States," http://clinton.senate.gov, September 22, 2005.
12. Press release, "Statement of Senator Hillary Rodham Clinton on the Nomination of General Michael Hayden to be Director of the Central Intelligence Agency," http://clinton.senate.gov, May 26, 2006.
13. Ryan Lizza, "The Abortion Capital of America: As the Pro-Life Movement Intensifies Nationwide, New York Contemplates Its History and Future as a Refuge," *New York Magazine*, December 12, 2005.
14. Robert Novak, "Rove's New Focus on Long-Term Political Planning Makes Republicans Happy," *Chicago Sun-Times*, April 23, 2006.
15. Harry Reid and Hillary Rodham Clinton, "Abortion Debate Shuns Prevention," *Albany Times Union*, April 18, 2006.

#7 – The Media File

1. Medea Benjamin, "Peace Activists at Hillary Clinton's Speech Try to Take Back 'Take Back America,'" http://www.counterpunch.org, June 13, 2006.
2. Carla Marinucci, "Hillary Ignores Question on N.Y. Gay Marriage Ruling; Tells Angelides at S.F. Fund-Raiser to Use Some Humor," *San Francisco Chronicle Online*, July 7, 2005.
3. "Transcript of the First Lady's Press Briefing on Millennium Project Part 5 of 5," U.S. Newswire, February 11, 1998.
4. "First Lady: Net News Needs Scrutiny," Wired.com, February 11, 1998.
5. Rebecca L. Eisenberg, "First Lady Just Doesn't Get It: Hillary Clinton's Call for Internet 'Gatekeeping' Reveals Lack of Understanding," *San Francisco Examiner*, February 22, 1998.

6. Greg Pierce, "Inside Politics; Boos for Hillary," *Washington Times*, October 23, 2001.
7. Richard Poe, *Hillary's Secret War* (Nashville: WND Books, 2004), 272.
8. Liz Trotta, "Sen. Clinton's Van Drives Past Security Checkpoint; Officials Claim 'Misunderstanding' at Airport," *Washington Times*, October 16, 2001.
9. Letter to the Honorable Hillary Rodham Clinton, "RE: Submitting Your Book Contract with Simon & Schuster to the Senate Select Committee on Ethics," http://www.essential.org, December 18, 2000.
10. Timothy J. Burger, "Hillary Deal by the Book," *New York Daily News*, February 15, 2001.
11. Press release, "CAGW: Senators Propose Redundant Media Research Study," PR Newswire Association, March 10, 2005.
12. Thomas B. Edsall, "Democrats' Data Mining Stirs an Intraparty Battle; With Private Effort on Voter Information, Ickes and Soros Challenge Dean and DNC," *Washington Post*, March 8, 2006.
13. Jeff Jacoby, "The Right's Balance," *Boston Globe*, June 2, 2005.
14. See Exhibit J.
15. John F. Harris, Sharon LaFranier, "Clinton Aides Shared Data With DNC," *Washington Post*, January 31, 1997.
16. Glenn F. Bunting and David Willman, "Mrs. Clinton Linked to Database Merger; Politics: Confidential Memo Shows She Endorsed Plan to Use White House Resources to Update DNC Information," *Los Angeles Times*, March 4, 1997.
17. Michael Weisskopf, "A Secret Cash Link; A White House Operation That Tracked Donors Was Extensive, Top Secret and Pushed by the First Lady," *Time*, February 3, 1997.
18. John F. Harris and Sharon LaFranier, "Clinton Aides Shared Data With DNC," *Washington Post*, January 31, 1997.
19. Glen F. Bunting and David Willman, "Memo to First Lady Told of Database Ambitions; Politics: In Confidential Document, Aide Suggested Using White House Resources to Update DNC Information," *Los Angeles Times*, March 4, 1997.

#8 – The Immigration File

1. Maggie Haberman, "GOP Would Have Booted Jesus: Hill," *New York Post*, March 23, 2006.
2. Calvin Woodward, "Bush and His Critics Have Both Overreached in Immigration Claims," Associated Press, May 16, 2006.
3. Press release, "Statement from Senator Hillary Rodham Clinton on Passage of Legislation to Extend Immigration Filing Deadlines," http://clinton.senate.gov, March 15, 2002.
4. Michelle Malkin, "Thwarting Homeland Security: Hillary Amendment Undermines Immigration Enforcement," *Human Events*, February 17, 2003.
5. Press release, "Corzine, Clinton Win Protection For Immigrant Families of September 11 Victims," http://clinton.senate.gov, January 23, 2003.
6. Press release, "Statement of Senator Hillary Rodham Clinton on Comprehensive Immigration Reform," http://clinton.senate.gov, March 8, 2006.
7. Press release, "Statement of Senator Hillary Rodham Clinton on the Emergency Supplemental Appropriations Conference Report and Real ID Act," http://clinton.senate.gov, May 10, 2005.
8. Jeffrey S. Passel, "Size and Characteristic of the Unauthorized Migrant Population in the U.S.," Pew Hispanic Center, March 7, 2006.
9. Regina Medina, "Hillary's Speech Is a Latino Hit," *Philadelphia Daily News*, July 19, 2005.
10. Ibid.

#9 – The 9/11 File

1. Russ Beutter, Heidi Evans, Robert Gearty, Brian Kates, Greg B. Smith, Richard T. Pienciak, "9-11 Money Trough," Parts 1–7, *New York Daily News*, December 5, 2005–December 11, 2005.
2. Russ Beutter, Heidi Evans, Robert Gearty, Brian Kates, Greg B. Smith, Richart T. Pienciak, "Billions in Liberty Bonds Go Unspent: Controversy Swirling Around," 9-11 Money Trough: Part 5, *New York Daily News*, December 8, 2005.
3. Geoff Earle, "Million-$$ Greedy Grab-Vegas Salon Among 1,000s of Businesses Caught Hogging Fed Aid," *New York Post*, December 29, 2005.

4. Press release, "Clinton Calls for Bush Administration Investigation and Congressional Hearing into Misuse of Critical 9/11 Small Business Assistance Program," http://clinton.senate.gov, December 30, 2005.
5. Russ Beutter, Heidi Evans, Robert Gearty, Brian Kates, Greg B. Smith, Richart T. Pienciak, "A Feeding Frenzy for FEMA Funds—Plan Wasn't Helping People: Bizman," 9-11 Money Trough: Part 4, *New York Daily News*, December 7, 2005.
6. Russ Beutter, Heidi Evans, Robert Gearty, Brian Kates, Greg B. Smith, Richart T. Pienciak "FEMA's 9-11 Grief Money Misused: Counseling Program Didn't Follow Rules," 9-11 Money Trough: Part 6, *New York Daily News*, December 9, 2005.
7. Russ Beutter, Heidi Evans, Robert Gearty, Brian Kates, Greg B. Smith, Richart T. Pienciak, "'Feel Free to Feel Better,'" 9-11 Money Trough: Part 6, *New York Daily News*, December 9, 2005.
8. Russ Beutter, Heidi Evans, Robert Gearty, Brian Kates, Greg B. Smith, Richart T. Pienciak, "Plenty of Hand Stirring Pot: Projects Already in Great Shape Still Snagged Millions," 9-11 Money Trough: Part 3, *New York Daily News*, December 6, 2005.
9. Press release, "Senator Hillary Rodham Clinton's Statement on the Floor of the United States Senate in Response to the World Trade Center and Pentagon Attacks," http://clinton.senate.gov, September 12, 2001.
10. John Machacek, "White House Spokesman Criticizes Hillary Clinton," Gannett News Service, May 18, 2002.
11. Press release, "Remarks of Senator Russ Feingold Introducing a Resolution to Censure President George W. Bush," http://feingold.senate.gov, March 13, 2006.
12. David Limbaugh, "Arrogance and Duplicity," *Washington Times*, March 10, 2006.
13. Dick Morris, "Bill and Hillary Clinton Are on Both Sides of the Issues," Newsmax.com, March 8, 2006.
14. Ian Bishop, "Hillary on Bubba: Dubai-ai-ai Admits She Didn't Know He Advised Port Bigs," *New York Post*, March 3, 2006.
15. Ibid.

#10 – The Iraq File

1. Ann Coulter, "Firemen Beware: Here Come Susan and Hillary," *Human Events*, March 3, 2003.

2. Marc Humbert, "Hillary Clinton Prefers 'Peaceful Solution' in Iraq," Associated Press, March 3, 2003.
3. Stephan Dinan, "Hillary Says 'No' But Acts Like a Candidate," *Washington Times*, September 25, 2003.
4. James Gordon Meek, "Hil Hits W on Iraq, 9-11 Some Think Bush Whacks Tip Run," *New York Daily News*, October 30, 2003.
5. Editorial, "Doing the Hillary Shuffle," *New York Post*, March 4, 2003.